Acclaim for Dolores Hayden's

BUILDING SUBURBIA

One of PLANetizen's Top Ten Books on Urban Issues in 2003

"A lively and informative overview of the American mania for suburban living. . . . Fascinating." —*Audubon Naturalist News*

"Compelling and beautifully written. . . . It reads like a novel and at the same time offers an insightful social and political history of the rise of the suburbs in the United States. Hayden redefines the American Dream and critiques the rise of segregated housing and the isolated communities characteristic of the suburban landscape. There is no other book quite like this one because of its accessibility and breadth of scholarship." —Setha M. Low, author of *Behind the Gates: Life, Security, and the Pursuit of Happiness in Fortress America*

"Readable and revealing. . . . Insightful reading." —*Cape Cod Times*

"Wonderful—a great combination of human reaction and scholarly insight." —Virginia McAlester, author of *A Field Guide to American Houses*

"A rich and rewarding book with new and original material and surprising insights. . . . Beautiful and accessible writing . . . fascinating historical narratives. . . . Unlike most commentators, Hayden goes beyond analysis to propose solutions. . . . Welcome and significant." —*Constructs*

"Dolores Hayden shows us, for the first time, the remarkable diversity of suburban environments that Americans have produced over two centuries. Lucid, original, and abundantly illustrated, *Building Suburbia* is that delightful rarity: a scholarly book with a critical perspective and wide appeal." —Richard Harris, author of *Unplanned Suburbs: Toronto's American Tragedy, 1900–1950*

Dolores Hayden

BUILDING SUBURBIA

Dolores Hayden, an urban historian and architect, writes about American landscapes and the politics of design. She is a professor of architecture and American studies at Yale University. In addition to *Building Suburbia,* her books include *A Field Guide to Sprawl* and *The Power of Place: Urban Landscapes as Public History.* Hayden is also a poet whose work has appeared in *The Yale Review*, *Southwest Review*, *The Kenyon Review*, *Verse Daily*, *Witness*, and *Michigan Quarterly Review.* Her collection, *American Yard*, was published in 2004.

BUILDING SUBURBIA

BUILDING

Dolores Hayden

SUBURBIA

Green Fields and Urban Growth,

1820–2000

VINTAGE BOOKS
A DIVISION OF RANDOM HOUSE, INC.
NEW YORK

FIRST VINTAGE BOOKS EDITION, NOVEMBER 2004

Copyright © 2003 by Dolores Hayden

Acknowledgment is made for previous and forthcoming publications by the author: "Revisiting the Sitcom Suburbs," *Landlines: Newsletter of the Lincoln Institute of Land Policy*, 14 (March 2001): 1–3. • "What Is Suburbia? Naming the Layers in the Landscape, 1820–2000," copyright © by Dolores Hayden in *Smart Growth: Form and Consequences*, Terry S. Szold and Armando Carbonell, eds. (Cambridge: Lincoln Institute of Land Policy, 2002). • "The Enduring Crabgrass Frontier," in *Redefining Suburban Studies*, Barbara M. Kelly, ed. (New York: Greenwood Press/Hofstra University, forthcoming). • "Building the American Way: Public Subsidy, Private Space," copyright © 2002 by Dolores Hayden in *The Politics of Public Space*, Setha M. Low and Neil Smith, eds. (New York: Routledge, forthcoming).

The Library of Congress has cataloged the Pantheon edition as follows:
Hayden, Dolores.
Building suburbia : green fields and urban growth, 1820–2000 / Dolores Hayden.
p. cm.
Includes bibliographical references and index.
1. Suburbs—United States—History.   2. Urbanization—United States—History.
3. Land use—United States—History.   4. Real estate development—United States—History.   5. Suburban homes—United States—History.   6. Metropolitan areas—United States—History.   7. Suburban life—United States—History.
I. Title: American suburbia : green fields and urban growth, 1820–2000.   II. Title.
HT352.U5H39 2003
307.74'0973—dc21
2003042046

Vintage ISBN: 0-375-72721-3

Author photograph © Michael Marsland
Book design by M. Kristen Bearse

www.vintagebooks.com

Printed in the United States of America
10 9 8

For
Peter H. Marris
and
Laura Hayden Marris

CONTENTS

Preface and Acknowledgments   xi

Part One   THE AMERICAN METROPOLITAN LANDSCAPE

One   The Shapes of Suburbia   3
Two   The Suburban City   10

Part Two   HISTORIC PATTERNS IN THE LANDSCAPE

Three   Borderlands   21
Four   Picturesque Enclaves   45
Five   Streetcar Buildouts   71
Six   Mail-Order and Self-Built Suburbs   97
Seven   Sitcom Suburbs   128
Eight   Edge Nodes   154
Nine   Rural Fringes   181

Part Three THE NEXT SUBURBS

Ten   Nostalgia and Futurism   201
Eleven The Importance of Older Suburbs   230

Notes   249
Selected Bibliography   287
Index   303

PREFACE AND
ACKNOWLEDGMENTS

THIS BOOK IS AN EXTENDED ESSAY about 180 years of metropolitan development in the United States, decades that shaped the American landscapes we know today. Centered on the built environment, it explores life on the urban periphery, changing over time. It is addressed to the general reader and written from the perspective of an urban landscape historian who is also an architect, wife, mother, and suburban resident. Many Americans worry about planning and building because popular suburban patterns of houses, yards, shops, and workplaces form unequal, ugly, unsustainable metropolitan regions. As geographer Richard Harris has noted, "In the United States today, no place seems more familiar than the suburb. To appreciate the strange particularity of this place, we need to establish some imaginative distance...."[1] The book probes relationships between physical design, culture, and economic life that readers in the United States may never have questioned. I invite readers who have lived abroad, and may find American cultural landscapes bizarre, to explore why American tracts, malls, and highways look the way they do.

Part One, The American Metropolitan Landscape, poses the conflict between people who seek the triple dream of home, nature, and community, and entrepreneurs who search for profits through the development of greenfield sites. Chapter 1, The Shapes of Suburbia, argues that in the United States, this conflict has produced seven historic suburban landscapes between 1820 and 2000. Chapter 2, The Suburban City, outlines the attempts of historians, architects, sociologists, and geographers to conceptualize the physical and economic process of urbanization as it shapes the landscape. Even the words "city" and "suburb" are contested because recent economic growth on metropolitan peripheries has depleted older downtowns, reversing expectations that density decreases as one travels through city, suburb, exurb, and rural area. The term "growth machine" (or "sprawl machine") defines the political alliances exerting constant pressure for peripheral development.

Part Two, Historic Patterns in the Landscape, the heart of the book, traces the long trajectory of suburban expansion, from the borderlands and picturesque enclaves of the early and mid-nineteenth century to the streetcar buildouts that hyped homeownership for working families. It explores the chaotic mail-order and self-built suburbs of the early twentieth century, followed by Depression-era struggles for federal regulation, loan insurance, and mortgage subsidies that result in the postwar "sitcom" suburbs of small houses built at an urban scale without urban infrastructure. In the 1950s, federal subsidies for accelerated depreciation for commercial real estate and Interstate highways laid the groundwork for edge nodes and rural fringes, developed in the late twentieth century as the most visible expressions of urban growth.

The final section of the book, Part Three, The Next Suburbs, considers current building and planning. Chapter 10, Nostalgia and Futurism, explores the design of neo-traditional enclaves, digital houses, and "green" buildings to evaluate their potential as new construction. Chapter 11, The Importance of Older Suburbs, argues that reconstruction of the metropolitan landscape should prevail over new construction. Understanding the history of built space is crucial to contesting sprawl, because reconstruction should be tailored to seven kinds of historic landscapes. Examples of local economic development created within a more egalitarian building process suggest ways to braid physical, social, and economic strategies for renewal.

Writing about landscape history in a national context, I am grateful for the work of authors in a dozen disciplines who have studied housing, cities, and suburbs before me. Among the books I have consulted most frequently are three outstanding works from the 1980s, Gwendolyn Wright's *Building the Dream,* Kenneth Jackson's *Crabgrass Frontier,* and Robert Fishman's *Bourgeois Utopias.* Along with urban planner Tom Daniels's recent *When City and Country Collide* and Lizabeth Cohen's *A Consumers' Republic,* they were invaluable.

My book is written for the general reader, but for those who wish to pursue the subject, there are detailed bibliographical notes and a selected bibliography. In choosing suburbs to discuss, I looked for well-documented examples. Suburban history has been made everywhere. Readers will recognize thousands of local variations.

Funds for research were provided by the Graham Foundation for Advanced Studies in the Fine Arts, the Lincoln Institute of Land Policy, and the Griswold Fund at Yale University. At the Lincoln Institute, Armando Carbonell offered sound advice at many stages. Conferences and lectures at Lincoln, MIT, the Harvard Graduate School of Design, the Yale School of Architecture, the University of New Hampshire, Hofstra University, and the City University of New York Graduate Center offered occasions to debate findings with colleagues along the way.

Miriam Stewart, my Yale research assistant on this book and a previous one, deserves special thanks for her excellent editing, enthusiastic research, and persistence on the photo permissions. Other Yale research assistants who contributed over the years were Catherine Whalen, Sandy Zipp, Ethan McCusker, and Gabrielle Brainard. I also learned a lot from younger scholars who have recently completed their dissertations in American studies or American history at Yale—Catherine Gudis on roads and billboards, Jeff Hardwick on malls, Marina Moskowitz on mail-order houses and zoning laws, and Sarah Jo Peterson on World War II housing.

My husband, Peter Marris, offered wise counsel as both urban sociologist and writer. He provided detailed critiques of the text, as did Ann Forsyth, professor and director of the Design Center for the American Urban Landscape at the University of Minnesota, Elizabeth Blackmar, professor of history at Columbia University, and Setha Low, anthropologist of space and place, professor at the Graduate Center of the City University of New York. My daughter, Laura Marris, took notes in Tysons Corner while I drove, helped proofread, and attached captions to illustrations in the final days. I would also like to thank my editor at the Knopf Publishing Group, Jane Garrett; her assistants, Sophie Fels and Emily Owens; the designer, Kristen Bearse, and art director, Archie Ferguson; managing editor, Altie Karper, and production editor, Grace McVeigh. My agent, Ellen Levine of Trident Media Group, formerly the Ellen Levine Literary Agency, Inc., provided quick enthusiasm and consistent support.

Dolores Hayden
Guilford, Connecticut, July 2002

Part One

THE AMERICAN
METROPOLITAN
LANDSCAPE

Chapter One

THE SHAPES OF SUBURBIA

We're in the American Dream business.
—advertisement for Fannie Mae

FLYING ACROSS THE UNITED STATES, airline passengers look down on dazzling, varied topography, yet from Connecticut to California, monotonous tracts of single-family houses stretch for miles outside the downtowns of major cities. Subdivisions interrupt farms and forests. They crowd up against the granite coast of Maine and push into the foothills of the Rocky Mountains. Next to residential areas lie highways, shopping malls, and office parks. They overwhelm small town centers. More Americans reside in suburban landscapes than in inner cities and rural areas combined, yet few can decode the shapes of these landscapes or define where they begin and end.

Demographers still describe suburbs as "the non–central city parts of metropolitan areas," a negative definition, but suburbia has become the dominant American cultural landscape, the place where most households live and vote.[1] Describing suburbia as a residential landscape would be wrong, however, because suburbs also contain millions of square feet of commercial and industrial space, and their economic growth outstrips that of older downtowns. Most confusing of all, suburbia is the site of promises, dreams, and fantasies. It is a landscape of the imagination where Americans situate ambitions for upward mobility and economic security, ideals about freedom and private property, and longings for social harmony and spiritual uplift.

3

For almost two hundred years, Americans of all classes have idealized life in single-family houses with generous yards, while deploring the sprawling metropolitan regions that result from unregulated residential and commercial growth. With no national land use policy in the United States, single-family housing has often driven suburban planning by default. Between 1994 and 2002, real estate developers completed about 1.5 million new units of housing every year, most of them suburban single-family houses.[2] The production of millions of houses—involving massive mortgage subsidies by the federal government, huge expense to individual families, and extraordinary profits for private real estate developers—has largely configured Americans' material wealth and indebtedness, as well as shaped American landscapes. The metropolitan building process holds the key to many aspects of American culture, yet few know its social and spatial history.

This book is an account of suburbanization since 1820, exploring how entrepreneurs and residents have transformed fields, meadows, and woods into habitable space. The speed and spatial scale of land development have increased with each decade. In the earliest years of mercantile capitalism, a few suburban entrepreneurs launched isolated experiments in subdividing property and building new communities with the help of family and friends. Some real estate developers and boosters began to work together, forming political alliances called "growth machines." Between 1870 and 1920, at the height of industrial capitalism, developers extended their reach and promoted urban peripheries systematically, often working in partnership with transit owners, utilities, and local government. After the rise of a powerful real estate and construction lobby in the 1920s, the federal government took a major role—largely through tax, banking, and insurance systems—in subsidizing private development of residential and commercial property on a national basis. By the mid-1950s, federal tax supports for commercial developers and direct federal support for highways provided incentives for unchecked growth on a scale that earlier entrepreneurs could never have imagined. By the 1980s, state and local governments also frequently supported private commercial development with direct subsidies.

The history of suburban construction can be understood as the evolution of seven vernacular patterns. Building in borderlands began about 1820. Picturesque enclaves started around 1850 and streetcar buildouts around 1870. Mail-order and self-built suburbs arrived in

1900. Mass-produced, urban-scale "sitcom" suburbs appeared around 1940. Edge nodes coalesced around 1960. Rural fringes intensified around 1980. All of these patterns survive in the metropolitan areas of 2003. Many continue to be constructed.

Each pattern is defined by characteristic development practices, building technologies, marketing strategies, architectural preferences, and environmental attitudes. Despite some mid-twentieth-century claims that suburbia is a classless place, in each era of suburban life, economic class has affected residents' employment options, commuting choices, lot sizes, and house sizes, as well as favored shapes for houses, porches, and yards. There are working-class, middle-class, and upper-class configurations, as well as practices of racial segregation, intertwined with the seven suburban patterns.

Most previous accounts of suburban history have been organized around improvements in transportation technology, and explicitly or implicitly the authors suggest that transportation technology made residential growth inevitable. Categorizing places by commuters' choices—railroad suburb, streetcar suburb, automobile suburb—also leads to a focus on middle-class and upper-class male breadwinners and their housing. In contrast, this book highlights the complex relationships between real estate entrepreneurs and a wide range of suburban residents and workers. It explores the interplay of natural and built environments, considers women's and children's lives as well as men's, discusses working-class houses and yards as well as affluent ones, and explains why suburbia has been of great interest to political lobbyists.

Many different kinds of visual source materials reveal the precise shapes of suburbs, including maps, plans for towns, designs for houses, and photographs of households. The built places themselves provide material evidence used throughout the book, documented in both architectural and aerial photography. Low-level, oblique-angle aerial photography is especially useful for capturing the scale of recent developments in relation to older patterns.[3]

THE TRIPLE DREAM AND THE GROWTH MACHINES

The "American dream" is embedded in these seven evolving patterns of suburban development. Unlike every other affluent civilization, Americans have idealized the house and yard rather than the model

neighborhood or the ideal town.[4] From the beginning, the dream con-
flated piety and gender-stereotyped "family values." The ideology of
female domesticity, developed in the United States during the same era
when suburban borderlands were first attracting settlers, elevated the
religious significance of woman's work, defined as bearing and rearing
children in the strong moral atmosphere of a Protestant home set in a
natural landscape. The single-family house was invested with church-
like symbols as a sacred space where women's work would win a
reward in heaven. Catholic and Jewish immigrants also tied domesticity to religion.

The ideology of female domesticity, popular since the 1840s,
was wedded to a cult of male home ownership, extended to include
working-class men around the 1870s. Over the years, developers
embellished the religious imagery. In 1921 an editorial writer for the
National Real Estate Journal told readers that the Garden of Eden was
the first subdivision.[5] While Eden also took the fancy of the editors of
American Architect and Building News who claimed that Adam and
Eve built their home in Short Hills, New Jersey, a perfect town, many
more developers have sited their new houses in heaven. An angel with
a sword of justice delivered developer Samuel Gross's "home at $10
a month" to a Chicago workman. A *New Yorker* cover showed a
new house floating on pink clouds, above a husband, wife, and child
ascending into the sky in 1946, holding their blueprints. (The artist,
Constantin Alajálov, included one sharp detail: outside the back door
of this upper-middle-class house, an African-American cook chats
with a Fuller Brush salesman.)[6] More recently, heavenly notes were
sung by architects Andrés Duany and Elizabeth Plater-Zyberk when
they announced "The Second Coming of the American Small Town"
at Seaside, Florida. A memoir by D. J. Waldie evoked Lakewood, California, as *Holy Land*.[7]

Occasionally, developers have relocated the sales pitch for heaven in
the secular landscape of happiness. William F. Chatlos built one thousand "Happiness Homes" in Williston Park, Nassau County, Long
Island, in the 1920s. His three-bedroom Tudor and Dutch Colonial
houses occupied an alphabetical grid of streets named for prominent
colleges and universities, including Amherst, Brown, and Cornell.[8] In
the 1940s, advertising copywriters for General Electric promoted purchasing a home as "an adventure in happiness." Listing many electri-

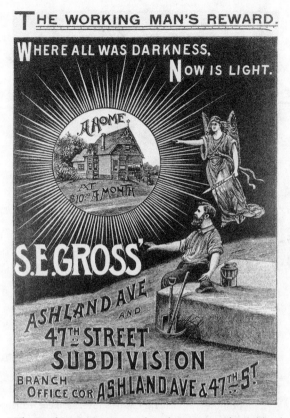

"The Working Man's Reward," advertisement for Ashland
Avenue and 47th Street subdivision, located close to factories
and stockyards, Chicago, Samuel E. Gross, builder, 1891.

cal appliances, GE told veterans, "It's a promise!" Most Americans
want to believe in a "Happiness Home." In the 1990s many flocked to
buy houses in "Celebration," a real estate development by The Walt
Disney Company, previously known for building theme parks advertised as "the happiest place on earth."

But for women, especially, the single-family suburban house implies
isolation, lacking physical and social context. For women, the dream
is house plus neighborhood sociability. Others have proposed a differ-

"It's a promise!" A General Electric advertisement from
World War II promises servicemen and their wives or
sweethearts "Victory Homes" filled with electric appliances—
fourteen are pictured at the bottom of the page—when the war
is won. Courtesy of General Electric Company.

ent double dream, a house set in unspoiled nature.[9] The result is a
triple dream, house plus land plus community, the kind of neighborhood space represented in Phyllis McGinley's charming poem about
Larchmont, New York, "I Know a Village." She observes that "streets
are named for trees," gardens hum with bees, and "people visit on
their porches."[10] This triple dream encompasses both the private and
public pleasures of peaceful, small-scale residential neighborhoods.

For the most part, the physical realization of this dream has been in the hands of developers trying to turn a profit through suburban growth. Conflict has characterized every era of development, as green fields have attracted residents to the peaceful outskirts of cities but also drawn promoters. In addition to those directly involved in the building process, the boosters of growth have included lawyers, owners of suburban transportation companies (including ferries, railroads, and streetcars), owners of utilities, and owners of local newspapers, supermarkets, and big-box stores. They have handled house purchases, punched commutation tickets, generated electricity, increased total circulation, marketed cornflakes, and sold screwdrivers. Once a suburban area is established, growth promoters usually seek greater and greater levels of density. The residents' hope of unspoiled nature fails because open land vanishes with increased development. Their hope of community is betrayed when tracts of houses, hyped as ideal "communities," lack social and economic centers, parks, schools, and necessary infrastructure. Contestation—between residents who wish to enjoy suburbia and developers who seek to profit from it—lies at the heart of suburban history.

Chapter Two

THE SUBURBAN CITY

It is the city trying to escape the consequences of
being a city while still remaining a city. It is urban
society trying to eat its cake and keep it, too.
— HARLAN DOUGLAS, *The Suburban Trend,*
1925

W HEN KENNETH T. JACKSON PUBLISHED his prize-
winning history of suburbs, *Crabgrass Frontier,* in 1985,
he concluded, optimistically, that the United States was
turning away from suburbia. He suggested that "the long process of
suburbanization ... will slow over the next two decades." He pre-
dicted that rising energy and land costs would lead people back to
urban centers.[1] Instead, in the last two decades, Americans have settled
on the distant fringes of metropolitan regions faster than ever before,
while older downtowns have lost population, jobs, and economic
vitality.[2] Downtowns with offices, stores, museums, and entertainment
drew Americans from the 1870s to the 1950s, but a suburban trend in
the mid-1920s became a suburban tide in the 1950s. By 1970, more
Americans lived in suburbs than in either central cities or rural areas.
By 2000, more Americans lived in suburbs than in central cities and
rural areas combined. The United States had become a predominantly
suburban nation. Although inner cities still housed certain institutions
important to metropolitan regions, many key economic and cultural
centers such as corporate headquarters and regional theaters had relocated to suburbs.

After almost two centuries of steady growth, suburbs have over-whelmed the centers of cities, creating metropolitan regions largely formed of suburban parts. In the suburban city of 2003, all seven historic suburban landscape patterns continue to exist. Most political entities include the fragments, overlays, collisions, and erasures of more than one pattern, because suburban growth has been constant across the political boundaries of states, counties, cities, towns, and villages. Metropolitan regions reveal what critics call suburban sprawl, the lack of land use controls or environmental planning.[3] They also reflect a culture of easy obsolescence, where yesterday's picturesque enclave may be sliced by today's new highway leading to tomorrow's edge node.

There have been many efforts to rename the spread-out suburban city. "Galactic metropolis" taps a word from outer space. "Regional city" combines spread and center. So does "sprawl city." "When Suburbs Are the City," the title of a paper by historian Sam Bass Warner, Jr., captures the problem in words that everyone understands.[4]

In the spaces of the suburban city lie metropolitan complexities. American suburbia has always been physically and socially diverse.

The triple dream of house, yard, and neighborhood,
with backyard pools and flowering trees. Small ranch houses,
raised ranches, and colonials, Bridal Path Lane,
West Haven, Conn., 1998. Alex S. MacLean, Landslides.

The suburban city, where older single-family houses exist in a metropolitan
landscape of apartments, arterials, offices, and big-box stores. North Haven,
Conn., 1998. Alex S. MacLean, Landslides.

The outskirts of mid-nineteenth-century cities housed noxious industries like slaughterhouses and glue factories, social reform establish-
ments such as poorhouses, orphanages, contagious disease hospitals,
and prisons, plus temporary sites for camp meetings and traveling cir-
cuses.[5] There were suburban temperance communities, as well as
squatters on marginal land. Although the history of the suburbs
includes countless examples of exclusion implemented through developers' deed restrictions, bankers' red-lining, realtors' steering, government lending policies, and other discriminatory practices, not all
nineteenth-century suburban residential areas were white, Protestant,
and elite. From about 1870 on, many working-class and lower-
middle-class families were attracted to the periphery of the city, where
land was cheap and houses might be constructed with sweat equity.
While nineteenth-century immigrants often spent time in inner-city
tenements before moving out to streetcar suburbs, today some new
immigrants to the United States head straight to the suburbs to live
where jobs are easier to find.

Some affluent suburban communities remain almost entirely white and Protestant, but there are also Irish-American suburbs, African-American suburbs, Polish-American suburbs, and Chinese-American suburbs, as well as older streetcar suburbs like Boyle Heights in Los Angeles, a place that has welcomed successive waves of new immigrants from Mexico, Russia, and Japan.

Sometimes the impact of ethnic diversity can be seen and heard in the suburban landscape. New Haven's Italian-American neighborhoods reveal gardens of basil, tomatoes, and oregano, as well as yard shrines honoring the Virgin. Latino families in East Los Angeles decorate their front yards with traditional *nacimientos*. Sikhs have renamed a street in Fremont, California, for their Gurdwara Temple. Polish-Americans have established talk radio in Polish from suburban Pomona, New York; Chinese-Americans offer news and entertainment in Chinese out of Freeport, Long Island; and Indian immigrants broadcast from a radio station in Metuchen, New Jersey.[6]

The diversity of suburbia is evidence of assimilation and a source of conflict. Suburban residents from different ethnic backgrounds have purchased older single-family houses and yards only to use them in new ways. In Silver Spring, Maryland, planners are reexamining the term "household" to deal with perceived overcrowding by extended families from Latino backgrounds. In Fairfax County, Virginia, Vietnamese, Indians, Arabs, Pakistanis, West Africans, and East Africans have joined Latin Americans looking for affordable shelter near their suburban jobs. Many households are large, multigenerational groups, with aunts, uncles, brothers, sisters, cousins, and grandparents helping to pay the rent or make the mortgage. Their cars crowd small driveways. Dozens of these immigrant families have paved over their front lawns to make it easier to park, offending their neighbors. In June 2002, Fairfax County passed a controversial regulation forbidding homeowners to pave their front yards.[7]

If suburban space has sometimes resisted ethnic diversity, it has been even less accommodating to changes in household composition and women's roles. Men of all classes have portrayed the suburban home as a retreat from the cares of their jobs. But since the time of the borderlands, houses have been workplaces for millions of women of all classes and all ages—paid cooks, cleaning women, and nannies, as well as unpaid housewives and mothers.

Almost two centuries later, household composition has changed.[8] Married couples with children are no longer dominant in suburbs. They are outnumbered by young singles and the elderly living alone. As suburban families have become more diverse and millions of housewives have found paid work, the male-breadwinner family with stay-at-home mom and two children, in a peaceful three-bedroom colonial with a leafy yard and sociable neighbors, predominates only in reruns of old sitcoms. Still, gendered work often remains the rule. Women lug groceries, push strollers, make meals, and serve as "taxi parents." Men do yard work and maintenance. New nurturing roles are evolving in new kinds of households, including those of employed women, single parents, single people, same-sex partners, and two-worker couples, but millions of suburban women have moved into the paid labor force while retaining their "second shift" at home. Because women hold jobs in every economic category, the roads are filled with women commuters as well as taxi parents. "I drove on down the Trail of Errands," sighs the main character in *Carpool,* a novel by Mary Cahill.[9] The "Trail of Errands" is far longer than it needs to be because single-family zoning is often too rigid and the regulatory system in mortgage banking has been formed around the sale or resale of one kind of house for one kind of family—a male breadwinner, a female housewife, and their young children.

DISMISSING AND REDISCOVERING SUBURBIA

Suburbia conceals as well as reveals its complexity. For years, when urban historians wrote about the "city," they meant the center, the skyline, downtown. Suburbs were left out of traditional "city biographies," which emphasized economic development, population growth, and the achievements of business leaders and politicians. Everyone knew that large suburbs existed and had something to do with the process of urbanization. But most historians thought they were less significant than the city center: spatially, because they were less dense than centers; culturally, because more of their attractions involved nature than architecture; and socially, because their daytime activities involved women and children more than men.

Because of prejudices about density, high culture, and gender, suburbia resisted scrutiny. It evaded art-historical analysis, derived from the aesthetic assessment of outstanding buildings, and urban analysis, based on demographic and economic statistics. As a result, many urban historians were surprised that the consistent spatial push for residential development at the very edge of the city finally brought about the dominance of a suburban pattern in the metropolitan landscape as a whole. They were intellectually unprepared for the shift.

In the 1970s and 1980s, architects and urban theorists also largely ignored suburbs or lambasted them as banal areas of tract houses. Artists and writers tended to agree, perhaps because television, films, and advertising often represented American family life in comfortable suburban houses as a mindless consumer utopia. Synonyms for "suburb" in the 1970s included "land of mediocrity," "middle America," and "silent majority," as well as outskirts, outposts, borderlands, and periphery.[10]

In 2003 there is far more interest in suburbs and less agreement about their character. Beginning in the 1980s and 1990s, architects and landscape architects started to reconsider the American suburb as a built product. Some studied the social and cultural history of vernacular building and landscapes.[11] Others argued that better design was the key to better suburbs. These "new urbanists" designed model developments, rewrote zoning codes, and attacked highway engineers who encouraged traffic.[12]

During the same decades, a group of sociologists, geographers, and planners created new urbanist sociology, unrelated to new urbanist architecture.[13] They analyzed the forces driving urban growth. While suburbs and greenfield construction were not their main focus, they studied the political economy of places, researching how the built environment had been financed, planned, designed, constructed, and marketed. Harvey Molotch's 1976 essay "The City as a Growth Machine" called attention to the ways local elites dealt with land as "a market commodity providing wealth and power."[14] These social scientists attacked "planned sprawl" and wrote about "growth machines" or "sprawl machines," suggesting that pro-growth lobbies were comparable to the corrupt urban political machines that figures like Boss Tweed forged in the mid-nineteenth century.[15]

New urbanist sociology has directly influenced community organizing. "The engine of growth is powered by the fortunes resulting from land speculation and real estate development," wrote activist Eben

Fodor of Eugene, Oregon. "The primary business interests are the landowners, real estate developers, mortgage bankers, realtors, construction companies and contractors, cement and sand and gravel companies, and building suppliers."[16] In *Better Not Bigger,* Fodor concluded that professionals whose jobs depend upon growth—including planners, architects, landscape architects, surveyors, interior designers, and engineers—tend to support new development. He argued that planners and members of the design professions have often chosen not to criticize their clients for fear of losing them.[17]

Along with historians, sociologists, planners, and architects, geographers have joined suburban debates. Years before Kenneth T. Jackson defined the suburb as a community of middle-class commuters' residences, many geographers asserted that the American suburb had "evolved" beyond being a "bedroom suburb" for workers who commuted to the center for their jobs. The geographers studied jobs in the periphery. As early as the 1960s some of them claimed that they saw enough new employment at the outer edge of metropolitan areas to call the fabric that was thriving "urban." Could a booming place be suburban and urban at the same time?

Urban historian Robert Fishman said yes. In 1987 he startled readers by announcing the era of "the suburb" was over. He defined the American suburb as a place for commuters, as Jackson had, but he defined it even more narrowly as an exclusive and leafy residential enclave of male-headed upper-class and upper-middle-class families, a "bourgeois utopia," primarily Protestant and white. For Fishman, a "classic" suburb was a Main Line Philadelphia railroad suburb between the 1920s and the 1960s.[18] What existed in the 1980s, he thought, was a "post-suburb" or a "technoburb."

The rush was on to invent new terms: outer city, shock suburb, out-town, edge city, boomburb, and exopolis. *American Quarterly* sponsored a debate about the redefinitions, "Bold New City or Built-Up 'Burb?"[19] Did scholars and planners need new words? New words often obscure old problems. Words like post-suburb, techno-burb, and exopolis suggest that ordinary citizens will not understand issues. They imply that massive new construction is inevitable, and they encourage designers and planners to develop futuristic solutions for fringe areas.

Urban growth has been a continuous economic and political

process. Because federal supports for private real estate development, throughout the eras of the sitcom suburbs, the edge nodes, and the rural fringes, have consistently favored new construction, Americans have abandoned existing built environments, willingly or unwillingly. The conservation and repair of urban and suburban fabric depends on a fuller understanding of why unplanned growth has prevailed.

Arguing for the metropolitan context of suburban landscapes, this history attempts to reconnect city and suburb, showing that since the early nineteenth century, suburbs have been important to the process of urbanization and economic growth, perhaps as important as the crowded centers of cities. Defining the seven historic landscapes of urban expansion can lead to more precise proposals for their reconstruction. The vernacular houses and yards of suburbia, the older suburban and small-town centers, so long overlooked by urban historians, are an essential part of American life. Their fabric could be preserved by sympathetic practitioners, skilled developers, architects, planners, and public historians, who mend and reweave landscapes while adding new housing, services, and amenities. This would demand both political insight and cultural understanding.

In 2003, when most Americans live in suburban cities, many of the spatial conventions and social expectations of the nineteenth and early twentieth centuries remain tangled in memory and manners. Change is difficult when suburban houses and yards are infused with the pieties of Protestant, Catholic, and Jewish "family values" and also contain the purchases of a society inundated with advertising and consumer culture. Long ago, Catharine Beecher promoted the "Heaven-devised plan of the family state" with a Gothic cottage. In the 1950s Elizabeth Gordon championed "the architecture that will encourage the development of individualism" in *House Beautiful,* calling modern family houses and private gardens a bulwark against communism. Both authors saw private housing as a stage for middle-class consumption, and consumption as the route to economic prosperity, a view they shared with developers, manufacturers, and utilities. This is the "Consumers' Republic" historian Lizabeth Cohen has defined, but not the side of suburban life twenty-first-century environmentalists wish to preserve.[20]

At every stage of suburban development in the United States people created more frugal patterns, places where earning and nurturing were essential parts of daily life. Some of these patterns appeared in working-class suburbs. Some appeared in communitarian settlements, new towns, Greenbelt towns, and cooperative multifamily housing projects. All were part of suburban choices before the 1950s, and they are alternatives to remember. In most cases, designs to conserve energy and land had merit, and some, like the solar houses of the 1940s, were brilliant. Excessive private consumption was not inevitable. It was the result of sustained pressure from real estate interests and their allies in government to marginalize the alternatives to unlimited private suburban growth. As the production of built space came to dominate the economy, replacing the production of manufactured goods, the pressures increased.

Current environmental campaigns aim to increase sustainability and reduce the consumption of nonrenewable resources. These campaigns to halt unchecked growth will fail unless most Americans know the complex history of their own suburbs, and how major developers, with increasing collaboration from the federal government, have mass-marketed ever-larger private developments while neglecting to consider the environmental consequences or to build infrastructure for public life. Politicians of both major parties have supported hundreds of antisprawl initiatives across the country. The next step is to understand how, over almost two centuries, sales of model houses for the millions have overwhelmed more sustainable alternatives for housing and urban design. Seven historic patterns of suburban neighborhoods embody the material history of Americans' private dreams even as they form complex and problematic urban realms.

Part Two

HISTORIC PATTERNS
IN THE LANDSCAPE

Chapter Three

BORDERLANDS

Economical, healthful, beautiful, and Christian
homes.
—advertisement for *The American
Woman's Home*

AROUND 1820, IN PORT CITIES SUCH AS New York and
Boston, wharves, houses, shops, offices, factories, livery stables, and markets were crowded together for the convenience
of buying and selling. Buildings of wood, brick, and stone rose no
more than three to five stories. The steeples of churches and the masts
of sailing ships defined the skyline. In this era, the owners of businesses, their families, employees, and servants lived in close proximity
to each other as well as to the waste products of workshops and factories. Rough wooden wagons jostled elegant horse-drawn carriages in
muddy streets strewn with filth and rubbish. Pedestrians crowded
onto sidewalks if they could find them, or kept to the sides of the
streets. Respectable girls and women were very restricted in their
movements, lest they be considered prostitutes or "public women."
Peddlers shouted their wares while beggars moaned for alms. There
were no public parks. Trees and grass were scarce.

One by one, American middle-class families chose to reside at the
edge of the city rather than in the center. The edge of the city was just a
mile or two away. Depending upon topography, it might be reached by
boat, on horseback, by private carriage, or by an energetic walker.
Historians have debated what the edge was like. Some have written

of the "borderland" as a place where prosperous families who disliked urban congestion might set up housekeeping, lured by the scenic
charm of living near farmers' fields and woods.[1] These affluent families sought more delicate amenities than noisy urban centers could
offer—pure air, pure water, access to fields and gardens, meadows
where children might play, lanes where women might walk, trees that
would offer shady relief from the stifling summer heat of the city. Were
the families who thought they were moving to "the country" on the
borders of the city misled?

The periphery of the city in this era was not the country. The edge
was neither rural nor urban. It formed a distinctive gateway zone
between city and country. Entrepreneurs in this zone ran industries
that required extensive space, such as ice gangs, glassworks, and rope
walks, and more noxious ones such as tanneries, soap factories, glue
factories, powder works, slaughterhouses, and brick factories. In the
summers, religious revivals staked their tents in the borderland. In
addition, the periphery included small businessmen who handled traffic to and from the rural hinterland, carters and wheelwrights. "The
scattered centers, the absence of dense settlement, the fuzziness of
boundaries, the bucolic appearance of the landscape—all these bore a
resemblance to the country," Henry Binford observes in his study of
Boston's first suburbs of Cambridge and Somerville. "To many outside observers, the suburbs of this period seemed an economic back-
water." It was easy to misread the "awkward embrace" of city and
country. Residents might have entertained bucolic fantasies about
moving to the countryside, but they entered a zone of "improvement
enterprise and the fringe economy," where shrewd local business people calculated how to turn them into customers.[2] Borderland bankers,
real estate salespeople, transit owners, and landscape gardeners were
among the earliest suburban growth promoters.

Contest over land defined the borderland. This contest began as a
cultural tension between rural farmers who wanted to farm and more
sophisticated residents who worked in the city but wanted to live amid
fields, woods, and meadows. It became a sustained economic conflict
between those who viewed the landscape as a place to rest from profit-
ing elsewhere and those who viewed it as a place to make a profit.
Sooner or later, the quest for borderland life in a pastoral setting and
the growth of hinterland enterprises led to the systematic subdivision,

sale, and development of residential property. With new residential development, debates about public transportation intensified. Would residents patronize the steamboat, steam railroad, omnibus, horsecar, and, eventually, electric streetcar? Would they accept supporting infrastructure such as piers, tracks, paving, rails, and wires?

None of the new transportation technologies caused suburban development. Transportation technology enabled rival groups of businessmen to push lines out of the city or pull them into fringe areas in order to maximize their investments in land. From the commuter's point of view, early suburban transportation was often arduous and irregular. First the omnibus carried small groups on an infrequent basis. Then steam railroads or horsecars served larger groups on more regular schedules, but they were still prone to accidents and delays. The fare determined which class would choose to travel, and how far. As transport started to carry people to the periphery on a regular basis, more systematic selling of land occurred. Sometimes businessmen who developed the transportation subdivided the land, while at other times different entrepreneurs were involved. Public transport always provoked local debates on how borderland residents could "control the degree of their urbanization."[3]

By the 1840s, around Boston, New York, and many other cities, the borderland was both fiercely protected and actively developed. Residents who favored retaining pastoral charm opposed those who had a financial stake in expanding their business interests. Class, crosscut by occupation, influenced citizens' positions on future development. While all classes lived in the borderlands, the rich had two houses, one on the fringe and one in the city. The poor were farmers or farm workers with small dwellings. Only middle-class men and women tried to have it all, to sustain a country ambiance near the city with just one residence. They struggled with the difficult commutes and became the most ardent defenders of building single-family houses among the trees and flowers, removed from the pollution, epidemics, and economic stresses of the city. Rejecting the urban row house and looking down on the country farmhouse, they invented a new approach to residential space located on the borders of the city.

By boosting a new style of suburban life, middle-class illustrators and writers also made important contributions to emerging suburban growth machines. Nathaniel Parker Willis's *American Scenery* of 1840 celebrated the visual pleasures of the urban fringe as well as more remote places. Borderland residents delighted in natural settings where they could look back at the city they had escaped, yet they savored being close enough to engage with urban life on a regular schedule. In Bartlett's scenic view of the broad Hudson River from the rocky heights of Weehawken, New Jersey, the careful observer can discern a small sailboat approaching a pier where passengers wait in line to be ferried across the water to the distant buildings of Manhattan. In his view of the Brooklyn ferry, farmers with carts of hay share the ride with fashionably dressed women who might be going shopping.

The new suburban way of life appeared in manuals of advice for homeowners and prospective owners. Middle-class families who

Church steeples and ships' masts are the tallest structures in distant Manhattan.
Detail of *View of New York, from Weehawken,* steel engraving
from a drawing by W. H. Bartlett, in Nathaniel Parker Willis,
American Scenery, vol. 2 (London: G. Virtue, 1840).
Beinecke Rare Book and Manuscript Library, Yale University.

Farmers with carts of hay share the deck with well-dressed women heading
for the city. Detail of *The Ferry at Brooklyn, New York,* steel engraving
from a drawing by W. H. Bartlett, in Nathaniel Parker Willis,
American Scenery, vol. 2 (London: G. Virtue, 1840).
Beinecke Rare Book and Manuscript Library, Yale University.

sought out the borderland needed to define the material culture appropriate for new settings. Two inspirational leaders produced best-sellers
about suburban properties. Although all prescriptive literature needs
to be read with a skeptical eye, one man and one woman offered
exceptional insights about the possible configurations of suburban
space. Andrew Jackson Downing achieved renown for his landscape designs for middle-class suburban properties. Catharine Esther
Beecher achieved an even greater influence with designs for houses to
support middle-class women. She offered technologies for heating,
ventilating, cooking, and bathing, as well as instructions on spiritual
guardianship of family life. Together they had a broad influence in
shaping the romantic, remote yards and houses favored by middle-
class suburban families whose gender roles were thought to derive
from divine authority.

MR. DOWNING'S GOSPEL OF TASTE

Born in 1815 in Newburgh, New York, a small town on the west side of the Hudson about fifty miles north of Manhattan, Andrew Jackson Downing was the youngest son of a prosperous wheelwright, nurseryman, and modest real estate investor. While his father was a borderland entrepreneur who had risen from fixing wheels to selling land, Downing had much more ambitious ideas about his own upward mobility. He attended an exclusive boarding school where, among other subjects, he learned drawing. His formal education ended at age sixteen, when he resisted his mother's advice to clerk in a store and joined his older brother in running their late father's nursery. Downing cultivated wealthy and aristocratic friends, including Baron Alois von Lederer, Austria's consul general in New York.[4] In 1838 he married Caroline Elizabeth DeWint, the daughter of a wealthy land speculator with investments in the local railroad and ferry lines. With the backing of her father, the young couple built an elegant Gothic revival house on land Downing inherited from his parents.

Downing published *A Treatise on the Theory and Practice of Landscape Gardening* in 1841. The book borrowed heavily from *The Suburban Gardener, and Villa Companion,* published in 1838 by British author J. C. Loudon, and was aided by six illustrations of the work of the innovative American architect A. J. Davis, author of *Rural Residences.*[5] Downing's work could not be called original, but it was popular. The New York firm of Wiley and Putnam put out Downing's book for $3.50, a relatively expensive item on their list, which included horticulture, farming, Christian virtues, and household topics. The book brought customers to his Botanic Garden and Nurseries and drew new clients for his landscaping services. He began shipping plants all over the United States and had clients asking for help in laying out grounds. "Landscape Gardening bids fair to become a *profession* in this country," he exulted late in 1841.[6] He was a mail-order pioneer as well as a landscape gardening entrepreneur.

Downing promoted the picturesque—defined as a style emulating wild or natural beauty with irregular and broken lines—as well-suited to the scenery of the United States, especially the hills of the Hudson Valley. Enthusiasm for picturesque landscape design, expressed in terms of recent commissions executed for the wealthy, was familiar fare in England. Years earlier, Lancelot "Capability" Brown, the great British designer, had earned his nickname by saying that all of his clients' estates were "capable of improvement." But the adulatory publication of details about rich men's new estates and their new houses was a fresh way of looking for design commissions in the United States in 1841. When his work was praised in England and Germany, Downing was pleased, commenting that his book "seems to have startled the Europeans, who can hardly believe that we have anything but log cabins."[7]

Perhaps the most interesting images in the *Treatise* show how to convert an ordinary farm into a gentleman's estate or "Country Seat" with ten years of planting and work.[8] These sketches suggest that in the borderlands, buying a farmer's land and turning it into a suburban property was what men and women of this era—and indeed every succeeding decade—needed to do. After Downing's suggested improvements, there would be few right angles. A farmer's fields, with a straight access road, would give way to lawns divided by a curving drive and strategically situated trees and bushes. An orchard and a kitchen garden could be added at the rear. The farmhouse itself, if built in some foursquare colonial or federal style, would get a new roofline, almost putting on a new hat, in order to appear fanciful and pointed, with Gothic dormers, accentuated chimneys, and a front piazza adorned with decorative plantings. Downing's obsession with setting a suburban residence behind a wide swath of lawn and his insistence on exaggerated rooflines as proof of "style" are still part of suburban house design today.

In his first book, Downing gave most of his attention to the landscape, but in later books he developed a didactic, missionary zeal for improving the spareness of American farm life, although only the most prosperous farmers could afford his suggestions. He addressed a middle-class audience by talking about upper-class and upper-middle-class properties. For the farm worker or the restless city worker, Downing provided few examples of houses and yards that would be affordable. He claimed that home life would encourage young men to settle down, rather than migrate west in search of opportunity, but offered no suggestions about how to manage the cost of land and building. In *Cottage Residences,* published a year after the *Treatise,* his

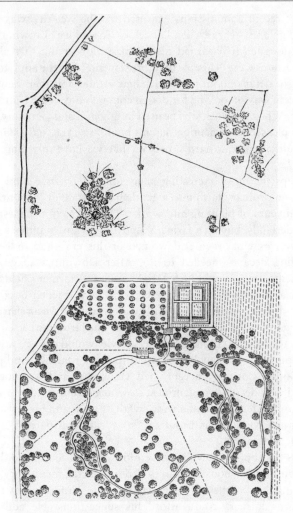

"Plan of a common Farm, before any improvements,"
and "Plan of the foregoing grounds as Country Seat,
after ten years' improvement," from Andrew Jackson
Downing, *Treatise on the Theory and Practice
of Landscape Gardening*, 1841.

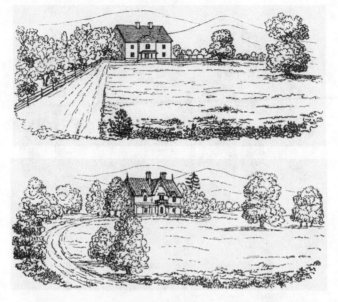

"View of a Country Residence, as frequently seen, and as improved," from Andrew Jackson Downing, *Treatise on the Theory and Practice of Landscape Gardening,* 1841.

design for "A suburban cottage for a small family" appeared. To be located "in the suburbs of a town or village," this house was placed on a lot 150 feet by 75 feet (about a quarter-acre). It included seven rooms and over 1,760 square feet of space. The estimated cost was $1,800. When Downing described this as a "simple cottage" of "very moderate size" for a "family of small means, leading a comparatively retired life," he spoke the coded language of *Pride and Prejudice,* where Elizabeth Bennet's house is modest only in contrast to Mr. Darcy's vast estate.[9] Downing's condescension becomes grating as he quotes Abraham Cowley, the seventeenth-century poet: "I must confess, I love littleness almost in all things. A little cheerful house, a little company, and a very little feast."[10]

Downing claimed that he wanted ordinary Americans to live more tasteful and fashionable lives. Unfortunately, he actively disparaged excellent American vernacular architecture. He did not care for coun-

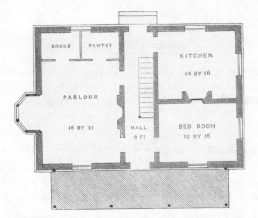

BOOKS | PANTRY

KITCHEN

14 BY 16

PARLOUR

16 BY 21

HALL

6 F⸱

BED ROOM

12 BY 16

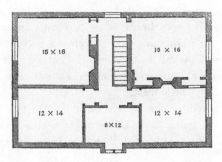

15 × 16

15 × 16

12 × 14

8 × 12

12 × 14

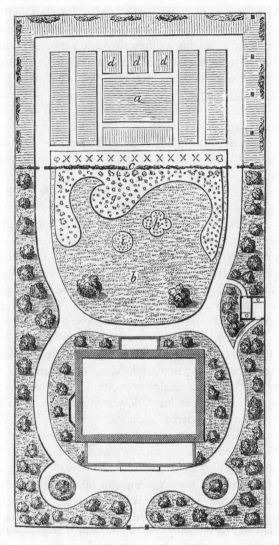

"A suburban cottage for a small family," Andrew Jackson Downing, *Cottage Residences,* 1842, including main floor plan, second floor plan, and landscape plan for the yard. The kitchen garden with vines at right contains an asparagus bed (*a*), herbs (*d*), rhubarb (*x*), lawn (*b*), ornamental trellis (*c*), outer border of trees and shrubs (*e*), turf border with fragrant shrubs (*f*), arabesque border of perennials (*g*), bed of roses (*h*), and bed of mignonette (*i*). The yard also includes a two-seat outdoor privy at right.

try builders' farmhouses and barns in New England and New York, designed with a strong sense of proportion based on the golden section. Downing urged his readers to demonstrate personal style by remodeling or replacing the local builders' neoclassical houses. Despite "the almost universal prevalence of wooden country houses in the United States," Downing did not like wooden houses, preferring stone, brick, or stucco, very Anglophile choices. He hated white houses, preferring grays and tans, "cheerful mellow hue[s] harmonizing with the verdure of the country."[11] For domestic architecture he recommended "Rural Gothic" and "Italian" styles. Everything else was uncultured and obsolete.

Downing was not a good amateur architect.[12] He lavished his energies on the landscaping of his "Suburban Cottage." One-third of the lot was given over to the kitchen garden, where fruits and vegetables could be grown. Around the kitchen garden he placed a border of fruit trees—pear, peach, plum, cherry, and apricot—and a selection of four vines bearing different kinds of grapes. A trellis covered with honeysuckle, wisteria, clematis, and roses screened the kitchen garden from the ornamental yard. The ornamental grounds were to be planted with shrubs, trees, and flowers. Each area was vividly described. Downing specified nine varieties of plants to keep the grounds in bloom from May to December and suggested twelve perennials to make the flower border at the rear of the house "deliciously fragrant" from March to November.[13] No garden catalog ever offered more seductive copy. His description of a suburban lot as flowering paradise appealed to families everywhere who ordered his plants.

Downing knew a fabulous garden required labor. To the man of the house, he assigned the heavy work, "managing the kitchen garden, the fruit trees, the grass, and the whole of the walks. . . . with perhaps the assistance of a common gardener, or labouring man, for a day or two, at certain seasons of the year." To the wife and daughters he assigned the ornamental side. Downing supposed women "to have a sufficient fondness for flowers, to be willing and glad to spend three times a week, an hour or two, in the cool mornings and evenings of summer, in the pleasing task of planting, tying to neat stakes, picking off decayed flowers, and removing weeds from the borders."[14] Men were instructed to hone their skills at yard work. In Downing's time, the lawn, or "management of a dressed grass surface," was "a somewhat ill-understood subject" for Americans, but Downing endeavored to correct this.[15] Over the next few decades, more and more companies started to cash in on the lawn. A fashion for lawns led to sales of grass seed. After the lawn mower was patented in 1869, some manufacturers promoted it as a romantic device for courtship or equated the ownership of a modest lawn mower with the proprietorship of a vast estate—a sales pitch quite in the spirit of Downing's original *Treatise*.

In *The Architecture of Country Houses,* published in 1850, Downing covered cottages, farmhouses, and villas. A cottage was a small house (starting price, $400); a farmhouse was a substantial rural house (starting price, $1,200); and a villa was a country house for a person of wealth ($4,300 and up). Downing estimated prices for every design (with allowances for different regions of the country and different materials) and also listed prices for the items of furniture, most of them ornate, pictured in a chapter at the end. Everything became a commodity. While promoting his wares, Downing claimed to be writing about culture: "a good house (and by this I mean a fitting, tasteful, and significant dwelling) is a powerful means of civilization."[16]

Much has been written about Downing's expressed desire to en-

"The Archimedean Lawn Mower," 1878 model, produced by Amariah Hills of Hartford, Conn. Trade card, Warshow Collection, Archives Center, National Museum of American History, Smithsonian Institution.

courage restless Americans to settle down, cultivate gardens, build homes, and develop a sense of place. He encouraged "love of home, and with it all the tender affections bound up in that endearing word," saying that the love of home "will be sure to grow with every step we take to add to its comforts or increase its beauty."[17] He connected the good house to the good family as the "best social form" and saw "moral influence in a country home."[18] "The family, whose religion lies away from its threshold, will show but slender results from the best teachings, compared with another where the family hearth is made the central point of the Beautiful and the Good."[19] He gushed about God as the "Great Master whose words, in all his material universe, are written in lines of Beauty."[20] When Downing idealized rural life as a model for suburban residents, his views must have seemed nostalgic to some of his younger colleagues who critiqued the rural life of isolated farm families and discussed social opportunities in the city.

Downing's decision to write about gardens and houses for the American client, not for the builder, marked him as unusual. He supplanted earlier American builders' handbooks, filled with construction details and profiles of moldings, with much more persuasive prose about taste and style addressed to the owners. In the same way, he made scientific material on botany more accessible. Throughout his career, he cultivated the image of a gentleman of leisure. He may have been the first American designer to use his own home as the showcase for all of his ideas, a technique Martha Stewart exploited in the twentieth century. But Downing's Hudson River estate was beyond his means. Difficulties with his wealthy father-in-law about financial matters led to a lawsuit and Downing had to sell his tree nursery to settle his debts. He had a secret door constructed in his library so that he could slip away to another room to write or design while guests never suspected his long hours of work, straining to pay his bills.[21]

Steamboats enabled New Yorkers to reach desirable country properties in the Hudson River Valley, Staten Island, and New Jersey. This early and expensive form of commuting could be dangerous, but the world of second homes and suburban residences it served was essential to Downing's influence. He and his wife boarded the *Henry Clay*, a steamboat stopping at Newburgh on its way to New York in July 1852. The *Henry Clay* was racing the *Armenia* from Albany down the Hudson River, until the *Henry Clay* developed an engine room fire near Yonkers and ran aground. At least seventy people died. Downing was said to have rescued several people before he sank. His wife, Caroline, survived but lost both her husband and her mother in this disaster. Nine weeks later, Downing's heavily mortgaged estate—a model of all the genteel living this tastemaker had preached—had to be sold. His biographer comments, "Ironically, Downing had advised against building large houses because of the transience of wealth and the restless mobility of the American people, yet the property he had inherited from his parents, the house and gardens he had designed and loved, quickly passed to another family."[22] Downing's architectural partner, Calvert Vaux, his friend A. J. Davis, and many other friends and associates would continue his work.

MISS BEECHER'S HOME CHURCH OF JESUS CHRIST

Catharine Beecher's numerous books were read even more widely than Downing's. While he praised the contemplation of God in the cultivation of natural beauty, she pressed her readers to find salvation in the perfection of family life. Author of a *Treatise on Domestic Economy for Use of Young Ladies at Home and at School* (1842) and coauthor of *The American Woman's Home* (1869), Beecher urged women to take charge of the suburban house and family, which she called "the home church of Jesus Christ." She instructed them to stay home and master efficient house design and gardening, as well as the spiritual nurturing of large families.[23] Beecher was the first American writer to produce a manual of domestic life including architecture, landscape architecture, interior design, cooking, cleaning, and child raising. Her books were broader than Downing's in that she addressed nurturing within the home as well as the shaping of domestic space. She was a far more skilled amateur architect than Downing and designed spaces for a range of housekeeping activities in a very precise and innovative way. Her potential audience included every American woman, young and old. Her vision of domesticity was explicitly gendered: women were to create a peaceful domestic world, removed from the stresses of work in the city, and although women would find themselves excluded from the political and economic arenas of public life, they would receive a reward in heaven for their self-sacrifice.

Beecher's family retreat was architecturally very specific. By 1869 it

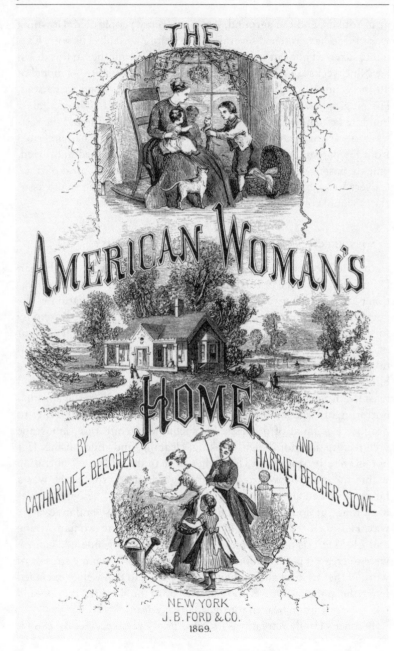

THE
AMERICAN WOMAN'S
HOME

BY
CATHARINE E. BEECHER

AND
HARRIET BEECHER STOWE.

NEW YORK
J. B. FORD & CO.
1869.

Title page, frontispiece, and view
of "A Christian House,"
from Catharine E. Beecher
and Harriet Beecher Stowe,
The American Woman's Home
(New York: J.B. Ford, 1869).

was definitively suburban: "applicable to the wants and habits of those living either in the country or in such suburban vicinities as give space of ground for healthful outdoor occupation in the family service." She allowed that "railroads, enabling men toiling in cities to rear families in the country, are on this account a special blessing."[24] A Gothic cottage, set on a riverbank amid verdant foliage, adorned with images of women, children, pets, and flowers, decorates the title page of the 1869 book, coauthored with Harriet Beecher Stowe, her sister. The frontispiece shows a woman at the center of a three-generation family, reading in front of a hearth. The chapter entitled "A Christian House" begins with an enlarged exterior view of the house, showing three crosses located on the end gables and over the front door.

Unlike Downing, who was launched into horticulture at age sixteen, Beecher arrived at her interest in architecture more slowly. Eldest daughter of Lyman Beecher, a prominent Congregationalist minister, she was born in 1800 in East Hampton, Long Island, the eldest of eight children. She assumed a substantial share of domestic responsibility after her mother died when she was sixteen. At Miss Pierce's

School in Litchfield, Connecticut, her daily journals won prizes, displaying her skill in writing about personal life for public audiences.[25] She and her sister, Harriet, watched all of their brothers depart for college and careers in the ministry. Catharine Beecher then became a drawing instructor in New London, Connecticut. At age twenty-three she established her own school for young ladies in Hartford, Connecticut; at thirty-two she founded the Western Female Seminary in Ohio. Her first book, in 1831, argued for the moral superiority of women, based upon women's dedication to self-sacrifice. She was forty-one when she published the *Treatise,* which sold so well that it assured her financial independence.

A lifelong single woman, although engaged in her youth to a young Yale professor who died on a sea voyage, Beecher advised marrying early, giving up worldly activities, having ten children, and going without servants. She defined household work and nurturing as "woman's true profession," speaking of woman as a "minister." In part this was a response to her own somewhat disappointing experience of organized religion. Beecher never experienced a religious conversion. She felt that by staying clear of religious theory, a woman could gain salvation by practical dedication to the needs of others in a "home church" of her own creation.[26] In part Beecher was also responding to the stirrings of a new movement for women's rights. She launched an assertive call for women's authority in the domestic sphere, but she had in mind a conservative version of women's lives, one that specified women's competence at home but surrendered it in public life. Hers was a "domestic feminism" in contrast to the "social feminism" of temperance advocates like Frances Willard, and the "material feminism" of women who advocated pay for housework, like Melusina Fay Peirce.[27]

Carrying on a busy schedule as an author and lecturer, Beecher never practiced the domestic feminism she preached. Her intense energies were applied to giving hundreds of practical directions. Her book was encyclopedic: how to take care of an invalid, how to plant a garden, and above all, how to build a healthful home which eased a woman's labors. Here she was decades ahead of any professional architect or designer. Having studied the best manuals of architecture, sanitation, and mechanical engineering, as well as books on medicine and etiquette, she applied her own inventive mind to creating dozens of small-scale solutions to the "close packing of conveniences." Over several decades she refined the conventional sketches of Greek revival and Gothic revival houses in the first edition of her *Treatise* so that the final designs in the 1869 book were very advanced. She solved design problems architects were working on well into the twentieth century. During the process, Beecher renamed the rooms where housework would become a kind of liturgy, with its seasonal variations: the parlor became the "home room," the kitchen became the "work room," the dining room became the "family room."[28]

Inside her 1869 house, every square foot was carefully designed by this former drawing instructor. At approximately 2,100 square feet, it was a little larger than Downing's "Suburban Cottage," far more comfortable, and also more fluid in its flow of space. Beecher offered two major parlors to Downing's one. Because she mastered central heating by inserting cast-iron Franklin stoves connected to a central hot-air furnace in the basement, she could avoid small rooms and use space freely. One of the parlors could be subdivided with a novel movable wall. Both parlors included conservatories, windows, and porches. Fresh air was drawn in through ingenious ventilating tubes and foul air extracted through others. In every sense, Beecher's comfortable house anticipated the work of twentieth-century designers.[29]

Most of all, Beecher redefined the kitchen, devising a single-surface workspace with storage for tools and supplies, while hiding the heat of the cooking stove behind sliding glass doors. The "roasted lady" protested by women of the 1840s had no place here. Beecher supplied a kitchen sink with running water. She developed a special counter for making pastry and another for cooking. She organized the storage of dishes and pots. Her shelves were orderly and tools hung on hooks. She paid close attention to modern plumbing. Her house had two indoor bathrooms, one in the basement and one on the bedroom level, at a time when many people were still using "outdoor accommodations" such as Downing had prescribed for his 1842 cottage.[30] In the basement she also organized efficient space for the heavy work of doing the washing and ironing, storing ice, and canning fruits and vegetables.

Beecher's house was clearly a workplace. With Bibles and trundle beds, shelf boxes and sewing boxes, a woman's work was never done. And neither was a man's. Her tone was direct: "Let your men-folk knock up for you, out of rough, un-planed boards, some ottoman

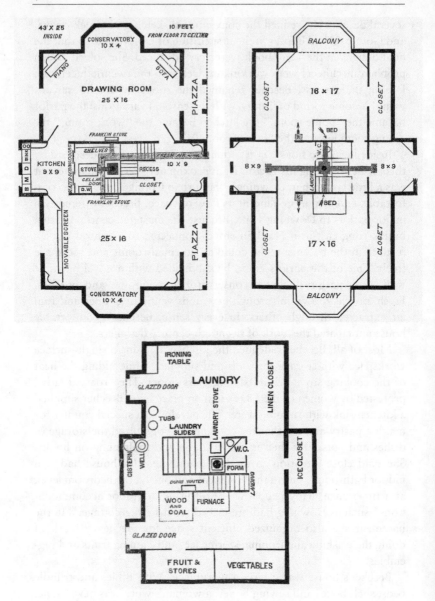

Plans of main floor, second floor, and basement,
from *The American Woman's Home.*

Movable wall with decorative panels (closet space behind),
from *The American Woman's Home.*

frames . . . stuff the tops with just the same material as the lounge, and cover them with the self-same chintz."[31] After making these lambrequins and some white muslin curtains, the housewife could start reupholstering an old, broken-down armchair. *The American Woman's Home* was promoted as "The Cheapest and most Desirable Book of the Year" and as "a Book that should find its way into every Household in the Land." The publishers, J. B. Ford, suggested that "ONE HINT FROM THIS BOOK MAY BE WORTH MANY TIMES THE PRICE OF THE BOOK," which sold for $2.50 in 1869, "replete with the latest and most authentic results of science applicable to domestic life."

After her system was completely worked out for the ideal suburban house, Beecher did note that it might have to be adapted to other circumstances in city or country. She sketched an inner-city apartment and miniaturized some of the furniture so that a resident of a city tenement could still practice being a "home minister." She also designed a combination of house, school, and church for missionary teachers. These were single women who might go to the Southern states after the Civil War to teach in remote communities. The school could be converted to a church if a traveling preacher came by to offer services, and the missionary teachers lived in quarters upstairs over the schoolroom. This schoolroom could be divided with a movable wall. Beecher also became an early advocate of household consumption as necessary to a capitalist economy, recommending the use of multiple consumer

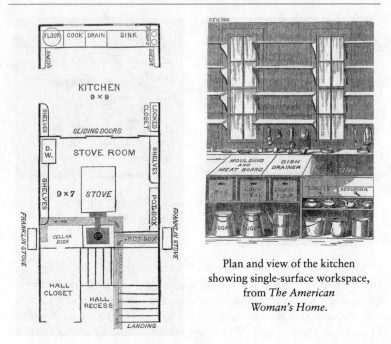

Plan and view of the kitchen
showing single-surface workspace,
from *The American
Woman's Home.*

goods, or "superfluities," in order "to promote industry, virtue and religion" by keeping people employed in diverse kinds of production.[32]

LEGACIES OF PRESCRIPTIVE LITERATURE

It is hard for Americans to remember that before Downing and Beecher, most families lived in city centers or rural areas, the man was assumed to be head of the house in all matters, and most middle-class families had domestic servants. The gendered, pious approach to middle-class suburban life—man nurturing the yard, woman the house and family—first laid out by these two best-selling authors, stands at the heart of our culture. Their views of the proper ways to build and decorate have remained influential, especially Beecher's designs for a well-plumbed, well-heated, well-ventilated set of spaces for work and family life.

Yet these authors from the era of manual mania tied themselves in knots. Downing was a social climber whose run-on sentences took on a snobbish, pious tone; Beecher grew up debating theology with highly educated men of the ministry and strove for a more chatty, gossipy voice. He knew his fruits and fruit trees and flowering vines, but aspired to aristocratic architecture; she knew how to open up space but could not resist suggestions for decorating that made her handbook look more Victorian. He was a relatively poor man struggling for social position and economic security. She was an intelligent middle-class woman who wanted a public life. Both hid their anxieties behind piety. Family life eluded them at times. Downing was not interested in children. Beecher claimed that women should devote themselves to the nurturing of children, though she herself had a busy public schedule.

Contemporaries showered praise on these two writers, so very little criticism of their idiosyncrasies appeared. In the borderland, women did complain of "Lonelyville" for the next several decades. Suburban living left more than one mother bereft, complaining, "The busy men leave on early trains and are at once plunged into the rush of their accustomed life among their usual associates, while the suburban woman remains at home, standing beside the struggling young vines of her brand new Piazza."[33] Both Downing and Beecher thought about this problem of isolation in a very tentative way. He suggested public parks surrounded by romantic houses in rural towns. She said women might benefit from neighborhood laundries and other shared services. For Downing and Beecher, the borderland was a place where families chose to go, one by one. Their main topics were the yard and the house, enhanced by broad discussion about taste and spirituality. The neighborhood, with its potential for conflict and discord, was not a congenial topic. They articulated two parts of the dream, house and nature, but failed to understand the intense desire for community on the part of potential suburban residents.

In their fixed attention to space at the scale of the yard and house, Downing and Beecher also missed a chance to point out the inherent contradictions of the borderland. These advice givers could not solve the key problem facing borderland families: the advance of the city. Once-remote houses in pastoral locations were, sooner or later, perceived as not so distant. The landscape could be invaded by new industries. The residents could be surprised by the shanties of squatters, who might keep goats and pigs or steal their middle-class neighbors' timber.[34] Over and over, dwellers in the fringe reinvented themselves as advocates of a pastoral life, but again and again their landscapes succumbed to the pressures of new development. Downing's Newburgh, a quiet town in the 1830s, acquired a cotton mill in 1845 staffed by three hundred unskilled women workers, located just three blocks from Downing's own house. This distressed him, but the owners of the Newburgh Steam Mills used their profits to commission his new services as a landscape consultant for their private residences.[35] Like many architects and landscape architects, he straddled the contradiction and perhaps liked to pretend he didn't notice the mill or the poor women who worked there. Factories would continue to locate in metropolitan peripheries, and many would continue to ignore them. When some speculators laid out a crude grid on the banks of the Hudson near Irvington (then called Dearman) in 1850, they decorated their plat with images of a couple of his "cottage residences." Downing had to notice. He published a piece about better ways to deal with "Our Country Villages," but he never designed one.[36]

Borderland ideals have lasted. Many Americans still believe in an endless amount of available land. They hope for new technologies of transportation and communication that will overcome the friction of distance. Always reinvented, always unsatisfactory, the borderland advanced as affluent residents converted farms to houses in every succeeding decade. In the first half of the nineteenth century, residents, designers, and pattern book writers forged enduring ideals of romantic houses set in picturesque terrain. Many of the spatial conventions that Downing and Beecher established remain to the present day, tangled in religious piety and middle-class manners.

The borderland has always existed more vividly in prescriptive literature than in the lives of real families. The old advice manuals created an imaginary place where houses existed as drawings that each reader could enter and inhabit, images of family togetherness enjoyed in a leafy pastoral setting. When real houses were built or remodeled, one at a time, inevitably they changed the character of the borderland landscape. The most desirable attribute of the borderland, closeness to nature, was also its greatest vulnerability because of the pressure to develop land. The rustic landscape could not bear sustained observation because of its inherently unstable character, but the generation after Downing and Beecher thought they might be able to improve the borderland, so they designed the enclave.

Chapter Four

PICTURESQUE ENCLAVES

No great town can long exist without great suburbs.
— FREDERICK LAW OLMSTED

A RCHITECTS AND LANDSCAPE ARCHITECTS began to design picturesque enclaves in the 1850s. These were entire new communities with curving roads that followed irregular local topography. Houses were sited amid heavy planting adjacent to shared parks and other common spaces so that they appeared to be wrapped in greenery. The residents who purchased building lots in these enclaves were responding to the social isolation experienced by families in borderland locations. The designers of enclaves added a sense of community to the borderland goals of house and land, becoming the first to express the triple dream. Picturesque enclaves were the most important secular manifestation of a wider communitarian movement whose adherents believed that building a model community in a natural setting led to the reform of society. Designers and developers of two of the earliest and most important picturesque suburbs, Llewellyn Park in West Orange, New Jersey, and Riverside, Illinois, had strong personal connections to the Fourierist branch of the communitarian movement. These designers believed that shared open space was essential to a new kind of community life.

THE ORIGINS OF PICTURESQUE ENCLAVES

In debates about the precedents for the design of the earliest American picturesque enclaves, the communitarian settlements of the 1840s and 1850s have often been neglected. Architectural and cultural historians say that British designers of "villa parks" spurred the fashion. Landscape historians have cited picturesque cemeteries and parks as possible influences. Real estate historians argue that urban land speculators led the way. Dozens of communitarian socialist experiments, built in both religious and secular forms in the United States, received far more publicity at the time and were more directly influential. Locating the origins of contemporary suburbia in popular social movements of the 1840s begins to explain why community became an enduring part of the triple dream. It also highlights how much has been forgotten.

Subdividers of Urban Real Estate

Throughout the 1820s, 1830s, and 1840s, developers subdividing land in locations adjacent to the centers of New York and Boston looked for ways to promise middle-class community to potential customers. Subdividers of real estate—urban or suburban—never liked to sell land one plot at a time. A large concentration of affluent residents committed to building houses provides a much safer investment for new buyers and a better return on the project. Around 1820, Hezekiah Pierrepont, a backer of Robert Fulton's steamboat in 1814, turned sixty acres in Brooklyn Heights into lots measuring 25 by 100 feet (the typical size for Manhattan, calculated for masonry row houses with rear yards).[1] Although the location was a rocky, agricultural area, views across the East River provided a sense of open space. Some houses were built on double lots at the start, gaining wider frontages and vistas, but the pattern of development turned to a grid of narrow urban row houses. Similar developments were launched in Boston in the 1850s with the filling of the Back Bay and the South End. Generally, the Boston developers also platted grids of narrow lots for row houses. While there were some squares with green space in the South End, and public parks drew buyers of lots to the Back Bay, the shape these neighborhoods took was defined by the middle-class urban row house.[2] Although some historians have called Brooklyn Heights the first suburb, neither Brooklyn Heights nor the Boston projects provided models for the picturesque enclave. They are better understood as extensions of urban housing models from the affluent neighborhoods of Manhattan and Beacon Hill.

Villa Parks

"Villa parks" were launched by developers in England as clusters of detached single-family houses situated on substantial private lots around shared landscaped settings, which might be public parks. Situated outside the large industrial cities, they changed the earlier image of the suburb as a "licensed stewe" of crime or a place for "suburb sinners," slang for prostitutes. The villa parks followed the informal example of late eighteenth-century Clapham, outside of London, where wealthy families who shared evangelical religious beliefs had created an enclave.[3] John Nash designed the Regent's Canal Village in London of 1823 and then collaborated with James Morgan on the Newbold Comyn Estate at Leamington in 1827. Richard Lane created Victoria Park in Manchester in 1837. Joseph Paxton and James Pennethorne designed Prince's Park in Liverpool in 1842 and Paxton began Birkenhead Park outside Liverpool the following year. As John Archer has documented, villa parks provided views of trees and grass for affluent families, but the houses were not always immersed in privacy amid lush greenery. Sometimes they included row houses or semidetached houses, and they appealed to residents who found a suburban community more desirable than an isolated rural house. John Claudius Loudon's *The Suburban Gardener* of 1838 advised, "One immense advantage of a suburban residence over one isolated in the country consists of its proximity to neighbors, and the facilities it affords of participating in those sources of instruction and enjoyment which can only be obtained in towns." He went on to promote the benefits of social homogeneity in a suburban neighborhood and the possibilities such a location offered for the personal appreciation of nature.[4]

By the mid-1830s, American architects were designing developments of single-family detached houses with gardens on the outskirts of cities. In 1836, a development at New Brighton, on Staten Island, attributed to British émigré architect John Haviland, arrayed three rows of villas on a hillside overlooking the water and advertised direct access throughout the day by steamboat to lower Manhattan. The design included bathing houses (for swimmers) and two resort hotels. In the late 1830s and 1840s, the resort hotels were drawing visitors

George A. Ward, *Description of New Brighton on Staten Island . . .
New York 1836.* Lithograph by P. Mesier, detail. Milstein Division of U. S.
History, New York Public Library, Astor, Lenox, and Tilden Foundations.

who might eventually wish to live there. A landowner just to the west
of New Brighton then commissioned a plan for several houses from
American architect William H. Ranlett in 1847.[5] While Haviland's
and Ranlett's designs are charming, and resort hotels often did become
part of the promotion of affluent enclaves, these two plans did not
engage the topography, aside from positioning houses for water views.
Haviland's plan offered three parallel rows of buildings, while Ranlett's can be described as houses and gardens inserted into a grid.

Picturesque Cemeteries and Parks

In the 1830s more elaborate examples of picturesque landscape design
began to appear in the new cemeteries of Boston, New York, and
Philadelphia, where naturally varied topography was enhanced by
winding roads, ponds, streams, and groves of trees. The movement
for suburban "rural" cemeteries was supported by authorities in medicine and health, such as Dr. Jacob Bigelow of Harvard University,
who helped to create the Mount Auburn Cemetery in Cambridge in
1831. Green-Wood in Brooklyn was established in 1838. The rural
cemetery was also a result of rising prices for inner-city real estate,
which pushed less profitable uses to the edge. The cities that established cemeteries as green spaces with heavy picturesque planting

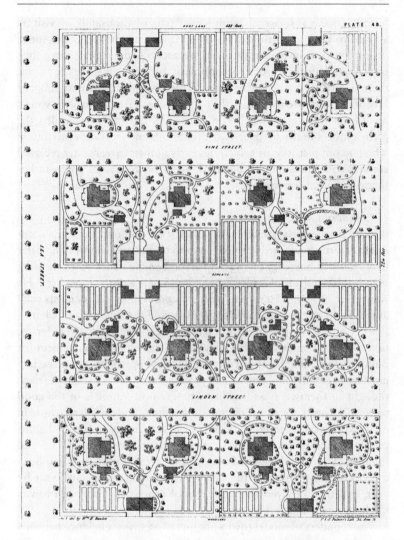

Design for houses west of New Brighton, Staten Island,
for Col. N. Barrett, by William H. Ranlett, *The Architect*, vol. 1
(New York, 1847). Beinecke Rare Book and
Manuscript Library, Yale University.

found—to the surprise of many—that tens of thousands of visitors arrived to walk amid the gravestones. Transcendentalists could speak of finding God in nature in these precincts. A movement for public parks was launched from the popularity of the cemeteries, but was there a direct connection between cemetery and residential suburb? Historian John Archer argues the negative, because the imagery would have been too lugubrious.[6] The cemeteries movement preceded the picturesque suburb by over two decades. Some landscape architects who laid out picturesque cemeteries early in their careers later received commissions for suburbs, but most went on to design parks rather than residential communities.[7]

Communitarian Settlements

A more persuasive argument can be made for the founders of communitarian settlements, who aimed to combine city and country and offer new forms of housing. In 1840 Emerson commented, "Not a reading man but has a draft of a new community in his waistcoat pocket." He was referring to materials published by communitarian socialists such as the Shakers, the Oneida Perfectionists, and the followers of Charles Fourier at the North American Phalanx, near Red Bank, New Jersey, or at Brook Farm in West Roxbury, Massachusetts. The movement for building communitarian towns in the United States began in the late eighteenth century and reached its peak in the 1840s. Communitarians thought of themselves as building "patent office models of the good society."[8] They strove to perfect their dwellings and their landscapes in order to display material evidence of the superiority of their religious beliefs or their political views. Communitarians, both native-born and immigrants, chose the United States as the location for over two hundred experiments because the frontier was moving westward, year by year, and they believed that residents of other new American towns might copy their example.

The founders of model towns attempted to strike a balance between agriculture and industry, so very difficult to create in the industrial cities of the Eastern seaboard. Their site plans suggested that innovative combinations of the country and the city could be achieved. All of them also offered new forms of public space and living quarters, from private apartments to communal dwellings of various kinds. Many argued that more imaginative dwellings could improve women's status by providing technological support for laundry or food preparation, or by arranging space for collective child care. Dealing with complex issues of authority and participation, community and privacy, uniqueness and replicability, the most successful communitarians set high standards of village design. Tourists from around the nation and from Europe often journeyed to see their towns.[9]

The communitarians' claims to sanctity were all different, but perhaps the most persuasive were the Shakers, who claimed to be turning the earth into heaven at twenty-one different villages in New England, New York, and the Midwest.[10] The largest Shaker village, with its expansive model farm at New Lebanon, New York, and the nearby Shaker settlement at Hancock, Massachusetts, were places of great charm. Beautifully proportioned dwellings, barns, and workshops stretched in linear villages near fields and woodlands, supported by agriculture, an herb and seed industry, and chair-making and brick-making factories. In the 1840s each Shaker village also established a holy mountain sanctuary where the residents celebrated the beauties of nature. These mountain sanctuaries were places of intricate landscape symbolism, used for rituals representing the experience of heaven. From the mountains, Shakers could look down to admire their considerable skills in village design.

While the Shakers' celibate villages were severe in their basically federal forms and proportions, eclectic Italianate architecture characterized John Humphrey Noyes's "mansion house" with landscaped grounds in Oneida, New York. Here, several hundred Oneida Perfectionists practiced "complex marriage" beginning in 1848. They raised their children in common. Andrew Jackson Downing's "Southern Villa, Romanesque Style," was the model for the elaborate second mansion house at Oneida by architects Erastus Hamilton and Lewis W. Leeds of New York.[11] They also favored viewing places. This building included a tower so that community members could climb up to admire their picturesque grounds.

Many influential intellectuals and artists were drawn to the secular equivalents of these religious communitarian settlements, especially the communities following the ideas of French social theorist Charles Fourier. Fourier suggested that settlements of sixteen hundred people could combine agriculture and industry and work toward "Harmony." Fourier's leading American disciple, Albert Brisbane, was the son of a wealthy land speculator from Batavia, New York. Brisbane began to popularize "Association" on Fourier's principles as a form of social evolution that could lead to the improvement of society and the disappearance of class conflict through gradual stages of voluntary cooperation. He made it sound a little like a joint-stock corporation. Beginning in 1842, Brisbane wrote a column on the front page of Horace Greeley's *New York Tribune,* and launched over twenty experiments in community building. Some of them adopted the ideal of a "Unitary Dwelling" rather like an apartment house or hotel, but others began to experiment with private houses as part of a cooperative association.

One such experiment was called "Industrial Home Association Number 1," a suburban community in Mount Vernon, New York, headed by John Stevens, a tailor. The association, which included Greeley as a sponsoring member, purchased five farms totaling 370 acres. The common purpose was "protection against the unjust power and influence of capital, and against land monopoly as the efficient cause of poverty." The land was to be divided into quarter-acre lots with no member having more than one share. Four half-acre lots were allocated for schools, and a half-acre for a railroad station on the New York, New Haven, and Harlem Railroad. By 1852, about three hundred families were in residence or constructing their houses.[12] Plans for the school were neoclassical, the town was on a regular grid, and only the railroad station partook of the Gothic revival. Many of Mount Vernon's members sold their lots to outsiders by the 1860s, but it is a strong example of the connections between the founding of secular cooperative communities and suburban towns.[13]

Efforts to build according to Fourier's theory of "Association" involved leaders who later worked on picturesque suburbs. One of Brisbane's many converts was Marcus Spring, a wealthy dry goods merchant from New York. Spring became a patron of the North American Phalanx, an experimental community in Red Bank, New Jersey. In 1852, he built a private cottage in the Gothic style, right on the grounds next to the community dwelling, which included many private apartments. Spring also founded another Fourierist community, the Raritan Bay Union at Eagleswood, New Jersey, in 1853. Again Spring insisted on a single-family house for himself. He lived in the house of the original owners of the estate, while across the lawn he erected an elaborate Italianate collective dwelling designed by A. J. Davis.[14] The residents at Eagleswood included Angelina and Sarah

Grimké, noted advocates of both women's rights and abolition, and Theodore Weld, abolitionist husband of Angelina Grimké. Elizabeth Cady Stanton visited them and considered joining the community herself.[15] She enrolled two sons in the school run by the Grimkés.

Marcus Spring carried Fourier's ideas to broad intellectual and artistic circles. Spring visited Downing and Fredrika Bremer, Swedish author of a volume called *Homes of the New World,* in Newburgh. Bremer was one of many journalists who visited the North American Phalanx to report on the household arrangements of "Association." Landscape designer Frederick Law Olmsted, who knew Spring, Downing, and Davis, also visited the North American Phalanx and came often to Eagleswood. He lived on Staten Island just across Raritan Bay and wrote testimonials for the Associationist movement. Olmsted spoke well of the North American's political atmosphere, though not of the economic resources for aesthetic development.[16] All of these intellectuals believed that the reform of society was tied to the development of appropriate "social architecture" in natural settings.[17] Environmental determinism united them, as well as a preference for the picturesque. They also believed that the reform of society would progress in stages, and that each stage might involve different levels of sharing, moving from the individual to the collective. In the national debate about model homes and model families launched by Downing

Raritan Bay Union, Eagleswood, New Jersey (near Perth Amboy). View of the house of Marcus Spring and the new phalanx designed by Alexander Jackson Davis. Detail of a map of Perth Amboy, Staten Island, and South Amboy, by Thomas A. Hurley, 1858. From the collections of the New Jersey Historical Society.

and Beecher, Davis and Olmsted were prepared to weigh in on the side of collective life rather than the isolated family. But it was not just the fully collective life of Fourier's phalanx they promoted. Instead they worked out steps on the road to collective life, expressed as the development of public parks in Olmsted's case and as the creation of individual homes, shared grounds, and community rituals for the model suburb by both Olmsted and Davis.[18] Thus, some picturesque enclaves were designed with the same communitarian fervor and environmental determinism as the phalanxes, even if the underlying economic force was understood as the development of borderland real estate.

LLEWELLYN PARK, WEST ORANGE, NEW JERSEY: "HAPPY PARTNERSHIP"

Llewellyn Haskell, a successful wholesale pharmaceuticals magnate and the developer of the first picturesque enclave, was a religious Perfectionist who believed that by right living one might attain a spiritually perfected existence on earth. Haskell grew up in New Gloucester, Maine, near the Sabbathday Lake Shaker community established in 1794. As a youth, he admired the evolution of the Shaker settlement. As an older man, he tried to achieve a secular, marketable version of this process at Llewellyn Park, New Jersey, advertising "Country Homes for City People." He attracted wealthy businessmen, social reformers, and religious enthusiasts. Transported twelve miles from the center of New York by ferry and train to a former spa located in mountainous terrain south of the Palisades, residents expected this new community would give them a healthy and uplifting connection to nature. Unlike most communitarians, the founder and residents of this picturesque enclave were rich.

Haskell hired Alexander Jackson Davis, the most brilliant and original designer of his time, an architect who had decades of experience designing both public buildings and private villas along the Hudson, in Staten Island, and in Connecticut. Davis had produced a beautiful guide to *Rural Residences* in 1837, including an "American Cottage," a "Farmer's House," and a "Villa" with wife on the porch and husband wheeling a child in a stroller.[19] In 1841 Davis had contributed examples of his many elegant country houses to illustrate Downing's *Treatise*. Haskell first hired Davis to build a speculative house near

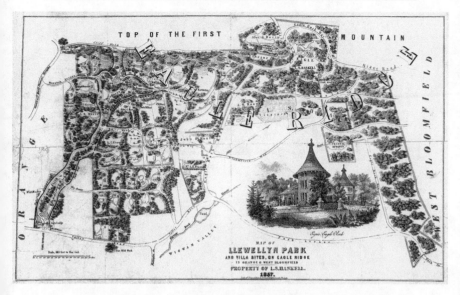

"Site of Llewellyn Park, and Villa Sites on Eagle Ridge in Orange and West Bloomfield, New Jersey, 1857." The Eyrie, Haskell's home, is pictured at bottom right. Site plan by Alexander Jackson Davis. Lithograph, The Metropolitan Museum of Art, Harris Brisbane Dick Fund, 1924.

Belleville, New Jersey, in 1850. The two became close friends, and Davis designed a house for Haskell's own use, labeling the salon, the dining room, and the parlor, Mind, Body, and Soul.[20] He got on so well with his client that his next job in 1852 was to remodel an old farmhouse for him on a wild tract of land. This turned into a commission to design an entire new community at Llewellyn Park, at a time when Davis had a simultaneous commission for the Raritan Bay Union phalanx just a few miles away in Eagleswood, New Jersey.[21]

Haskell's mountainous land on Eagle Ridge, about twelve miles from New York City, offered breathtaking views, steep cliffs, waterfalls, and ponds. Haskell and his friends had the funds to hire Davis to work with the craggy terrain. He surrounded the houses with nature while achieving Victorian comfort with full-time, live-in servants. Davis designed the site plan. His other architectural projects there included his own house, Haskell's house, speculative houses for

AMERICAN COTTAGE Nº I

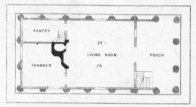

FARMER'S HOUSE

FIRST FLOOR.   SECOND FLOOR.

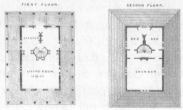

VILLA. DESIGNED FOR DAV. CODWISE. ESQ., BY A.J.DAVIS, ARCT.

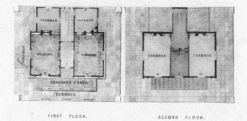

FIRST FLOOR.   SECOND FLOOR.

"American Cottage," "Farmer's House," and "Villa Designed
for David Codwise, Esq.," by Alexander Jackson Davis, from
Rural Residences (New York, 1837). Hand-colored lithographs,
Beinecke Rare Book and Manuscript Library, Yale University.

Haskell, small structures for the community (two gate lodges, the gate,
rustic settees, rustic kiosks, a "wigwam," and all the bridges) as well
as houses for many private clients there. The work continued over several decades.

Haskell's fabulous house, The Eyrie, sited in a spectacular spot atop
Eagle Rock, was an older house extended with new structures made of
the local stone and cedar boles. As Susan Henderson describes it:
"Vertical siding made from the bark of tulip trees, carefully procured
to insure that the fragile mosses and lichens would remain intact, covered the wooden tower and the body of the house. Atop the wooden
tower three lens windows in the conical roof magnified the view:
reportedly one could read the names of the ships in New York Harbor

E. W. Nichols House, designed by Alexander Jackson Davis,
Llewellyn Park, N.J. Watercolor, The Metropolitan Museum
of Art, Harris Brisbane Dick Fund, 1924.

Wildmont, Alexander Jackson Davis's summer cottage,
Llewellyn Park, N.J. Pen and wash drawing, The Metropolitan Museum of Art, Harris Brisbane Dick Fund, 1924.

and the time on the clock of City Hall."[22] The thirty-foot-high viewing tower, equipped with a powerful telescope, enabled these borderland residents to look back at the city in a theatrical manner. A. J. Davis built his own weekend house on twenty-five acres next to his best client. Called Wildmont, it was a board-and-batten structure in the Gothic style, a summer cottage with a fanciful tower. Davis surrounded it with a picturesque garden.

The building process intensified in the late 1850s. At its height, around 1870, Haskell owned about 750 acres, and was planning to sell home sites of one to twenty acres to about one hundred families. By that time, perhaps fifty lots had been sold and thirty families were in residence.[23] Lots were not standardized but purchasers did sign a covenant: minimum land purchase was one acre; each owner would have one vote per acre concerning the management of the commonly held land; fees for maintenance were ten dollars per acre owned, per year; commercial land uses were prohibited. No fences would be built. One commentator called it a semipublic or "social park."[24] One landowner, editor Theodore Tilton, said: "Each estate being isolated from the next, yet each, by a happy partnership with every other, possessing the whole park in common, so that the fortunate purchaser of two or three acres becomes a virtual owner of the whole five hundred; a plan by which a poor man, for a few thousands of dollars, may buy a country seat that challenges comparison with the Duke of Devonshire's."[25] While this comment seems a bit naive, it suggests the Associationist spirit of the place.

Within the park, Davis and others who collaborated on the landscaping, including Haskell, Eugene Baumann, and Howard Daniels, developed a narrative sequence that could be experienced from the ten miles of carriage ways that wound around the community. Anyone lucky enough to be invited to Llewellyn Park would have a series of distinct landscape experiences. The drives offered views of distant landscapes as well as close-ups of forests and meadows. Thousands of trees were imported. Shrubs and flowers were situated in appropriate spots. A brook falling down a 650-foot cliff provided drama.

Particular landscape effects were developed at distinctive sites. Susan Henderson has discussed the design and plantings in detail. Willow Pond graced the area immediately adjacent to the Gate Lodge. Weeping trees were found at the water's edge, cascades tumbled over rough stones at either end. Beyond Willow Pond was a forest mixing deciduous and evergreen trees of both native and exotic kinds along a carriage way leading to Glen Ellyn, the most rugged and indigenous area, where oaks and elms towered over a path that ran along the ravine and past waterfalls, ponds, and rustic bridges. From Glen Ellyn one came to the Ramble, a series of forests interspersed with meadows. A final meadow was reached at Loch Elm. Winding stairs led to a walk along the cliff edge called the Rocks and Cliff Walk. Because so much energy, money, and talent were expended on shaping mountainous terrain with many spots for contemplation, each one a landscape of a different kind, Llewellyn Park introduced to the United States a new residential idea: the heavily landscaped suburb with substantial private houses next to shared parks. One hundred households had taken themselves away from the bustle and contagion of New York City to live on this remarkable mountain. Haskell and Davis introduced a scheme for retreat that was no longer about a single family, but about the shared experience of community. Whether or not Haskell remembered the Holy Mountain sanctuaries of the Shakers, he had outdone them.

In the park called the Ramble, Llewellyn Park residents celebrated May Day in 1860. They were accompanied by reporters and a crowd of "a thousand to fifteen hundred ladies and gentlemen of breeding and fine manners and deportment" who observed an elaborate festival of flowers.[26] But the community never finished building Davis's designs for the Lyceum (schoolhouse, lecture hall, and library), the greenhouse, and other community facilities promised at the start. Haskell ran into financial difficulties in 1870. The inhabitants also changed. The earliest residents, while affluent, included abolitionists, two journalists connected to *The Nation* magazine, a painter, a homeopathic physician, and a poet—collectively described by a journalist as "longhaired men and short-haired women."[27] Mixed in were successful businessmen whose fortunes came from shoe jobbing, insurance, dry goods, and hardware. Over time, the grandeur and seclusion of the place attracted a very different set of wealthy industrialists, including Thomas Edison, George Pullman, and Elisha Otis. Some of the new magnates tore down the charming cottages of earlier times in order to build larger structures. Eventually the communal space was no longer heavily used, and three lakes were filled. By 1941 rezoning for con-

"May Festival at Llewellyn Park, Orange, N.J., on May 30th, 1860,"
from *New York Illustrated News,* June 23, 1860.

struction on half-acre lots enabled the building of smaller houses. A
highway reduced the size of the community in 1972, but Llewellyn
Park remains an exclusive, gated enclave, and anyone wishing to visit
must write for permission to enter.[28]

RIVERSIDE, ILLINOIS: "HARMONIOUS ASSOCIATION"

After the success of Llewellyn Park, picturesque enclaves were promoted in newspapers, popular magazines, novels, and plays as models
for American life. When landscape designer Frederick Law Olmsted and his partner, Calvert Vaux, were asked to design Riverside, Illinois, in 1869, they were already well known for their work on New
York's Central Park. Olmsted held a critical view of many of the subdivisions going up on the outskirts of cities after the Civil War. He

called them "a series of neighborhoods of a peculiar character," some "rude, over-dressed villages," others "fragmentary half-made towns." Yet he thought a few offered "the most refined and the most soundly wholesome forms of domestic life, and the best application of the arts of civilization to which mankind has yet attained." He concluded, "No great town can long exist without great suburbs."[29]

While this sounds like real-estate-speak for the promoters, Olmsted also used language familiar to the communitarians. He wrote about "the harmonious association and co-operation of men in a community." Next to "Association," the favorite terms of the Fourierists were "harmony" and "cooperation." "The families dwelling within a suburb enjoy much in common," Olmsted said, "and all the more enjoy it because it is in common, the grand fact, in short, that they are Christians, loving one another, and not Pagans, fearing one another, should be everywhere manifest in the completeness, and choiceness, and beauty of the means they possess of coming together . . . and especially of recreating and enjoying them[selves] together on common ground, and under common shades."[30]

The land at Riverside—the former David Gage farm, nine miles from the business center of Chicago—was far from choice. It was graced with a new station on the Chicago, Burlington, and Quincy Railroad. Olmsted described this 1,600-acre tract of prairie as "miry" and "forlorn," but he used the unbuildable wetlands around the Des Plaines River for a park and dammed the river to create a lake. He added winding roads bordered by trees to break up the featureless prairie. The Riverside Improvement Company—often prone to wild overstatement—claimed to have planted "47,000 shrubs, 7,000 evergreens, and 32,000 deciduous trees . . . some of them 19 inches in diameter . . . and 80 feet high." The company boasted of using "50,000 cubic yards of MacAdam stone, 20,000 cubic yards of gravel, and over 250,000 cubic yards of earth" to transform the bleak land into a desirable area for middle-class residence.[31]

Unlike Llewellyn Park, where no commerce was allowed, at Riverside, Olmsted designed a small business district around the railroad station. He also planned a wide pleasure drive for carriages connecting back to the city, but this was never built. Lots were fairly regular and boosting the price of lots was his job. He was sure some owners would build ugly or unsuitable houses, but "they shall not be allowed to force them disagreeably upon our attention."[32] He wrote a covenant

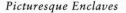

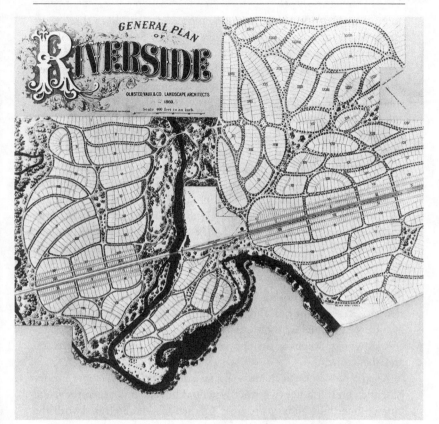

"General Plan of Riverside," by Frederick Law Olmsted and
Calvert Vaux, 1869. Courtesy of the National Park Service,
F.L. Olmsted National Historic Site.

requiring that houses be set back thirty feet from the road and that
each owner have one or two trees in the planting strip between the
house and the street. This was the first of many restrictive covenants
for suburban communities drafted by the Olmsted office over the next
decades.[33]

Olmsted's plan looks much more contemporary than Llewellyn
Park because it is a plan for 2,250 salable lots, about 100 by 200 feet
(half an acre, with room for a barn, stables, and a garden), rather than
a plan for an elaborate, shared communal life. Vaux's letter book

noted that the price of lots increased more than tenfold in three years "from $300 (and no sales) on a paper plan to $40 a front foot. . . . Fifty private houses already built or building."[34] While public park areas along the river were defined by the design, private lots covered most of the available land for building, and private investment in lots was key to the developers' financial success. If the dozens of eclectic villas at Llewellyn Park were "almost swallowed up in nature," the hundreds of houses at Riverside were merely set back a minimum of thirty feet and separated from the road by the required trees. Olmsted did suggest that "at frequent intervals in every road, an opening large enough for a natural group of trees, and places for croquet[,] for ball grounds, sheltered seats, drinking fountains" be provided. Landscape architects Kenneth Helphand and Cynthia Girling have noted, "the boundaries between roadway and park were muted."[35] Yet Riverside, with double the acreage of Llewellyn Park, held twenty-one times as many houses as well as a business district, so density was much higher. The Riverside plan offered an outline for an entire new town where the residents would not all know each other. Still, it had charm. Olmsted marked out one island in the Des Plaines River as a "Picnic Island" and named many roads for naturalists and landscape designers: Downing, Repton, Loudon, Kent, Uvedale, Audubon, Bartram, and Shenstone.[36]

As a community, Riverside was a speculation. The developer Emory E. Childs built a hotel to attract potential buyers and issued the usual inflated handbills about "progress." When Childs interfered with the public spaces in the design, Olmsted was infuriated:

> Dear Sir,
> I have just been informed that a private house is to be placed in the midst of the Long Common. I can not express to you how much I am shocked and pained to hear that such a suggestion could for a moment be entertained. It is not a matter for argument. It sets aside at once all the study which we have given to your enterprise as of no value and breaks the plan in its most vital point. . . . I entreat you to give it up.[37]

Worse was to follow. The promoters seemed to have deep pockets, but turned out to be crooks. Robert Fishman has reported what most other historians have failed to discuss—Olmsted's sour view that his clients were perpetuating a "regular flyaway speculation." One of the promoters, the city treasurer of Chicago, stole $500,000 from the city to cover overruns in the construction of Riverside. Even this did not save the day. The company went under in the Panic of 1873.[38] A period of uncertainty followed, but as years passed, Riverside incorporated as a village and filled out. It has survived to this day as a picturesque enclave of handsome houses. Although in his younger days he might have wanted a more collective solution to the problem of the suburb, by 1869 Olmsted was conceding to a friend, "the laws of supply and demand compel me to work chiefly for the rich and to study rich men's wants, fashions, and prejudices."[39]

The Olmsted office designed many similar landscaped enclaves with winding streets, including Druid Hills in Atlanta, Fisher Hill in Brookline, Massachusetts, and Sudbrook Park outside Baltimore. They set the standard for many other architects, landscape architects, and builders throughout the country. When developers imitated Olmsted's plans, sometimes they worked them out on tight budgets. Typical was the case of a seventy-acre farm in Westchester County, New York, owned by an insurance company after foreclosure. This became Rochelle Park, a railroad suburb designed by Nathan Barrett in 1886. It offered "The Lawn" and "The Court," two central green spaces totaling about six acres, surrounded by about 115 half-acre lots. Some pleasant houses were erected, including several by architect Wilson Eyre, and Nathan Barrett himself moved in. Residents formed an association to handle the maintenance of the common land and the roadways, working also with town authorities on streetlights and the extension of sewers. Legal negotiations about the divisions between private and public were extensive, since residents paid fees to the community as well as taxes to the town, and wanted to get infrastructure from both.[40] Although pleasant, Rochelle Park lacked the scale and complexity of Olmsted's 1869 project, but it suggests how frequently Riverside was imitated.

LEGACIES OF COMMUNITY AND EXCLUSION

The picturesque enclave was launched in the 1850s, the product of an era when debates about the construction of community filled the pages of popular magazines and daily newspapers. It came at a time when Americans discussed moving beyond the private house to share space with one's neighbors and build physical community in far more complex ways than Americans do today. Early examples of the picturesque enclave show a substantial park as common territory, and some communities also developed rituals for their common parks. Enthusiastic residents of Llewellyn Park got married at dawn under a great tree in the open space.[41] In the early picturesque enclaves, the exploration of community and privacy, as a part of spiritual life, was as important as the negotiation of city and country, or the development of personal taste and style.

As decades went on, the picturesque enclave, carefully fitted to its hilly terrain with winding and well-graded roads, augmented with handsome community parks, appeared in more and more reduced form as a flat subdivision with just a suggestion of two-dimensional curvature to the streets. By the 1920s, design of the picturesque enclave was routinized. Every new suburb included the word "park" in its name, whether it had a park or not. Developers swapped schemes for increasing lot frontage. Designers in the Olmsted office published a chart of provisions for restrictive covenants, thinking of this as a way to help others practice landscape architecture more efficiently.[42] When the Federal Housing Administration suggested rules for *Planning Profitable Neighborhoods* in 1939, the grand shared mountain park of Llewellyn Park, the riverbank park of Riverside, and even the much more modest green spaces of Rochelle Park had been pared down to a tiny strip. The builders of picturesque enclaves were creating a triple dream, house plus nature plus community, that required a large investment at the start. Since the buyers of houses had to bear the financial burden of maintaining a community's public lands and agree to participate in its rituals, they had to believe in this triple dream as well. Not surprisingly, when the attempts to achieve adequate community space in new enclaves conflicted with the need to make them highly profitable, profit often won out.

Enclaves for the affluent continued to be developed during the Gilded Age, some noted for their snobbishness as much as for their spectacular scenery. The country club, with its golf course, tennis courts, swimming pool, and exclusive social functions, began to take the place of the picturesque park as the center of a community. Outdoor festivals like the May Day event at Llewellyn Park began to be replaced by debutante balls and social affairs characterized by the exclusiveness of high society. In 1886 architect Bruce Price designed the resort of Tuxedo Park, New York. Massive stone gates and a large clubhouse sat on six thousand private acres surrounded by a barbed wire fence eight feet high and twenty-four miles long, guarded by private police. Tuxedo gave its name to the fashion for men's short dinner jackets less cumbersome than white tie and tails. Residents included Wall Street millionaires and tobacco barons, who built vast country houses in the English style on the mountains overlooking three lakes. Many inhabitants occupied their houses only during a short stretch of fall, between summer in Newport, Rhode Island, and the start of the social season in Manhattan. It was never casual, although Price's daughter, Emily Post, the prolific author on etiquette, called it an "American rural community."[43] An "unabashed upper-

Closing the gates at a private residence in Tuxedo Park, N.Y., 1906–07. Within a gated community, this was a gated estate. Museum of the City of New York.

class social whirl" was also typical of Lake Forest, Illinois, north of Chicago, where golf, polo, horse shows, steeplechases, and traditional hunts kept residents busy. The town center created in the Tudor style between 1912 and 1916 included the Onwentsia (a club), a bank, post office, and small arcades with over two dozen stores located around a fountain, trees, and parking.[44]

Other developers sought exclusivity as a route to profitability, although the residents might not all be listed in the Social Register. In the age of the automobile, Palos Verdes, California, was designed by Frederick Law Olmsted, Jr., who created a site plan for a community of Spanish colonial houses on dramatic hills overlooking the Pacific Ocean. Equipped with a golf club and nursery school, happily celebrating Mexican feast days as local rituals, residents saw no irony in adopting deed restrictions to prohibit Mexican-Americans from buying houses.[45] Near Kansas City, beginning in 1923, J. C. Nichols developed the Country Club District with "1000 Acres Restricted," prohibiting billboards and African-American residents. He also built a larger commercial development than the one at Lake Forest. His

"1000 Acres Restricted, Country Club District," Kansas City, Mo.,
J. C. Nichols, builder, c. 1905–10. Western Historical
Manuscript Collection, Kansas City.

Country Club Plaza is often cited as the forerunner of the shopping mall. Nichols introduced Christmas lights at the Country Club Plaza in 1929, promoting a commercialized Christmas with electricity and setting a national trend in shopping.[46] He was active in the National Association of Real Estate Boards (NAREB) for many years.

Developers of affluent suburbs increasingly wished to exclude potential buyers on the basis of race, religion, and social class. On the residents' side, the quest for spirituality and new forms of community were replaced by the routines of buying into a leafy place with big houses and affluent neighbors. John Archer has suggested that early British colonial suburbs became sites for the "establishment and augmentation of a person's individual identity, architecturally celebrating the alienation of wealth and privilege from the process of production, although dependent upon it."[47] Robert Fishman, who has also studied many of the English precedents for American suburbs in this era, has described the suburb as "bourgeois utopia," the "triumphant assertion of middle class values" accompanied by "the alienation of the middle classes from the industrial world they themselves were creating."[48]

Fishman's discussion of the "classic suburb" of Chestnut Hill, outside Philadelphia, documents the importance of a resort hotel, a country club, and an Episcopal church to the definition of membership in this elite Protestant community. Many Americans found this way of life boring. Haskell, Davis, and their friends at Llewellyn Park had established a unique enclave on the mountain, much more daring. But if the intense excitement of establishing a new community was part of the attraction of Association in the 1850s, the problem many communitarian settlements faced was how to sustain the unique experiment after the founding generation. The picturesque enclaves shared this problem. If people tired of the same faces and the rules began to seem overly complicated, then the next generation might fall back on exclusivity without any community activities. Or they might substitute architectural preservation of their suburban enclave for active social life within it.

It is a complex task to unravel the racism and snobbery of certain picturesque enclaves from the positive aspects of communities designed with respect for the natural landscape of rocks, hills, rivers, lakes, wetlands, and wildlife. As historian Mary Corbin Sies has observed, some residents' effective strategies for the preservation of physical character (strategies many other Americans can learn from) were often accompanied by extremely narrow views of social coherence, with negative lessons to teach.[49] Yet at the same time that developers with substantial capital were attempting to sustain markets for expensive suburban property in picturesque enclaves, other developers had very different ideas about promoting suburban dwellings as the "workingman's reward."

Chapter Five

STREETCAR BUILDOUTS

The little yellow, blue, green, white, and brown
streetcars which he saw trundling here and there,
the tired, bony horses, jingling bells at their throats,
touched him. They were flimsy affairs, these cars,
merely highly varnished kindling wood with bits of
polished brass and glass stuck about them, but he
realized what fortunes they portended if the city grew.
— THEODORE DREISER, *The Titan*

FROM THE 1870S ON, subdividers of land near city centers
provided a cut-rate version of the verdant residential ideal
expressed in the picturesque enclaves. Served by the omnibus,
the horsecar, and the electric streetcar, these new buildouts began as
linear real estate developments along expanding transit lines. Sometimes they were adjacent to urban or suburban industries. Owners of
large tracts of land subdivided and marketed lots to many second-
generation Americans, children of immigrants who had grown up in
inner-city tenements. Subdividers sometimes organized construction
of houses, but more commonly small builders took over, or the owners built themselves. Houses were usually on a modest scale. They
included single-family, two-family, and three-family dwellings, plus
some commercial and apartment structures. New England was home
to the triple-deckers, three-story dwellings on narrow lots, gable end
to the street. In the Midwest and West, single-family cottages or
bungalows were often preferred. During economic boom times, met-

Streetcar suburb. Fair Haven area, New Haven, Conn., April 1997.
Alex S. MacLean, Landslides.

ropolitan areas doubled and tripled in size because of the buildouts, but when a crash came, tens of thousands of newly platted lots might remain unsold.

In the streetcar suburbs, residents were never as separated from paid and unpaid work as the owners of houses in picturesque enclaves pretended to be. Multiple workers in families included women and children; multiple units included arrangements for kin and boarders. If the wives in the streetcar suburbs were not in paid employment, they might raise chickens, grow food, or take in laundry. For men, often sweat equity was part of the deal. Owner-builders were common in some cities. Often ethnic clubs and churches—Irish-American, Polish-American, Italian-American—provided social centers. Involvement by trained architects in streetcar suburbs was minimal, but the local government's engineers might eventually organize the physical infrastructure (water pipes, gaslights, sidewalks, macadamized roads, and electricity), if the areas were annexed to a city.

Today the streetcar buildouts may not be thought of as suburbs, because of their density and proximity to the center of the city. Sociologists in the early twentieth century called them the "zone of emergence," because layers of streetcar settlement reflected emergence from tenements in the center of the city. The cost of fares might determine just how far out from the center a family could afford to go.[1] In Boston, although the subdividers owned large tracts, the owner-builders were often operating on a very small scale, producing two or three wooden triple-deckers in a career. Often they chose to live in the neighborhoods they constructed. In Chicago, a developer like Samuel Eberly Gross operated on a much larger scale, subdividing lots and building thousands of brick and frame houses which could be purchased on long-term plans.[2] In San Francisco, in the Sunset district, an unusual streetcar suburb was made out of streetcars themselves, older models taken out of service and converted to funky dwellings at the bottom of the market.[3] In Chevy Chase, Maryland, an unusually upscale streetcar suburb was established in the 1890s by two United States senators from Nevada with fortunes from the Comstock Lode, Francis G. Newlands and William M. Stewart. An electric streetcar line, built by the developers, served large houses and a club devoted to riding, hunting, and polo.[4]

Since streetcar suburbs vary in form and age in different parts of the country, it is hard to generalize about their residents, but in most parts of the country, they consisted of dwellings for skilled workers and people of modest middle-class status. The small front gardens and rear yards in streetcar suburbs were often intensively cultivated. Different ethnic neighborhoods could be identified by their plantings, and the varied delights of ethnic kitchen gardens contrasted with the exotic landscapes and flower gardens of the elite in the borderlands and picturesque enclaves.[5] Streetcar suburbs offered options for the elderly and the three-generation family unmatched in other suburbs. Where streetcar suburbs have been well maintained, they offer livable patterns worth reexamining for their compact land use and good public transit.

MASS TRANSIT AND THE SHAPE OF THE SUBURBS

Over the course of the nineteenth century, both suburban and city entrepreneurs engaged in developing public transportation, often as an adjunct to the land business. At first, service was primitive. The omnibus of the early nineteenth century was an urban version of the old-fashioned stagecoach. Drawn by a pair or a team of horses, the omnibus jolted along rough roads, carrying passengers to residences in outlying parts of a settlement. It was usually a small business run by a borderland entrepreneur. In Boston, omnibus service was available starting in 1826 to carry passengers to outlying towns such as Cambridge and Somerville. Uncomfortable, inconvenient, and expensive, the omnibus was not easy for the daily commuter. By 1835, a steam railroad was also serving the Boston area. It was fast but made few stops and was far too expensive for most workers.[6]

As the omnibus became more crowded, it was replaced by a slightly longer vehicle, the horsecar, sometimes still called an omnibus and sometimes called a "car." Launched in New York in 1832, the horsecar could attain greater speed if the horses pulled it along a metal rail placed in the street. By 1852 the first horsecar street railway in the Boston area was operating between Harvard Square in Cambridge and Union Square in Somerville. With the success of this enterprise, several rival firms entered the field in different parts of town. Ultimately the Henry M. Whitney syndicate bought up all the smaller firms and merged them into one operation with a uniform fare of five cents.[7] Larger cities had more horsecars, which meant more passengers stuck in traffic. The congestion in New York City was severe. A reporter standing on Broadway in 1867 counted 3,672 horsecars passing by in thirteen hours. One rider complained: "Modern martyrdom may be succinctly described as riding in a New York City omnibus. . . . It is in vain to seek relief in a car. People are packed into them like sardines in a box with perspiration for oil. Passengers hang from straps like smoked hams in a corner grocery. . . . pickpockets ply their vocation. . . . The foul, close air is poisonous."[8] Thousands of overworked horses died straining to haul the cars. Their carcasses were left in the gutters. Streets were also fouled by hundreds of tons of horse manure dropped every day.[9]

While the centers of cities might be crowded with horsecars, one horsecar clopping by at five miles per hour in areas outside of the centers of cities did not impede peace and quiet. The construction stimulated by horsecar lines tended at first to be linear. Builders mixed mom-and-pop shops with apartments and more conventional one-, two-, and three-family residences. Fronting a main street was conve-

The John Mason, pioneer horse car. It began carrying
New Yorkers to and from work in 1832, over the first
railway chartered exclusively for city passenger traffic.

Enter suburbs—exit slums

You will find the mon-
ogram of the General
Electric Company on
the motors of elevators
which made possible the
skyscraper, as well as on
the motors of the trol-
leys which created the
suburb. And on *little*
motors, also, which do
the burdensome part of
housework for a wage
of 3 cents an hour.

Suppose our cities still depended upon horse cars. Workers would live huddled under the shadow of their factories. Children, who can now reach the cool beaches for a few pennies, would be condemned to the hot pavements all Summer.

The trolley car has transformed the conditions of city life. With its coming the suburb started to grow and the slum to go.

GENERAL ELECTRIC

"Enter suburbs, exit slums," 1923 General Electric advertisement
showing an early New York horsecar of 1832 and its replacement,
an electric streetcar. GE sold the motors for streetcars and claimed
that streetcars enabled workers and their children to
live in comfort. Courtesy of General Electric Company.

nient, especially if side roads were not paved. The shift to the electric streetcar (also called a trolley, a tram, or traction) changed this pattern in the late 1880s. The electric streetcar traveled at ten or fifteen miles per hour and required numerous poles with cumbersome wires supplying current. Residents along major lines no longer found those streets desirable. Some engaged in unsuccessful litigation to halt the nuisance. Merchants were less likely to object. Since major streets no longer offered the most attractive residential lots, new streetcar suburb housing was located off the major streets carrying the trolleys and developed in concentric rings around downtown. Sam Bass Warner, Jr., estimated that the electric trolley tripled the area of metropolitan Boston between 1890 and 1900. Calculating the cost of transit fares and the cost of lots by size, he showed that class-graded bands of settlement emerged, with more affluent middle-class families farther away and on larger lots.[10]

In return for establishing service, city governments usually gave a particular company the exclusive right to operate a line along a given street. "Bribery and political favoritism were the most common requisites of successful applications," according to Kenneth Jackson. He found much more careful government control of routes, fares, and service in European cities than in American ones, where the "robber barons" of the street railways—Peter Widener, Henry and William Whitney, Charles Yerkes, Borax Smith, and Henry Huntington—made immense fortunes.[11] In Europe, owners of streetcar lines were forbidden to engage in land speculation, but most American companies were involved in subdividing and selling land near their routes. As the streetcars proved fast and profitable, with eight hundred street railway lines established in the United States by 1902, much wider areas were opened up to subdivision.[12] Some reformers called for municipal ownership of public transportation, as part of a larger program of "sewer socialism" designed to benefit working people, but the profits were so high that the streetcar barons fought to retain control. When workers who ran the streetcars engaged in strikes and other demonstrations, some line owners employed men to beat them up. It was an ugly business.[13]

NINE THOUSAND SMALL BUILDERS

After large-scale land subdivision had taken place, the construction of houses remained a small business in some cities like Boston. Sam Bass Warner's *Streetcar Suburbs* follows the trail of building permits in three areas to the south of the city, Roxbury, West Roxbury, and Dorchester. Between 1870 and 1900, their population grew from 60,000 to 227,000. He traces 9,000 individual builders sheltering 167,000 people by constructing a total of 22,500 houses. This total included 2,000 single-family, 6,000 two-family, 4,000 three-family, and 500 multifamily structures, as the shape of the land was buried under a jumble of streets and buildings. Each buyer wanted to think for five or ten years that the house he or she had purchased was in the country. For the most part, the builders were very small operators, and 70 percent were building in the towns where they lived, 40 percent within two blocks of their own residences. Carpenters and draftsmen from rural backgrounds, most of them built between one and four dwellings. There was no public control over subdivision or zoning. In the second half of the nineteenth century, the city of Boston was investing over half of its annual budget in services—paved roads, piped water, and electric lights. In the suburbs, residents had to organize and tax themselves to obtain infrastructure.[14]

In central Dorchester, Warner found that builders of one-family and two-family wooden houses on former farmland occasionally inserted a dwelling and store unit at transport nodes, or put low-cost houses on small pockets of bad land. One area became an Irish, middle-class neighborhood centered on a church. Over several decades, the middle class gave way to a working-class population, but the dimensions were adequate for higher densities and adaptation. In the Tremont Street area of Roxbury, Warner noted a more risky investment, with very closely calculated, cheaper housing for the lower middle class. The smaller houses here, some of them wooden row houses, were below the common understanding of what constituted a decent home, although better than the dark and airless tenements of the central city. The lot sizes were cramped and too tight to be adaptable. This neighborhood could only go downhill.[15]

Characteristic of the densest areas studied by Warner was the triple-decker, a detached wooden house with apartments for three families. Triple-deckers could provide income for a resident owner, or offer the chance for a three-generation family to unite parents, children, and grandparents. Often they were constructed with the new products available to builders through the development of large lumberyards—stock moldings, window sashes, and doors, and elaborate precut wooden ornament. Architectural historian Gwendolyn Wright has traced the development of new mass-production techniques in the manufacture of building materials in this era. Everything from ready-mix plaster to plumbing fixtures became the subject of new entrepreneurial efforts aimed at increasing demand. Wood was the material of choice for housing. Standards varied widely, but what was considered modern "American" construction was often a sentimental Victorian hodgepodge of forms borrowed from Gothic, Renaissance, Egyptian, and other traditions. It could be lively, but it never had the integrity of older New England houses, which were often said to lack "style," as in Andrew Jackson Downing's day.

Occasionally Warner's "weave of small patterns" was interrupted by a larger development, such as Robert Treat Paine's philanthropic development of 116 one-family and two-family houses, constructed in 1891, offered to buyers with a novel amortizing mortgage.[16] Recognizing the need for mortgages to support home ownership for people of modest means, workers had begun to form new kinds of cooperative organizations to finance home ownership as early as the 1830s. Paine's publication of 1881, *Own Your Own Home,* stressed the importance of thrift to solid family life, and encouraged residents of streetcar suburbs to become members of building-and-loan associations. By 1893 over one and a half million members belonged to building-and-loan associations in every state. Every member was a stockholder, paying dues and electing directors, and close to a third had received mortgages. Historian and architect David Handlin has traced this process. A typical ad showed a suburban house with a porch and lawn: "The occupant of this house is paying for it through the Co-operative Bank." Pictured below it was a row house with a line of washing next to a saloon: "The occupant of this house has not yet heard of the Co-operative Bank." Usually the association inspected the house and lot, offered a mortgage, and calculated family budgets, including streetcar fares, before making the loans. At times mortgagees who had fallen

behind in payments might be fined or visited by the association's directors in an attempt to apply peer pressure.[17] Ads might run like this:
"the association has kept our boys' money safely invested, and they are
$925 better off than two years ago. (These boys had formerly spent
all their money for drink.)"[18] The cooperative appealed to potential
homeowners in an era when banks often failed. It helped working-
class families gain decent shelter without paying excessive amounts of
interest.

"THE LARGEST REAL ESTATE BUSINESS IN THE WORLD"

An alternative pitch for ownership in streetcar suburbs, without the
work involved in a cooperative association, came from a subdivider in
Chicago who was also a builder and a financier. The sales brochures of
Samuel Eberly Gross still exert a "magnetic" attraction. *Famous City
Subdivisions and Suburban Towns* (1891) begins with two pages of
fan letters:

> Dear Sirs—The *best investment* that I *ever* made, was the purchase
> of one of your houses. Yours, Jacob H. Layer, 423 Gross Parkway

> Gentlemen—I am perfectly satisfied with the cottage I bought from
> you two years ago. I consider that I have that much saved. *It is better
> than a bank for a poor man.* Respectfully, D. H. Brookins, 389 Gross
> Parkway

Compliments flow: "The house is well built . . . warm and comfortable. Wm. Clair." "Our property has increased in value at least 15 per
cent since we purchased it. Lizzie Root." Others testify to buying several lots for investment, including a lieutenant in the Fire Department
and a principal at the Ogden School. Last but not least come letters in
German and Swedish.[19] Gross follows the effusive testimonials with a
map of Chicago locating his principal subdivisions and towns along
the "Street and Steam Car Lines" leading to them. Gross boasts: "I
have, within the past ten years, sold more than 30,000 lots, built and
sold more than 7,000 houses, and located and built 16 towns and
cities." He styles himself "the World's Greatest Real Estate Promoter"
and claims he runs the "Largest Real Estate Business in the World."[20]

Born in 1843 in Dauphin County, Pennsylvania, Gross grew up in
northern Illinois and served with distinction in the Civil War. After the
war he returned to Illinois, earned a law degree at the University of
Chicago, and was admitted to the bar in 1867. For the next six years
he was active in the real estate market, surviving the Chicago Fire
of 1871 by taking to the river in a tugboat with his deeds and legal
papers, then struggling to hang on during the Panic of 1873. He spent
the lean years of the mid-1870s writing a play and patenting systems
for paving streets.

Back again in real estate in 1879, Gross platted several subdivisions
in southwest Chicago, launching over two decades of intense building
and financing activity directed at both working-class and middle-class
purchasers of homes.[21] He subdivided tracts, sold lots, and also built
houses, offering buyers mortgages he carried himself. He worked close
to the stockyards as well as in emerging suburbs, and during his career
built on the north, south, and west sides of the city. Early in his career,
Gross decided that building houses could increase the profitability
of an entire speculative tract. He was the kind of developer who
would later be called a "community builder." While later "community
builders" received production advances and loan guarantees from the
federal government, Gross had no government support, so his extensive operations had no security net, except for revenues from his
earlier projects.

Gross put at least as much talent into the design of his sales materials as into his houses. Since he was a playwright, it seems appropriate
to view them as theatrical. First comes the cast of characters. He identified "Persons Who Should Buy Property" as including "The Man
of Family," "The Business Man," "The Young Man," "The Lady,"
and "The Renter." For the last he recommended "A GOOD TITLE TO A
HOUSE AND LOT, instead of a package of worthless rent receipts."[22]
For the other "home-seekers and investors" who had capital or were
regular earners, he offered payment plans—a low down payment (usually 10 percent, sometimes waived if people promised to build immediately) and the balance in monthly payments. He claimed never to have
had a foreclosure or a lawsuit against a buyer.[23]

Gross's little booklets and handbills were distributed outside factory
gates, since he located subdivisions near the Union Stock Yards (New
City), brickyards (Gross Park), and the Deering Harvester Works

"Outside FIRE Limits. You can build Wooden Houses."
Advertisement for Gross Park, Chicago, Samuel E. Gross, builder,
1885. State Historical Society of Wisconsin, PAM 75-2121.

(Gross Park).[24] He became an advocate of the eight-hour day, partly because this would allow a workman enough time to manage a long commute.[25] Gross advertised in a wide variety of newspapers, including labor papers and foreign language papers, and his graphics often had the punch of a strip cartoon. One of his pamphlets contrasted prudent Andrew, who buys a home, with the improvident "Hardup" Ben-

"The First of May." Advertisement for Samuel E. Gross, builder, 1889.
Chicago Historical Society, ICHi-28168.

jamin, who spends on frolics and has to deal with a landlady. In "The
First of May" this theme continues: the owner of a home sits reading
with wife, two children, and elderly relative, while the unfortunate
renter must load his trunks and chairs into a broken-down cart and
find new lodgings. In a short story, *The House that Lucy Built, or, A
Model Landlord*, a young woman persuades her husband that buying
from Gross is the answer to all their problems.

A particularly effective graphic illustrates the subdivision building
process as if it were a vaudeville show on a stage. "Virgin Soil" appears
first, then "Prospecting" in a sleigh, "Placing the Corner Stakes,"
"Putting in Water Pipes and Planting Trees," "Summer Home Building" (frame and brick houses go up), and "Autumn, The Home Completed." Finally, "Winter Again—Our Home," a cozy indoor scene, is
flanked by twin medallions inscribed "One of My Easy Payment Plan
Houses" and "One of My Easy Payment Plan Cottages." Gross was
first to use the building process itself as the focus of a dramatic sales
pitch, a technique William Levitt later made famous. At the very end of

"Scenes Illustrating S. E. Gross' Enterprises," 1889. Chicago Historical Society, ICHi-28166.

this sequence an angel slips a deed into a man's pocket as he stands next to railroad tracks, throwing away a rent bill.

Gross knew that the dramatic handbills and stories might get prospective purchasers interested, but he still had to clinch the sales. He advertised "Grand Free Palace Excursion Trains" so that potential buyers could ride out to see his properties, and these excursions were carefully scripted performances. Brass bands might be seated on the roofs of the railroad cars, sounding the overture to a festive day. Arriving on one of these trains to "Magnetic" Grossdale, passengers would see a substantial railroad station and a meeting hall and store constructed by the developer. Accompanied by the band, they would march on into a circus tent where they might listen to more music, have food and refreshments from wagons loaded with barrels of

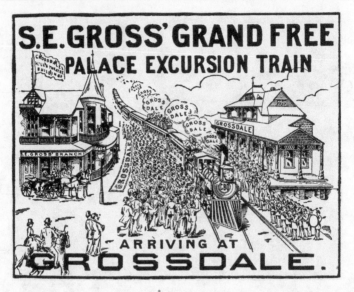

"S. E. Gross' Grand Free Palace Excursion Train," "Scene in the Pavillion," "Plat of Grossdale," and "One of my Grossdale Houses," $4,400, with 50 feet of ground, from *Tenth Annual Illustrated Catalog of S. E. Gross' Famous City Subdivisions and Suburban Towns* (1891). Collection Centre Canadien d'Architecture/Canadian Center for Architecture, Montreal.

PLAT OF GROSSDALE,

Showing Blocks 1 to 35.

BUSINESS LOTS IN BLOCKS 17, 18 and 19.

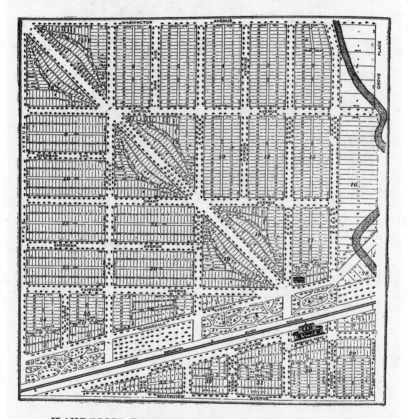

HANDSOME BUSINESS AND RESIDENCE LOTS.

On Grand Boulevard, a beautiful 80 foot macadamized and sewered street extending through the property and lighted for its entire length by street lamps.

ONLY 100 LOTS LEFT FOR SALE IN THESE BLOCKS.

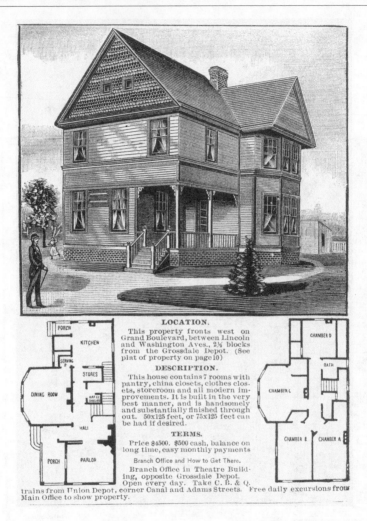

LOCATION.

This property fronts west on Grand Boulevard, between Lincoln and Washington Aves., 2¾ blocks from the Grossdale Depot. (See plat of property on page 10)

DESCRIPTION.

This house contains 7 rooms with pantry, china closets, clothes closets, storeroom and all modern improvements. It is built in the very best manner, and is handsomely and substantially finished throughout. 50x125 feet, or 75x125 feet can be had if desired.

TERMS.

Price $4500. $500 cash, balance on long time, easy monthly payments

Branch Office and How to Get There.

Branch Office in Theatre Building, opposite Grossdale Depot. Open every day. Take C. B. & Q. trains from Union Depot, corner Canal and Adams Streets. Free daily excursions from Main Office to show property.

beer, and talk to salesmen. "Entertaining Speeches are made." "Ample Time is given for Inspection of the Property."[26] Many visitors signed contracts.

Samuel Gross planned Grossdale (now Brookfield) in 1888 on five hundred acres just west of Riverside, Olmsted's town platted in 1869. In 1891, Gross's lots cost "$200 and upwards." They appear to have been about 50 feet by 250 feet, or a little more than a quarter of an acre.[27] Nowhere on the sales materials is the exact depth identified, and presumably it varied by location. Although he claimed it was like Riverside, Grossdale was a grid. One small strip of "parkland" buffered the lots for sale from the railroad line, which cut the development on the diagonal. Another diagonal "Grand Boulevard" was described as "a beautiful macadamized and sewered street extending through the property and lighted for its entire length by street lamps."[28] One suspects it was the only street with lights and a sewer. A future streetcar extension was promised. While Gross called it a "Most Delightfully Picturesque City" and drew many trees in the sales materials, Grossdale would not have been recognized as picturesque by any landscape architect. The gridded lots were long and narrow. Gross built a few houses himself, trying to stimulate buyers of lots to invest in construction. He also offered "400 designs" for houses free to those who would build. Overall, this was a speculative plan, as was Riverside, but it was a much less intelligent and generous plan, with much less landscaping and infrastructure provided.

The relationship between the residents of Grossdale and the developer became strained when Gross failed to pay property taxes and assessments on his holdings in a timely manner. Early residents decided to incorporate Grossdale as a village in order to tax themselves for paved streets, sewers, a waterworks, and streetlights that the developer had not provided. These improvements were paid for by property taxes and special assessments on the landowners, but they also benefited Gross, who had remaining lots to sell and could offer them at higher prices. Visitors to the World's Columbian Exposition of 1893 purchased some of his lots after participating in the train excursions, but many failed to build. Some were tourists who responded to high-pressure sales pitches. Others, who did buy and build, were in difficulties because of the Panic of 1893 and the subsequent depression and unemployment. Even if Gross had made many bad loans, the residents who did continue to make payments to him on their mortgages were angered by his failure to pay taxes because this meant potential bankruptcy for the whole village. By 1905, the locals voted to rename the village Brookfield.[29]

Historians who have written about Gross's career have argued that he was not only a bigger developer than many, but also a better one.

This is debatable. Gross was part of a Chicago growth machine that boomed new areas by planning streetcar lines and selling the surrounding property. He was a director of the Calumet Electric Railroad running to the southern side of the city, and he was in partnership with Charles Tyson Yerkes, the corrupt traction magnate, beginning in 1887, although the partners had a falling-out.[30] Yerkes ran a streetcar line north from the center of Chicago to Gross Park. In 1899 he sued Gross, complaining that Gross had not subdivided, improved, and sold the lots, while Gross contended that Yerkes had not provided streetcars running frequently enough to make his tract pay.[31] Since twelve years had elapsed, many of them bad years, the litigation suggests the vital importance of timing. Everything in a speculative tract had to come together at the same moment—transit had to be running, houses on lots had to be ready, and the economy had to be in a boom period with steady jobs to enable workers to meet their mortgage payments. Without any one of these, the developer was sunk. So, for any growth machine, advertising was essential. Intense sales propaganda could draw a crowd during boom times, but overselling could magnify the distress after a crash. In 1908, Gross filed for bankruptcy, the next year consoling himself at age sixty-six by marriage to an eighteen-year-old.[32]

THE "WHY-PAY-RENTS"

"Why pay rent?" campaigns tantalized Americans who had only known the tenements. They sounded even more reasonable to middle-class Americans with savings to invest. Large down payments were necessary and only short-term mortgages were usually available to ease the process of purchasing a home. Those buyers who managed to get cooperative mortgages were lucky. Others scraped together the short-term mortgage payments, made a final balloon mortgage payment, and held on to their streetcar suburb houses, sometimes with the help of family members who shared multiple dwellings. Still others learned about the negative side of home ownership when they were foreclosed, losing both their equity and their houses. As Matt Edel, Elliot Sclar, and Daniel Luria have argued, workers were struggling "up a down escalator," entranced with dreams of economic security, saddled with debt, and confused by a false sense of social mobility.[33]

Exaggerated sales pitches for suburban home ownership in many streetcar suburbs across the nation quickly became a subject of satire. Eugene Wood let it rip in *Everybody's Magazine* in 1910, mocking "quiet" streetcar suburbs built out to the maximum and long, crowded commutes. He parodied advertisements in the real estate section of the paper, "lovely houses, Easy Payment, Ten Cents Down and Fifteen Cents a Minute, Own Your Own Home, Why Pay Rent?" Wood described the "Why Pay Rents" as places located hours from town on the "Worry and Wait Avenue line," with unpaved streets full of puddles. All the streetcar suburbs had one thing in common, according to Wood: "They're a far, far ways from where you get your pay envelope." He commented, "Hop on any car whatsoever, transfer as often as I could, ride till if I rode no longer I should scream, then get off and face the wind. I'd snuff and snuff till I smelled fresh paint, then I'd follow my nose till I found the builder waiting for me." Horace Taylor's wonderful pen-and-ink sketches capture the monotony, the spindly trees, and the puddles. The houses differ only in the style of the attic window and in color, "pink, yellow, green, white, pink, yellow, green, white . . ."[34]

Wood criticized builders who asked too much and then added on a lot of extras. The house might be damp and settle badly. The doors and windows might stick. The first mortgage might be at 5 percent but renewable every three years. The buyer was under bond for twice the amount of the mortgage. If the buyer was ten days late on a payment—foreclosure. The second mortgage might be at 6 percent. The title search would cost money and needed to be done every three years, the buyer also had to pay the state mortgage tax, the notary public, and

Sketches by Horace Taylor, *Everybody's Magazine,* June 1910.
"Why Pay Rent?" "I'd Follow My Nose Till I Found The
Builder Waiting For Me." "Before You Get the Beds Up or the
Gas Cut In, The Nurseryman Calls," "Something That You Can
Work At Summer Evenings After Supper," "How Worn and
Thumbed Are All the Pages in the Cookbook."

other closing costs. Then, even before the buyer got the furniture ar-
ranged, the nurseryman arrived with a catalog of "apples and plums
and peaches and pears and cur'n's and goozeberries, and rosberries and
blackberries," all to be planted on a 30-by-100-foot lot, along with
hedges and saplings and roses and grapevines.[35] The landscaper was
always involved in growth promotion.

Wood's complaint was not limited to a financial critique. He
claimed it was just too exhausting for a couple to handle the housework and the yard work. Servants, he said, would not travel to remote
parts. The commute added two hours or more to the homeowner's
already long workday. One could not get to a play or the opera because of the transit delays at night. Henry Cuyler Bunner, author of
The Suburban Sage, a New Jersey chronicle of the same era, attacked
the inanity of suburban culture as well. He lampooned men standing
around trying to advise each other on the merits and problems of fur-

Suburban men discuss a broken furnace. Sketch by C. J. Taylor
in Henry Cuyler Bunner, *The Suburban Sage* (New York:
Keppler and Schwarzmann, 1896). Beinecke Rare Book
and Manuscript Library, Yale University.

naces. He bemoaned the male's endless chores with the lawn mower. A
new literary genre was established, making fun of suburban culture
and the gender roles it assumed. Mostly men told other men they were
the dupes of fast-talking real estate men, sleazy contractors, and door-
to-door salesmen. They sighed that they were henpecked husbands.
The genre later includes Eric Hodgins's *Mr. Blandings Builds His
Dream House* and John Keats's *Crack in the Picture Window*. Magazines addressed to women also carried material on home ownership,
but at the turn of the century they tended to give positive advice about
how to decorate the home and nurture the family rather than guidance
on how to achieve financial independence.

THE INTERURBANS

Electric streetcar syndicates had a profound effect on the shaping of
urban areas and metropolitan regions by the turn of the century. Entre-

Suburban men with lawn roller.
Sketch by C. J. Taylor in
The Suburban Sage. Beinecke
Rare Book and Manuscript
Libary, Yale University.

preneurs subdivided lots and
constructed houses on every
acre of buildable land within
an hour of the center of the
city. These residential areas
were never planned or de-
signed as urban development. Boom times always implied the possibility of a bust. The streetcar lines that had made fabulous fortunes for
their owners in the years between 1870 and 1900 sagged in profitability by 1920. The lines suffered from buildout (the end of nearby land
to subdivide), overextension (building unprofitable lines to further distant real estate operations), poor management, and aging equipment.

Signs of weakness in the streetcar companies were obvious for
decades, yet business continued because of the complex ways traction
companies could exploit electricity. As David Nye writes in *Electrifying America*, "a technology is not merely a system of machines with
certain functions; it is part of a social world." He suggests it is a mis-
take "to think of 'the home' or 'the factory' or 'the city' as passive,
solid objects that undergo an abstract transformation called 'electrification.' Rather, every institution is a terrain, a social space that incor-
porates electricity at a certain historical juncture as part of its ongoing
development."[36] Land subdivision practices were seen by businessmen
as related to the electric trolley business, like "two pockets in the same
man's trousers."[37] As long as the land business was good, developers
who also owned traction did not give any thought to the future of
public transportation.

Traction magnates who generated power to run the streetcars also
might sell electricity, but in the biggest cities utility owners could sell
power to the traction owners at a lower cost than the traction owners
could generate it themselves. A more common enterprise was con-

structing an amusement park at the end of the trolley line. This was usually profitable because people paid to ride at slow times, such as nights and on Sundays, and paid again for electrified spectacles with electrified rides. Trolley parks became a standard feature of remote streetcar suburbs. Coney Island was lit up so brightly by electricity that occasionally foreign ships seeking New York harbor mistook the huge amusement park for the city itself.[38]

By inventing the interurban, an electric trolley that would travel at high speeds between towns and cities, traction owners managed to stave off their demise with one final round of expansion. Transportation, power sales, and entertainment were all exploited to the maximum. The interurban challenged the steam railroad, carrying both passengers and light freight (groceries, newspapers, some U.S. mail, packages, some produce, and milk). The companies also sold electric power to towns under 100,000.[39] Interurbans stimulated regional tourism, connecting Boston with the New England countryside, for example, or New York with New Jersey and Connecticut. It provided one- or two-day excursions, giving small-town residents time to shop in the big city and inner-city residents hours to walk down shady lanes, climb hills, and rest by little brooks. Interurban cars could also be rented out for parties and excursions, taking large groups through the countryside for a day's outing. The entrepreneurs running the interurbans sustained the connection to pastoral landscapes at the edge of urban settlement, while reviving hopes for a borderland life that earlier dense streetcar suburbs had obscured. A whole new round of real estate subdivision followed the creation of each new interurban line.

LEGACIES OF MOVEMENT

The possibility of traveling through the urban fabric at a rapid pace changed the way that many Americans felt about housing and cities. Never again would working-class Americans feel obliged to live next to their workplaces, right under the smoke or the smells of industrial production, but there were costs to this new geographical freedom. Especially with the move from the horsecar to the electric trolley and the interurban, the paradoxes of transit began to be felt. Speed and movement connected diverse neighborhoods and made exciting new relationships possible, at the same time that they disconnected people from familiar places, destroyed the peace and quiet of older neighborhoods, and caused monumental traffic jams in the streets. City governments needed to regulate both the transit and the housing to secure public health and safety, but real estate entrepreneurs resisted regulation. Within widening built-up areas, little urban planning was taking place.

By the 1880s, housing had become a contested political topic. As industrial development took off and the demand for labor filled American cities with millions of new immigrant workers, it was as difficult to find a decent private rental apartment as it was to find an honest subdivider with a piece of land to sell. American reformers had criticized the lack of decent workers' housing for rent or for purchase since the 1840s, when Fourierists such as Parke Godwin suggested that workers add land reform and housing to demands for better wages and shorter hours. By 1879, Henry George was popular among workingmen for his extremely influential economic treatise *Poverty and Progress,* which explored why poverty persisted among workers in times of increasing affluence for capitalists and landlords.[40] George argued that land speculation was the cause of many evils and suggested a "single tax" on land as a solution. He believed that a more orderly suburbanization would result, with households spaced at reasonable distances. In 1886 he ran for mayor of New York City as an independent on a single-tax program.

George and his tax on land were defeated, but workers' movements continued to attack urban political machines for corrupt dealings with the streetcar and utility magnates and for lack of attention to workers' housing. In some cities of Europe, such as Glasgow in the 1890s, city government did own the transit networks and did undertake construction of multifamily housing. Transit and housing continued to be debated in the United States in the first decades of the twentieth century, both as part of a progressive agenda and in places where Socialist Party candidates won municipal elections, as they did in the "morning glory" cities of the Southwest.[41] But any kind of public involvement was hotly contested by the emerging real estate industry in the United States as infringing upon the private market.

Local growth machines composed of businessmen who profited from transit, speculating, subdividing, building, and landscaping were well established in American cities by 1900. The realtors and subdividers among them formed a National Association of Real Estate Exchanges (NAREE) in Chicago in 1908. It became the National Association of Real Estate Boards (NAREB) in 1916, and took its present name, the National Association of Realtors (NAR), in 1974. The group first tried to make landlords' rents exempt from taxes. When this effort was unsuccessful, NAREB campaigned to make home mortgage interest deductible from income tax and succeeded in the 1920s in winning this subsidy for their growing industry.[42] NAR ultimately became the largest trade association in the United States, working in partnership with government, proposing how government might best serve private interests. The era of the streetcar reached its peak around 1910, but extended by the interurbans and then by low prices for motorcars, waves of new subdivisions platted by private developers continued to create ever-larger metropolitan regions through the 1920s.

Chapter Six

MAIL-ORDER AND
SELF-BUILT SUBURBS

To get the most out of life as Our Creator
intended it to be, A HOME OF YOUR OWN
IS AN ABSOLUTE NECESSITY.
—Sears, Roebuck and Co.

B ETWEEN 1870 AND 1910, streetcars, subways, and interurban lines became part of subdividers' efforts to expand
residential areas distant from city centers. After 1910, entrepreneurs encouraged people with automobiles to reside in even more
remote areas than those transit had touched. "By 1930 every American city had rings of suburbs like the skins of an onion, and beyond
that, usually, other rings of platted fields," according to architectural
historian Alan Gowans.[1] As the size of American urban regions increased, options for constructing and selling houses also began to
change.

Most American working-class families wanted to move away from
airless, unhealthful tenements in the polluted centers of industrial
cities, if they could afford to do so. Developers like Gross had demonstrated that housing could be a very broad business spanning land
subdivision, construction, and mortgage lending. By the early twentieth century, many more entrepreneurs had launched projects aimed
at hundreds of thousands of potential customers. Hasty subdividers
called "curbstoners" proliferated, and so did speculative builders who
put up identical houses in a hurry. Large lumber companies also entered the field with mass-produced prefabricated construction materi-

als. The lumber companies targeted two different buyers—the home-owner, who wanted to save money on building one house, and the speculative developer, who wanted a fast way to develop a tract. All of the entrepreneurs engaged in intense competition to house both working-class and middle-class Americans. The only thing they could agree upon was the need for growth, but unplanned growth created very chaotic metropolitan landscapes.

In Los Angeles, which had developed 1,200 miles of streetcar lines by 1915, the platting of new suburbs was transformed into a giant land sale, setting the stage for mail-order and self-built houses. Sub-dividers in Southern California held huge barbecues with tables of roasted beef to attract potential buyers to auctions in empty terrain.

Prospective buyers of Southern California real estate on a streetcar excursion to an undeveloped area. Electric streetcar at rear. "Poppy Fields Near Mt. Lowe," about 1903. Seaver Center for Western History Research, Los Angeles County Museum of Natural History.

Tract Office, Van Nuys, Calif., 1911. Archive unknown.

Carriages and automobiles gather for a barbecue during land promotion, Montrose, Calif., 1913. Courtesy of University of Southern California, on behalf of the USC Specialized Libraries and Archival Collections.

Real estate barbecue, Santa Monica, Calif., 1875. Huge slabs of cooked meat
suggest a feast that will be a challenge for the woman in the white dress.
Courtesy of the Santa Monica Public Library Image Archives.

Buyers then decided how to build on their new suburban lots, and
many chose the mail-order option. Spanish colonial might rise next
to a Craftsman bungalow or a New England Cape Cod. Local vernacular building traditions suited to climate and natural materials faded.
Paradoxically, as the national and regional production of mail-order
houses became more standardized, sales pitches became more personal, appealing to do-it-yourself owner-builders to invest their savings
and their sweat in houses. Concern for the suburb as a particular place,
based on visions of natural landscape or ethnic community, began to
disappear in favor of regional and national advertising for the mass-
produced house.

FROM PATTERN BOOKS AND PLAN BOOKS
TO MAIL-ORDER CATALOGS

The development of national advertising for houses reflected a century
of improvement in printing technology that made illustrated materials

cheaper. Throughout the first half of the nineteenth century, small builders could consult pattern books such as Asher Benjamin's *The Country Builder's Assistant* (1797) and *The American Builder's Companion* (1827). These volumes were illustrated with simple wood engravings of plans, elevations, and details that builders could adapt to local projects such as country churches, schoolhouses, or dwellings. Architects began to enter this genre with portfolios that displayed their new designs, built and unbuilt, for potential clients, works such as A. J. Davis's *Rural Residences* of 1837–38, a hand-colored limited edition. A few years later, A. J. Downing broke new ground in the United States by offering a hefty volume of prose on taste and style addressed to the owners of modest gardens and houses, not to builders or architects. Downing stated an approximate price for constructing each design he published and often referred readers to local architects or furniture stores, but all he sold himself were plants from his nursery or his services as a landscape consultant. Beecher offered much detailed advice on design and construction, but limited her sales information to particular items such as up-to-date furnaces.

Downing's best-sellers—illustrated with wood engravings, steel engravings, and lithographs—were copied by both architects and builders. By the Centennial year of 1876, "a modern suburban house" might be Gothic, Italianate, or a highly eclectic Stick or Queen Anne style. Designers such as George Palliser of Bridgeport, Connecticut, saw profits to be made in offering more detailed plans and specifications to homeowners. For only twenty-five cents Americans could buy his pamphlet, *Model Homes for the People,* the first of over twenty plan books he published. First Palliser sold the plan book, then he sold more detailed working drawings and specifications by mail to both owners and builders, and finally, if he was fortunate, he reached clients who would pay him an additional fee to adapt one of his stock designs to their particular site.[2] Selling a plan book may have helped architects extend their practices by encouraging builders to attempt more complex designs. To this end, plan book architect Robert W. Shoppell claimed that older romantic house styles—Classic, Mansard, Gothic, and Italianate—were just boxes with different roofs and thus easy to build. In contrast, Shoppell claimed that a professional architect's advice was needed to guide the builder who attempted the complex, asymmetrical styles of the 1880s that involved "bewildering detail."[3]

Plan books like Shoppell's did not directly compete with local builders. He did not supply materials for construction or put the house together.

Large, color illustrated catalogs of mail-order houses for a mass audience changed everything. In 1896, the Rural Free Delivery Act greatly improved suburban and rural mail service, and the expansion of many different kinds of mail-order businesses followed. By the turn of the century, customers could order an entire house from a catalog. There were two kinds of mail-order buildings, panelized and ready-cut. Panelized (or portable or sectionalized) buildings were light-weight, small, and simple. In the United States they dated back to the 1840s, when John Hall of Baltimore advertised a portable cottage. The California gold rush stimulated demand for instant and movable shelter. So did the Civil War and the building of the transcontinental railroad.[4] Panelized buildings linked prefabricated walls with patented bolting systems. Advertising them as do-it-yourself projects was not unreasonable—they could be erected, dismantled, moved, and erected again without a great deal of skill. Often the job could be done in a day. In the early years of the twentieth century panelized buildings were popular as small gas stations. They were a fast way to add a garage to an existing house or build a small vacation cottage.

Most of the mail-order house business was not in panelized build-ings but in precut (or ready-cut) materials for permanent construction. Customers who owned a lot could browse through a catalog, pick out a plan, and then order every board, shingle, nail, and doorknob shipped to the site. Because a single-family house was usually a small job, the differences between a carpenter, a small builder, and a devel-oper, or between a draftsman and an architect, were not rigid. All of them could handle the design of a small house, although not always gracefully. When lumber companies and millwork companies wanted a share of the action, they advertised the high quality of their lumber and millwork (factory-made wooden structural components and deco-ration). They claimed that large companies could eliminate waste of time and materials by using sophisticated machinery for cutting basic lumber to size and shaping decorative trims. They also claimed to offer better designs. Many mail-order house companies employed teams of architects or "master builders" to provide their designs. They generally were anonymous in their work and conservative in their tastes. Aladdin called its team the "Board of Seven, master designers, builders, and manufacturers." They competed with many specialized local businesses—not just the architect, but the carpenter, the plumber, the builder, the lumberyard, the hardware store, and the supplier of lighting, paint, and decorative materials.

Part of the new sales efforts involved appealing directly to women as buyers. Pacific Ready-Cut Homes in Los Angeles stressed its architectural expertise in creating labor-saving kitchen designs to make work easier for the housewife, responding to the home economics movement.[5] For some, it made sense to hire women to design for other women. Sears described its "Architects' Council" as consisting of a "Chief Architect, and a corps of able assistants, including a woman adviser who understands the requirements of the housewife." An illustration in a Sears catalog showed a woman sitting at a conference table with five men in front of an all-male drafting room. For those inclined to doubt, architectural historians Stevenson and Jandl researched the team and found that "a club of women architects in Chicago listed Aileen Anderson as an architect working for Sears in 1937."[6] In addition to a few women designers in the mail-order business, one woman headed up a firm. In its early years, Adna G. Lewis was the president of the Lewis Manufacturing Company of Bay City, Michigan, which produced Easy-Built Homes, Lewis Homes, and Liberty Homes between 1907 and 1973.[7]

SEARS, ROEBUCK AND CO.

Sears, Roebuck and Co. was founded in 1886 and started its mail-order operations that same year with watches and jewelry. By 1907 it was sending out many specialized catalogs including ones for tombstones, washing machines, and millwork.[8] Between 1908 and 1912 Sears also sold its own brand of automobiles.[9] Millwork didn't turn a good profit until 1908, when Sears published its first catalog, *Book of Modern Homes and Building Plans,* and the Modern Homes division took off. Sears bought a lumber mill in Mansfield, Louisiana, in 1909, a lumber yard located on forty acres next to a rail line in Cairo, Illinois, in 1911, and a millwork plant in Norwood, Ohio, in 1912.

In 1911 Sears also entered the mortgage business, lending as much as 75 percent of the cost of a house, lot, and labor for construction. The page titled "Own Your Own Home" in the 1926 catalog was

Truck loaded with parts of a ready-cut house, Pacific Portable
Construction Co., Los Angeles, about 1910.

a cartoon just like the "Why Pay Rent?" put out by Samuel Eberly
Gross decades earlier: "Save Your Rent Money," "Give the Kiddies a
Chance," "Get Close to Nature," "Have Real Friends and Neighbors," and "Be Independent in Old Age."[10] Sears also used the Gross
technique of customer testimonials listing the names and hometowns
of buyers: "I am well pleased with the house and with your material.
My wife and I, who are nearing 60 years, built the house ourselves and
we saved about $1,300.00. W. E. O'Neil, 715 Maple St., Wamego,
Kan."[11] They had chosen "The Clyde."

A look at the forms to be filled out by Sears's potential customers
suggests that the mortgage loan business was even more profitable
than the mail-order house business. If a lot cost $500, a Sears kit
$2,500, and labor plus plumbing, heating, and masonry $2,000, then
a completed house and lot totaled $5,000. Sears would lend $3,750
for five years at 6 percent. Of course, this loan did not cover the cost.
Even if the lot was counted as a down payment, the owner somehow
had to save enough for a balloon payment to close out the deal. Otherwise the mortgage would have to be renewed or foreclosed.[12] In good

years, Sears built its business by easy credit. In 1930 it had sales offices in forty-eight cities, but after the crash of 1929, it was overextended. Stevenson and Jandl note that in 1929 Sears began to engage local building contractors to supervise construction. Perhaps this was the way that Sears dealt with a large inventory of precut houses as consumer demand declined. It is equally likely that Sears foreclosed on many loans and needed to finish hundreds of half-built houses in dispersed locations in order to resell them. By 1934, the Depression had intensified. Sears liquidated $11 million in mortgages and discontinued its Modern Homes division. It came back a year later with a curious design based on steel framing, steel roofs, and plywood walls, but closed down for good in 1940.[13]

How many houses did Sears actually sell? Maybe 50,000, although Sears liked to boast of 110,000. The cheapest cottage was a one-bedroom shack without interior plumbing for a few hundred dollars. One of the most expensive was "The Magnolia," a four-bedroom colonial revival that sold in 1919 for $7,960.[14] The most popular houses were the less expensive ones, yet the catalog was an invitation to overestimate a family's buying power. The kits did not include labor, of course, nor did they include supplies for plumbing, water heating, residential heating, materials for plaster or masonry, storm doors and windows, or screen doors and windows. Sears sold all of these parts at additional charges, and they might equal half of the cost of the house kit. Sears also hoped to sell house customers a complete set of home furnishings, including tables, chairs, carpets, beds, and bedding. The dream would recede rapidly for a buyer who added it all up before starting, but heavy advertising in mass-market magazines such as the *Ladies' Home Journal* and the *Saturday Evening Post* meant that many buyers were hooked before they ever priced the building project. In contrast to Sears, Pacific Ready-Cut Homes in Los Angeles, also known as Pacific Portable Construction, ran advertisements stressing practical arithmetic. They offered tables so that potential buyers could calculate rental costs over twenty years and compare them to house prices, both contractor-built and ready-cut.

Many of the Sears styles defy easy description in architectural terms, but the houses tended to be made of wood and utilize platform framing with standardized studs. Eclectic historicism characterized many of the bigger houses, styles half-understood piled upon other styles and then shrunken for cost savings. Over time, the Queen Anne

Home Ownership *plus* Secure Investment *plus* Highest Value

| *A Study in Rent Costs* | *Depreciation vs. Increment* | *A Study in Home Values* |

Your Automobile:
Original investment $1,500
Upkeep and depreciation at
$60.00 per month—in 3 years
costs you $3,660
It is then worth about............$ 350

When you buy a house already built:
Cost of lot, figured at................$1,800
Cost of constructing house by
ordinary method 4,000
Profit to speculator who builds
the house to sell to you   1,160
Incidental expenses   40
Real Estate man's commission   350
Approximate price you pay.....$7,350

Have you ever realized the high cost
of renting? These figures reveal the
loss of rent and interest thereon
compounded over a period of years.

Rent Paid Per Month	Loss in 10 Years	Loss in 20 Years
$ 20	$ 3,163	$ 8,828
25	3,954	11,035
30	4,745	13,242
40	6,326	17,657
50	7,908	22,071
60	9,499	26,485
70	11,071	30,899
100	15,216	44,142

Your Pacific Home:
Original down payment............$1,500
Monthly payments, interest and
taxes, in lieu of rent, at $60.00
per month including down payment—in 3 years total... ....$3,660
Your equity is then worth
about $5,500

When we build you a Pacific Home:
Cost of lot, figured at................$1,800
Actual cost of Pacific Home of
similar design, using same or
better grades of materials, com-
plete ready for occupancy.........$3,750
Total low cost to you.................$5,550
Approximate saving..... ... .$1,800

You Can't Afford Not To Own Your Home | *No Other Investment Pays Bigger Dividends* | *Cheaper to Build Than to Buy Already Built*

Advertisement for building a Pacific ready-cut house rather than
buying a home already built, about 1910.

faded. Tudor revival gave way to Williamsburg, and every now and
then someone ordered Spanish colonial revival or Dutch colonial revival. The more modest offerings were often better. The Four Square
(or Box) was two stories, four bedrooms over four main rooms with a
single-story porch on the front and a hip roof. Most popular were the
Bungalow and the Cape Cod. The Bungalow was a low house with
roofline parallel to the street, one front dormer, and a prominent front
porch. The Cape Cod was a one-and-a-half-story house with a central
chimney and dormers.

These were the houses that lined the streets of American small towns
before 1945. At the start, Sears houses were identified by numbers.
Soon a copywriter was giving them names as well as glowing de-
scriptions of their resemblance to more expensive houses: "The Prince-
ton possesses the dignity and charm of a high-class colonial home."[15]
Many of the names speak of the desire for assimilation. "The Yale,"
"The Franklin," "The Portsmouth," "The Hamilton," and "The
Atterbury" might be modest bungalows, colonials, or Cape Cods,

A GENERAL FAVORITE

The GLYNDON · Honor Bilt · $1,577.00
No. 2014 "Already Cut" and Fitted.

See Description of "Honor Bilt" Houses on Page 9.

At the above price we will furnish all the material to build this six-room bungalow, consisting of lumber, lath, shingles, mill work, flooring, porch ceiling, siding, finishing lumber, building paper, eaves trough, down spout, sash weights, hardware, sideboard and painting material. We guarantee enough material to build this house. Price does not include cement, brick or plaster.

A MODERN six-room bungalow, built along plain lines of high grade materials, yet at a price that is within reach of almost every purse. The numerous windows, some of which are double, make every room light and airy.

First Floor Front door leads into a parlor, which is connected with the dining room, directly in the rear, with sliding door. The dining room has plate rail and sideboard with small windows placed above plate rail at both sides of the sideboard and directly opposite the large sliding door, being plainly visible from the parlor. Directly adjoining the dining room is the kitchen with a large pantry. Glazed sash door leads from kitchen to back porch. A door leads from parlor to bedroom. The stairway leads from parlor to the second floor.

Second Floor At the head of stairs on the second floor is a hall which leads to front bedroom with closet, and rear bedroom with large closet. At the head of the stairs is a door leading to bathroom.

Height of Ceilings Ceiling on first floor 9 feet 2 inches high and on the second floor 8 feet 4 inches high.

We furnish our best "Quality Guaranteed" mill work, described on pages 120 and 121. Interior doors are five-cross panel, with trim and flooring to match, all yellow pine, in beautiful grain and color. Windows are made of clear California white pine, with good quality glass set in with best grade of putty. Porches have fir edge grain flooring.

We furnish two coats of paint for outside, your choice of color. Varnish and wood filler for interior finish. Stratford Design hardware, see page 129.

Built on concrete block foundation. Sided with narrow bevel clear cypress siding and best grade cedar shingles on the sides of dormer and on roof. All framing material, including joists, studding, etc., made from No. 1 yellow pine.

FIRST FLOOR PLAN.

SECOND FLOOR PLAN.

OPTIONS

Sheet Plaster and Plaster Finish to take the place of wood lath, $117.00 extra.
Fire-Chief Shingle Roll Roofing, Red or Sea Green in color, instead of wood shingles, $34.00 less.
Oak Doors, Trim, Stairs and Floors in parlor and dining room instead of yellow pine, $52.00 extra.
Maple Flooring for kitchen, pantry and bathroom instead of yellow pine, no extra charge.
Storm Doors and Windows, $39.56 extra.
Screen Doors and Windows, black wire, $26.63 extra; galvanized wire, $30.52 extra.
This house can be built on a lot 30 feet wide.
Double floor furnished for all "Honor Bilt" Modern Homes.

This house has been built at Indianapolis, Ind., Rocky River, Ohio, South Bend, Ind., Gary, Ind., Peoria, Ill., Elgin, Ill., Gibsonburg, Ohio, Lima, Ohio, Milan, Mich., and other cities.

Our Guarantee Protects You—Order Your House From This Book
Price Includes Plans and Specifications.

SEARS, ROEBUCK AND CO. CHICAGO

"The Glyndon," a precut bungalow, *Honor Bilt Modern Homes*, 1918.

Nantucket

The Cape Cod cottage design is the backbone of the Nantucket. It gives the house character—and a type of beauty and balance that cannot be achieved by any other kind of design. The Nantucket has one of those pleasant, unmistakable New England personalities. It impresses you definitely from the first moment you see it.

The Nantucket can be as large or as small as you want. You may finish only the first floor rooms and still have comfortable living quarters. You can finish the second floor any time in the future.

SECOND FLOOR OPTIONAL

FUTURE BED ROOM 14'2" x 11'7"

FUTURE BED ROOM 10'2" x 14'0"

PLAN No. 13719

KITCH 8'6"x10'6"

BED ROOM 9'4" x 12'0"

LIVING ROOM 18'6" x 12'0"

BED ROOM 9'4" x 12'0"

FIRST FLOOR

4 ROOM MODERN HOME

"The Nantucket," a precut house in a traditional Cape Cod style, *The Book of Modern Homes,* 1939. The design is similar to Levitt and Sons' first Long Island Cape Cod house.

Building From These Pages
on page 110

THE GOLDENROD.
55MH122   Price, **$403.00**

Three-Room Simplex Sectional House with porch. This house was erected by two men in one day. Size, 15 feet 3 inches by 21 feet 3 inches, outside. Floor plan to the right shows size and arrangement of rooms. Comes in ready made sections, as illustrated and described on page 110. Lumber strictly No. 1 grade throughout, and bright, clean new stock. Good grade hardware and galvanized iron chimney included. Roofing—Fire-Chief Shingle Roll Sea Green Slate Surfaced, 90-pound rolls. Guaranteed for seventeen years. (See inside back cover of this book.)

Brick, stone and cement not included.
Shipping weight, about 7,800 pounds.

The Goldenrod Floor Plan.

The Goldenrod.

THE STRAND. **$949.00**
55MH187   Price,

Five-Room Simplex Sectional House with large front porch. Erected by two men in three days, as shown by pictures on right hand side of page 110. Size, 27 feet 3 inches by 53 feet 3 inches. Floor plan to right shows size and arrangement of rooms. Comes in ready made sections. (See page 110.) Strictly No. 1 grade of lumber, bright, clean new stock. Good grade hardware and galvanized chimney included. Roofing—Fire-Chief Shingle Roll Sea Green Slate Surfaced, 90-pound rolls. Guaranteed for seventeen years. (See inside back cover of this book.)

Brick, stone and cement not included.
Shipping weight, about 18,700 pounds.

The Strand Floor Plan.

The Strand.

THE BOWER.
55MH189   Price, **$999.00**

Five-Room Simplex Sectional House with bathroom. Size, 24 feet 3 inches by 30 feet 3 inches. Floor plan shows size and arrangement of rooms. Comes in ready made sections. (See page 110.) Strictly No. 1 grade of lumber, bright, clean new stock. Good grade hardware and galvanized chimney included. Roofing—Fire-Chief Shingle Roll Sea Green Slate Surfaced, 90-pound rolls. Guaranteed for seventeen years. (See inside back cover of this book.)

Brick, stone and cement not included.

Shipping weight, about 18,000 pounds.

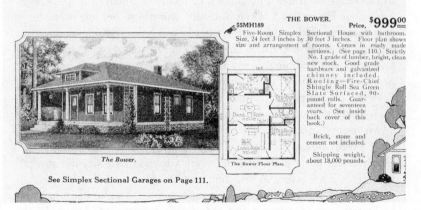

The Bower.

The Bower Floor Plan.

See Simplex Sectional Garages on Page 111.

"The Goldenrod," "The Strand," and "The Bower," cheaper, panelized houses on Sears's simplex system, from *Honor Bilt Modern Homes, 1921.*

but they had upper-class white Anglo-Saxon Protestant names. In the 1919 Aladdin catalog, even the small garages had names such as "The Peerless," "The Winton," "The Maxwell," and "The Packard."[16] There were also religious overtones to the sales pitches. A 1910 Sears catalog addressed "churchgoers": "To get the most out of life as Our Creator intended it to be, A HOME OF YOUR OWN IS AN ABSOLUTE NECESSITY."[17]

DO IT YOURSELF?

During its heyday in 1926, Sears was turning out over three hundred pre-cut houses a month from its Cairo, Illinois, lumberyard. A typical pre-cut house included over 30,000 pieces, excluding nails and screws. If shipped all at once it would fill two boxcars, but usually an owner received the parts in several shipments sent by rail to the location nearest the customer's lot. The owner was expected to record each shipment against a checklist and then find a way to haul the parts home along with a seventy-five-page construction manual. Every board was labeled with an identifying number. The catalog companies never published letters from those who gave up in frustration. Owners may have succeeded with the small bungalows, but it is safe to assume many who were not experienced in the construction trades themselves had to call in relatives, friends, neighbors, or local craftsmen to help. "Own Your Own Home" and "Do It Yourself" campaigns became prime targets for satire. Ring W. Lardner made fun of everything that went wrong on a $2,000 house in suburban Chicago in 1919.[18] After a certain amount of ribbing, many owners were unwilling to admit they had bought a mail-order house at all.

In the beginning, mail-order house companies hoped to appeal to do-it-yourself homeowners. One of Aladdin's first ads in 1907 offered a two-room "knock-down" house for $126. By 1914 they had a complete precut house for $797. The project appeared to be cheap—a family could get a piece of land, pour a foundation, and live in the basement, if necessary. When they were ready financially, they could order the kit and start to construct the first floor. The kit manufacturers stressed quality lumber, and encouraged customers to bypass local lumber dealers. But since these kits were very hard to put together, frustrated do-it-yourself homeowners often had to hire local carpenters to help them do the work. Some mail-order companies began pre-assembling discrete parts of the house, such as built-in cabinets or bathrooms, to make the job easier, but these came at an extra cost. Sometimes they also offered to send a crew to construct the house from the parts in thirty days.[19] Eventually, many local lumber dealers offered their own kits to compete with the regional or national mail-order firms.

Some homeowners stuck to self-building the kit from start to finish. Some bypassed the kits and simply built a house over time, using scavenged materials if necessary. This was particularly true for rural residents and migrants to suburbs from rural areas, who might have more skills in farmhouse and barn construction. It was also the case in many poor communities, such as the working-class suburbs of Southern California described in *My Blue Heaven* by Becky M. Nicolaides.[20] Self-building was also typical of African-American suburbs researched by Andrew Wiese. An African-American suburb outside of Cleveland, Chagrin Falls Park, was a source of pride to those who put it together, despite the lack of infrastructure: "The more prosperous hired builders and paid for new materials, but many more came out on weekends or in the evenings after work, building small homes with salvaged lumber and the help of friends and neighbors—literally, a paycheck at a time."[21] One resident said, "I think I bettered my condition. . . . I had nice, fresh air, and you could have vegetables and a garden."[22] An African-American growing up in Seattle in the 1940s and 1950s remembered: "My dad built our family home. He took on several jobs and earned the money week by week. He dug the foundation by hand. He built a cantilevered device so he could put up Sheetrock himself. He even bought a house that the state highway department was tearing down, took the nails out of the boards, and transported the boards to the site." While all of the family members worked on the project, this young boy was the "insulation specialist, crawling around in the rafters." He grew up to be the head of Fannie Mae, presiding over billions of dollars in government-sponsored mortgage guarantees.[23]

Self-building in the African-American suburbs around Detroit included many small houses in the Eight Mile–Wyoming area to the northwest of the city. As historian Thomas J. Sugrue described the area in the early 1940s, it was seen as a "slum" and an obstacle to white development. A developer who proposed an all-white subdivision to bankers was rejected because it bordered this African-American area. A compromise was reached and federal loans and mortgage guarantees were approved after the developer agreed to construct a concrete wall measuring one foot thick, six feet high, "running for a half-mile on the property line separating the black and white neighborhoods."[24]

John Vachon, a photographer employed by the federal government, documented the arrangement, as residents who hated the wall campaigned for some benefits for their own community, such as the extension of loans to African-American owners of small shacks. During the New Deal they did receive support for the construction of many larger and better-built houses. While this was a positive outcome for one African-American self-built neighborhood, ultimately it became a demonstration of "separate but equal," used to justify segregation.

Testimony from owner-builders in every kind of community is often positive, even when gathered after many decades. People who loved

Woman selling suburban lots along the highway near Detroit, 1941. Photograph by John Vachon, Library of Congress, LC-USF34-063745.

Self-built house in the Eight Mile–Wyoming neighborhood of Detroit, with concrete wall in background separating this African-American district from a white subdivision, 1941. The wall is a half-mile long. Photograph by John Vachon, Library of Congress, LC-USF34-063747.

house-building tell of doing carpentry, hiring skilled help in the other trades, and delaying the purchase of a furnace to keep to a budget. Others bought everything from Sears and then had a local contractor work out the physical end. W. Stephen and Beatrice Bordeaux wrote, "In 1933 we built a Sears home, an English-style four-room house, the Maplewood. We are still in it and love it. . . . We live on a hill just outside the village of Pleasantville, and there were so many Sears houses up here that it was known as Sears, Roebuck Hill."[25] While the people who put in sweat equity often became attached to their houses because of the labor invested, new owners could be equally nostalgic. Mary Anne O'Boyle said that her Maryland house is hard to heat and that roofers do not like to work on the roof. Still, "My Sears Modern Home No. 167 [the Maytown] is the kind of house you see in movies

Young residents of Eight Mile–Wyoming neighborhood next to the wall.
Photograph by John Vachon, Library of Congress, LC-USF34-063679.

about the good old days when virtue triumphed and the nice guy won
the girl, usually while sitting in the front porch swing. Visitors often
comment that there is something vaguely familiar about the house,
which is quite true. They have seen versions of it all over America, in
small towns and old suburbs, along streets lined with maple and elm
trees."[26]

Richard Harris's *Unplanned Suburbs* gives a more negative picture
of self-building in suburbs outside Toronto between 1900 and 1950.
Workingmen with jobs and long commutes to fringe locations took on
hours of additional construction work in order to be able to afford
home ownership. Some encouraged their wives to work for pay, and
others sacrificed their children's education to meet the mortgage payments. The men frequently were unavailable for family activities at
home because they were doing construction work. Sometimes they
asked their wives and children to work with them.

Houses that evolved from shacks often started out without paved streets, water and sewer hookups, or power lines. Doing without plumbing, heating, or electricity could be very difficult. Women might have to struggle with cooking and cleaning in crude conditions of the kind that Catharine Beecher had been eager to change in the mid-nineteenth century. There could be health problems as well if sites lacked sewers and piped water. Working-class, self-built suburbs might free residents from landlords, but incremental development had a downside.[27] In fringe neighborhoods, it might be a long time before infrastructure arrived. Installing utilities after the homes had been constructed was far more expensive than starting out with a plan for the area. Still, it was a common way to go, since Harris cites a federal government study showing that in the 1920s, 40 percent of new single-family homes in the U.S. cost under $4,000 and most of the houses in this price range were built by owners for their own use.[28]

When people of modest means failed to finish their houses, the result might be a "garage suburb." These were immense tracts around Los Angeles and Detroit, "fields subdivided into lots on which stood one-room structures intended one day to accommodate a car, but which temporarily (that is, for decades) accommodated families instead, with jalopy parked outside." How did people get into this predicament? "First you bought the lot; only when it was paid for did you put something on it, and often you wouldn't have enough to pay for your house, so you bought your garage instead and lived there until you'd accumulated enough for the house—which might be a long, long time."[29] Since mail-order garages were usually panelized buildings, at least the owners could put them together without too much of a struggle. Planners and town officials deplored garage suburbs because once established, they were expensive for towns to upgrade with standard utilities and services, yet the owners were determined to stay.

LARGER DEVELOPMENTS

Speculative developers sometimes used precut houses to construct subdivisions quickly. Sears, Roebuck's 1926 catalog included testimonials from twelve contractors who had erected between 6 and 257 "Honor Bilt" precut houses. All said they were made of high-quality materials and claimed that using the kits offered cost savings. Pacific Ready-

Cut Homes of Los Angeles, the largest mail-order house company in the West, sold between 40,000 and 50,000 bungalows in Los Angeles alone. The company kept about ten model houses furnished and ready for inspection at its exhibition grounds at 1330 South Hill Street in downtown Los Angeles. At first they were sending out panelized buildings and then they moved to precut lumber. Eventually they had a large staff of construction workers who assembled Pacific homes in rapidly developing neighborhoods. Both skilled union carpenters and small contractors disliked the competition the precut construction teams offered. Pacific continued its building operations in its own area, but also organized fifty "Authorized Builders" outside Los Angeles, who sold only Pacific Ready-Cut homes.[30]

Some company towns were constructed entirely of mail-order houses (either panelized or precut), including industrial towns with housing programs for skilled workers, boom towns, and mining towns. Sears sent several hundred houses to Carlinville and Wood River, Illinois, for Standard Oil, and to Hellertown, Pennsylvania, for Bethlehem Steel. Aladdin published a special catalog, *Low Cost Homes Designed for Industrial Purposes*. They shipped over 250 houses to Birmingham, England, for the Austin Motor Company in 1917, as well as sending DuPont workers' houses to Hopewell, Virginia, explosives workers' houses to Bacchus, Utah, brass workers' houses to Bristol, Connecticut, and miners' houses to Mt. Union, Pennsylvania.[31] Aladdin also did a lot of work for the U.S. government, advertising to potential customers that it had town planners and engineers available if customers required planning services.[32]

"CARPETECTS" VERSUS ARCHITECTS

With the rise of mail-order houses and the growth of companies such as Sears, Montgomery Ward, Aladdin, and Pacific Ready-Cut Homes, all selling tens of thousands of units apiece, the American house was disconnected from questions of site and neighborhood. In the 1920s members of the American Institute of Architects (AIA) deplored what they saw as the poor design of mail-order houses and made an attempt to win back recognition for the architectural profession. In that era, most trained architects wanted to see academic styles done correctly, with appropriate proportions and historical detail. Criticizing the "vicious architecture" of small homes "slapped" together by "carpetects," they founded the Architects Small House Service Bureau (ASHSB) and the Home Owners Service Institute (HOSI) as two attempts to recapture the middle-class customer.[33]

Unfortunately, their efforts did not often extend to designing entire suburbs, and even their house designs left something to be desired. Usually the architects criticized existing mail-order house plans and showed how to do a more "correct" design. Trying to enhance regional character by exploring vernacular styles of building, they found that buyers had other ideas. Small homes in the New England colonial and Dutch colonial styles did well everywhere, so did Tudor. Mediterranean, or "Spanish-Italian," was popular in the West and occasionally requested elsewhere. William Gray Purcell, an architect involved with ASHSB, complained in exasperation, "I see Colonial, English, Spanish built in New York, Florida, Los Angeles, Minnesota and I wonder."[34] In the end, these services couldn't satisfy AIA members who worried that inexpensive small houses lacked design quality, nor could they match the lower-cost products of Sears or the other big companies. These architects were competing on their opponents' ground, looking for financing for their publications from timber producers and seeking endorsement from the U.S. Department of Commerce. Of the eight million new dwelling units built in the United States during the 1920s, probably fewer than five thousand used ASHSB mail-order plans.[35]

HOSI architects Donn Barber and Whitman S. Wick achieved media coverage in 1922 when they were sponsored by Better Homes in America to construct the National Better Home in Washington, D.C., on public ground near the White House.[36] The architects created a "modernized replica" of a seventeenth-century saltbox from East Hampton, Long Island, but instead of executing it in wood, they chose concrete block covered in stucco! They changed the interior plans and furnished this strange object with colonial replicas. The colonial house chosen for re-creation as the "Better Home" was the birthplace of John Howard Payne, composer of the song "Home, Sweet Home." "Be it ever so humble, there's no place like home," was a classic.[37] "Nobody sings songs about a pile of rent receipts," was the slogan politicians used to justify a home ownership campaign. Better Homes in America was a politically conservative, pro-growth organization founded by Marie Meloney, editor of *The Delineator,* a women's magazine with a circulation of over one million female readers. A Republican administration was trying to woo women who had gained suffrage in 1920. Better Homes' National Advisory Council was chaired by the Secretary of Commerce, Herbert Hoover, and he had business objectives in mind. As Christine Frederick wrote in 1928 in *Selling Mrs. Consumer,* a book she dedicated to Herbert Hoover: "The founding and furnishing of new homes is a major industrial circumstance in the United States."[38] Cosponsors of the Better Homes demonstration included the General Federation of Women's Clubs, who used the house to train Girl Scouts of America in hostessing and housekeeping skills. Meanwhile, Republicans were repealing the post-suffrage legislation that supported maternal and infant health care.

Housing was one of the biggest businesses around. Better Homes in America worked closely with the federal government to develop "Own Your Own Home" campaigns.[39] Banks, realtors, timber interests, appliance manufacturers, and builders were the heart of these local growth lobbies. By 1930, the mail-order house was waning, although the growth coalitions were just beginning a new phase of mass-produced housing. The Depression reduced the big mail-order companies' operations. World War II brought extreme shortages in building supplies. Sears and Pacific shut down when there were no materials for civilian projects; Aladdin survived, but mostly by government work. Between 1900 and 1930, the mail-order house companies won a substantial share of the American housing market.[40] By successfully advertising houses as national brand-name products, these companies destroyed the livelihoods of many local architects as well as small builders and skilled carpenters. The national mail-order companies then declined, in competition with the vast site-specific real estate development firms that began to dominate the market in the 1940s.

UNREGULATED HOUSES IN UNPLANNED NEIGHBORHOODS

One lasting effect of the mail-order and self-built suburban houses was the dissolution of denser neighborhoods like the streetcar suburbs. Transit waned because once all of the lots were sold, many streetcar magnates who had been in the land business stopped running the lines. Kin networks loosened wherever the single-family house was accepted as the norm. Ethnic communities weakened as people sought out diverse locations where lots were cheap. In large, older cities such as New York and Chicago, many families still chose to live in a neighborhood of two-family houses, near a church or synagogue, and connected to transit, but in smaller or more lightly settled places, such as Los Angeles, buyers favored the single-family house. As suburban house lots became more remote from city centers, owners felt more connected to their houses than to their neighborhoods. This was particularly true if owners had to manage infrastructure themselves— connecting to water supplies, ordering electricity service—as well as investing sweat equity in construction after a load of materials was hauled to a site. The mail-order manufacturers recognized the loosening of neighborhood bonds implied by shipping houses to diverse sites. They formed clubs that held occasional picnics for their customers, but these were regional rather than neighborhood affairs.

By the 1930s, when the Depression slowed house-building and banks increased foreclosures, significant changes in the production of American residential space had already occurred. Lumber companies had mastered mass production so that the scale of house-building was conceived in terms of tens of thousands of units, even hundreds of thousands of units. With the timber producers in charge of design and mass production, Americans became used to looking at plans for houses made of wood, "stick-built" houses. They expected these houses to include many, many wooden parts, such as window frames, built-in cabinets, and exterior decoration, all promoted as expressions of individual style. These houses were low-tech compared with multi-family housing designed of concrete or brick, and they were often oddly proportioned and ornamented with cheap wooden trim.

When fitted into narrow sites badly planned by curbstoners, mail-order and self-built houses could be unattractive. A suburban landscape of this kind did not resemble a picturesque, large-lot enclave like Olmsted's Riverside, nor was it even a cheap copy of Riverside like Grossdale. It was a cut-rate approach to shelter that did not always meet basic requirements for sanitation, health, or efficiency, because all of the parts—the neighborhood, the lot, the house—were bought and sold independently. As a solution to housing the working man and his family, mail-order and self-built suburbs lacked public infrastructure and public space. Richard Harris notes that these chaotic suburbs have been very problematic for the United States: "To define them as working-class is to challenge the American myth of classlessness in ways that *immigrant tenements* does not." In some cases, a neighborhood of mail-order or self-built houses could improve with time and mature trees. Above all, when residents invested their energies in a social network connected to a place, a working-class suburb could support the aspirations of residents for a better life.[41] Harris reminds us to cherish "the values of thrift, mutual aid, and self-reliance which went into the making of unplanned suburbs,"[42] but some Americans thought this country could and should do better.

LEGACIES OF THE MAIL-ORDER AND SELF-BUILT SUBURBS: DEMANDS FOR PLANNING

Doing better involved planning—but there were competing ideas about what planning involved. Beginning in the streetcar era, local citizens' groups had often formed to advocate neighborhood planning. Some argued for amenities, such as new sewers, paved roads, and street lighting. Others campaigned against nuisances or overdevelopment. Historian Joel Schwartz has commented on suburban town improvement societies' struggles to protect property values by prohibiting saloons in the 1880s. Billboards were another target of many groups; some advocated the "Direct or Crowbar Approach."[43] Others tried to limit new transit routes because trolleys damaged trees, raised dust, and encouraged development of multiple dwellings. Schwartz notes that by 1912 the Massachusetts Civic League was developing legislation to regulate height, bulk, lot size, and the construction of certain kinds of wood tenements and three-deckers. The league drafted regulations that twenty-three towns had implemented by 1915.[44] Citizens' groups attacked self-built shacks and garage suburbs, claiming that visual blight, dust, threats to the natural landscape, and structures prone to fire all presented serious problems. What some considered "progressive" reforms to protect the local environment, others thought of as exclusionary tactics to raise the cost of property and discourage poorer residents. A mixture of environmentalism and social exclusion would roil private citizens' activist groups in the suburbs for many decades to come. Meanwhile, two very different approaches to planning were developed. Republicans thought about business plans, Democrats thought about shelter.

Herbert Hoover: Planning for National
Standardization on Behalf of Big Business

During the 1920s, the federal government began to engage directly with housing as an important area of national policy. Herbert Hoover, trained as an engineer, served two terms as Secretary of Commerce under Republican presidents Warren Harding and Calvin Coolidge. In 1921 Hoover established a Division of Building and Housing in the Commerce Department to stimulate consumption through the standardization of lots, houses, and building materials. The twenties were a time of boom for house construction as well as for sales of electrical appliances and automobiles. Although national mail-order house companies were achieving new levels of mass production of housing and new kinds of appliances were being manufactured, Hoover wanted to standardize the ways different localities regulated construction in order to maximize mass consumption.

Commerce first drafted a national model building code for localities to adopt in 1922. These laws set standards for electrical wiring and plumbing, consistent with new appliances and fixtures. They set structural standards for flooring and roofing. They assured that the components for a house produced in a factory in one state would be legal when erected in another. Model zoning ordinances in 1924 and 1928 complemented the building codes and attempted to rationalize land use so that local governments would be able to separate single-family residential, multifamily residential, commercial, and industrial uses. At a time when factories often spewed visible, noxious emissions, zoning prohibited industrial uses adjacent to housing. Zoning could also ensure that single-family residential districts did not permit multi-family dwellings (thought to be lower-class) or shopping (thought to generate traffic). The codes could also require that all structures be equipped with proper connections to sewers and water supply. They could also stipulate paved streets of a certain width and sidewalks. They could establish setbacks to ensure that light and air would reach every room in every structure. There was much common sense to zoning in the 1920s, so many cities and towns took it up, but the idea of separation of uses was often taken too far. A good pedestrian neighborhood mixes housing, schools, and shopping rather than segregating these uses into separate pods accessed by automobiles.

As the 1920s progressed, Hoover also played a central role in working with big business to define how the federal government could
promote business growth through real estate development. Through
the National Association of Real Estate Boards (NAREB), real estate
developers lobbied the federal government to establish a mortgage
interest income-tax deduction and to stimulate housing production
through loan guarantees and production advances for new projects. A
major effort to enhance the old game of land speculation with a new
game of federal subsidy gained momentum.

Many affluent Americans had acquired a taste for suburban houses.
Throughout the twenties, picturesque enclaves with elegant homes set
in elaborate landscaping continued to be built for the elite. However,
most of the large-scale land subdividers of the 1920s were real estate
brokerage firms who sold lots and left the building to small contractors, mail-order house companies, or the owners. By the late 1920s,
subdividers began to see that they could increase their profits by erect-
ing houses to enhance the image of community and stability they were
selling, an idea Gross had pioneered in the 1890s in Chicago.[45] Led
by affluent developers such as J. C. Nichols, developer of the Country Club subdivisions around Kansas City, a group within NAREB
began to call themselves "community builders" in an effort to distin-
guish themselves from the "curbstoners" who subdivided land hastily
and walked away. As Marc Weiss defines it, "A community builder
designs, engineers, finances, develops, and sells an urban environment
using as the primary material rural, undeveloped land. In the parlance
of the real estate industry, such activity is called the platting and improvement of subdivisions."[46]

Working closely with NAREB, Hoover's Commerce Department
began to craft supports for "community builders." In 1921 Hoover
had helped to establish and support Better Homes in America, Inc.[47]
Soon this had grown into an "educational" nonprofit that Hoover
called "a sort of collateral arm to the Housing Division of the Department of Commerce," with Hoover as president.[48] It was a propaganda
effort, a coalition of over seven thousand local growth machines composed of bankers, builders, and manufacturers supporting government
aid to private real estate development as a national economic strategy
to boost consumption.

In 1928 Secretary of Commerce Hoover ran for the U.S. presidency with the slogan "A chicken in every pot and a car in every garage." He beat Democrat Al Smith and took office in 1929. Following the stock market crash, Hoover developed a campaign for home ownership as a business strategy for recovery from the Depression. In 1931 Hoover's National Conference on Homebuilding and Home Ownership explored federal investment, discussing not only financing and construction of houses, but also building codes, zoning codes, subdivision layout, and the location of industry and commerce.

Hoover and NAREB agreed that federal sources of capital and mortgage guarantees could provide a safety net for subdividers who wished to increase the scale of their building operations. In 1932 Hoover signed the Federal Home Loan Bank Act to "establish a credit reserve for mortgage lenders" (and thus encourage home lending) and established the Reconstruction Finance Corporation (RFC) to issue bonds to banks to help them offer mortgages. Banks took 41,000 applications under the Federal Home Loan Bank Act but approved only three.[49] RFC created a scandal by bailing out bankers who were cronies of RFC directors.[50]

Although the legislation was enacted after his term, Hoover's influence on the Federal Housing Administration (FHA) was more lasting. With NAREB involvement, Hoover drafted the outlines of what would later become the National Housing Act of 1934, establishing the FHA. The FHA provided loans for owners to modernize existing houses and purchase electrical appliances. They also supplied funds for new home mortgages on favorable terms and supported new construction. They insured banks so that they could provide 80 percent production advances to developers who would purchase land, subdivide it, and construct houses on it with very little of their own capital. In return, developers had to submit site plans and housing plans for review by the FHA.

The FHA offered developers conservative advice about architecture and site design. Meant to correct the worst abuses of curbstoners and corrupt builders, manuals such as *Planning Profitable Neighborhoods* showed how to turn a grid of small lots (less than a tenth of an acre) into a modest subdivision of larger lots (about a quarter of an acre) plus street trees and a park. The new design was more spacious but it did not address the problem of affordability. In general, FHA rejected regional architectural styles, scorned modern architecture, and instituted what architect Keller Easterling calls low-quality "subdivision products."[51] Worst of all, the FHA followed the lead of another agency, the federal Home Owners Loan Corporation (HOLC) in determining creditworthiness. HOLC was established in 1933 to refinance home mortgages. HOLC defined the appraised value of properties by making

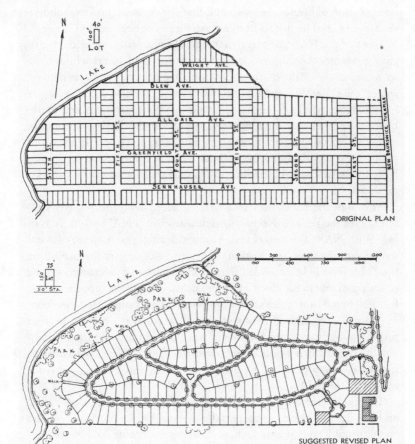

Plan for grid subdivision of 40-by-100-foot lots versus a recommended plan with parkland, street trees, more generous 75-by-100-foot lots, and community buildings, from *Planning Profitable Nieghborhoods*, Federal Housing Authority, 1939.

maps in various colors. They "red-lined," or prohibited mortgage loans, in neighborhoods inhabited by people of color.[52] Their highest classifications were reserved for all-white, all-Protestant neighborhoods, and they refused loans in racially mixed neighborhoods. Only segregated subdivisions, enforced by deed restrictions, and sometimes separated by walls from neighborhoods where people of color resided, could qualify for FHA support.

NAREB, through its Realtors' Washington Committee, lobbied for the FHA and against federal funding for any other approach to housing, including new towns and multifamily public housing in the cities. NAREB was also against prefabricated factory-produced housing (which would be produced by union workers and undercut the influence of the realtors and subdividers). Allied with NAREB were the U.S. Chamber of Commerce, the U.S. League of Savings and Loans, the National Retail Lumber Dealers Association, and the National Association of Manufacturers.

FDR: Housing Through Public Construction

Franklin Delano Roosevelt defeated Hoover in the presidential election of 1932 and took office in March 1933. With millions unemployed and many homeless, housing policy was highly contested. Roosevelt recast the programs for housing that Hoover had initiated, moving some in a more egalitarian direction, stressing cheap electricity as part of social modernization, and adding public construction. The New Deal legislation in planning and housing established the Home Owners Loan Corporation (HOLC) in 1933; the Federal Housing Administration (FHA) in 1934; the Resettlement Administration in 1935 to build the Greenbelt towns; and the U.S. Housing Act (Wagner-Steagall Act) in 1937, creating the U.S. Housing Authority to sponsor public housing.[53] Roosevelt was open to diverse strategies to shelter Americans, private and public. He did not challenge racial segregation in housing but made sure that some federal projects housed African-Americans.

Among the strongest Democratic advocates for public control of planning, design, and construction were the Regional Planning Association of America (RPAA) and the Labor Housing Conference. Housing activists such as Catherine Bauer and Edith Elmer Wood were members of the RPAA along with architectural critic Lewis Mumford, architect Clarence Stein, landscape architect Henry Wright, and planner Benton MacKaye.[54] They defined residential neighborhoods for the twentieth century as those that housed working families and preserved pedestrian access to schools, parks, shops, and transit, while accommodating the car. Throughout the late 1920s and 1930s, the members built successful demonstration projects in Sunnyside, New York, Radburn, New Jersey, and Baldwin Hills, California, which included both multifamily and single-family housing. The RPAA also supported the Resettlement Administration (RA), headed by Rexford Tugwell. Tugwell constructed over one hundred planned communities. Most famous were the Greenbelt towns. Twenty Greenbelt towns were authorized; despite intense Republican opposition, three were built before funding was withdrawn. Greenbelt, Maryland, outside Washington, D.C., included rental apartments, a cooperative drugstore, a cooperative grocery, and a cooperative filling station, demonstrating the survival of the communitarian spirit as an aspect of suburban design that had launched earlier places like Llewellyn Park and Mount Vernon, New York. Opponents on the right criticized Tugwell's projects as "communist farms."[55]

Bauer, author of the notable book *Modern Housing*, was also executive secretary of a group called the Labor Housing Conference. She and her colleagues linked multifamily housing with child-care centers and recreational amenities such as swimming pools and meeting rooms. They also believed in excellent architecture. Projects such as the Hosiery Workers Housing in Philadelphia, under the federal Public Works Administration (PWA) Housing Division, and the Harlem River Houses for African-Americans in New York, designed by teams of noted architects in the 1930s, pointed to what could be achieved for families of modest incomes. Bauer and Wood drafted the legislation for public housing. Conservative Republicans defeated the Wagner Act in 1935 and 1936, only to pass it in 1937 with severe cost restrictions, means testing for tenants, and slum clearance to protect private landlords. The Labor Housing Conference members called the result the Anti-Housing Act, and informally referred to the FHA as F——— Housing Altogether![56]

As Republicans and Democrats wrestled with housing alternatives throughout the 1930s, Republicans gained the upper hand because they promoted the ideal of home ownership without ever tallying the full physical or social costs of individual homes on separate plots of land served by roads, sewers, and parks. Democrats who built well-designed multifamily housing and complete communities with all of the necessary public amenities in place were told their plans were "too expensive." In fact, Tugwell was building for low-income families, and wisely "aimed to produce structures with low maintenance and replacement costs, so high-quality items were used in construction."[57] No one challenged the federal cost accounting to enlighten the warring political parties, because at bottom these debates were ideological. Would the federal government support real estate subdividers or construct housing? Would public subsidies back bankers' and businesses' efforts to build "profitable neighborhoods" or would they shelter poor people?

During the lean years of the 1930s, the subdividers' reach exceeded their grasp. Historian Joel Schwartz reports 375,000 newly platted lots around metropolitan Cleveland, almost half of them empty, and 1,250,000 lots around Detroit, enough for three times the city's population.[58] The planning effort consolidated by Hoover's National Conference was not derailed forever because many subdividers had made spectacular profits in the boom years of the twenties, building both upper-income picturesque enclaves and more modest subdivisions. Government had shown it was willing and able to intervene in the development process on behalf of finance, insurance, real estate, timber, manufacturing, and auto interests. The big firms could hold on, while the lean years wiped out the smaller builders, and the real estate lobby attacked new towns and public housing. A very powerful coalition had formed, one with close ties to the Republican Party, but also a lobby the Democrats would not be able to ignore. A new era of suburban development would soon emerge, dominated by large firms with federal backing.

Chapter Seven

SITCOM SUBURBS

You know, just because there's already a Forest Park
doesn't mean there can't be a Park Forest.
— CARROLL F. SWEET, JR., assistant to
developer Philip M. Klutznick

W ITH POPULATIONS BETWEEN FIFTY AND EIGHTY
thousand, the largest of the post–World War II suburbs
were the size of cities, but they looked and felt like overgrown subdivisions. In Levittown, New York, Lakewood, California,
and Park Forest, Illinois, model houses on suburban streets held families similar in age, race, and income whose lifestyles were reflected in
the nationally popular sitcoms of the 1950s and 1960s, including
Leave It to Beaver, Ozzie and Harriet, and *Father Knows Best.* The
planning of these postwar suburbs was often presented in the press as
hasty, driven by the patriotic need to meet the demand for housing created by the khaki-clad, beribboned heroes returned from the Battle of
the Bulge or Bataan. The press attributed problems in suburb design
to rushed planning, but this was not the case. Backroom politics of
the 1920s, 1930s, and early 1940s had shaped postwar housing and
urban design. There was no haste at all in the twenty years of lobbying for federal support of private-market, single-family housing development. The postwar suburbs were constructed at great speed,
but they were deliberately planned to maximize consumption of mass-
produced goods and minimize the responsibility of the developers to
create public space and public services.

Aerial view of Levittown. Courtesy of Nassau County Museum Collection, Long Island Studies Institute, Hofstra University.

In the vast new suburbs built in the late 1940s and 1950s, definitions of public and private were reshaped, as loans guaranteed by the federal government poured into private real estate development firms. Although many sociologists found it fascinating to interview suburbanites about issues of social conformity, surprisingly few detailed studies were made of the built environments of large, postwar suburbs. These places have not attracted architectural historians, because few well-known architects were involved, or planning historians, because they were not usually planned by noted practitioners. Historians of public policy have tended to trace legislation more than its implementation, so a critical look at how legislation was translated into three-dimensional living space is long overdue.

WARTIME

During World War II, the housing alternatives developed in the 1930s continued to spark debate. Housing shortages for war workers slowed the production of bombers and ships, so the federal government considered proposals for model cities for war workers, including housing, public transportation, and neighborhood amenities such as schools, child-care centers, and health clinics. At the Willow Run plant in Michigan, where Ford produced B-24 bombers, a proposal for "Bomber City," designed by Eero Saarinen, George Howe, Louis Kahn, and Oscar Stonorov, was defeated. Self-built slums and speculative tracts of small houses grew by default.[1] Similar speculation occurred around defense plants and military bases in California, along with the construction of temporary housing.

In other cases, industrialists such as Henry J. Kaiser stepped in to build war workers' housing. Although the federal government paid for some of it, real estate lobbyists argued that wartime housing funded under the Lanham Act of 1940 should be temporary, and they insisted that it be demolished or sold to private landlords at the war's end. Projects housing African-American war workers in Long Beach were dismantled.[2] Innovative Lanham Act housing in Vanport City, Oregon, providing women war workers with support services including around-the-clock child care and take-out meals, could have provided a model for postwar working families, but services were closed down and temporary structures were destroyed in a flood.[3]

Housing Hearings of 1947–48

Although they were disappointed by some aspects of the 1937 Wagner Act and by the defeat of some of the wartime projects, Catherine Bauer and other advocates of decent multifamily housing in sound residential neighborhoods did not retreat at the war's end. They campaigned for expanded public housing in the form of the bipartisan Taft-Ellender-Wagner housing bill, introduced in 1945 with support from the AFL, the CIO, and the Conference of Mayors. Advocates found themselves in a shouting match with NAREB lobbyists who were busy discrediting public construction of housing as "un-American" and promoting government subsidies for private housing development.

In *Picture Windows,* historians Rosalyn Baxandall and Elizabeth Ewen have analyzed the hearings on housing dominated by Republican Senator Joseph McCarthy in 1947 and 1948.[4] Before McCarthy gained fame hunting for moles in the State Department and reds in Hollywood, he developed his "sledgehammer style" attacking proponents of public housing and planned towns as socialists and communists. Lambasting one federally funded project for veterans, Senator

McCarthy claimed the government had paid for "a breeding ground for communists."[5] McCarthy hated multifamily designs as well as public funding for shelter. NAREB lobbyist Herbert U. Nelson, executive director of the Realtors' Washington Committee, was also sure that public housing was communistic. He testified that "public credit can properly be used to help sustain home ownership and private enterprise." In other testimony in 1949, he went on to attack the women housing reformers: "I do not believe in democracy. I think it stinks. I don't think women should be allowed to vote at all. Ever since they started, our public affairs have been a worse mess than before." Historians have noted Nelson had funds to spare: "More than $5 million was spent by homebuilders in the struggle over this act. So aggressive were their tactics that a full-scale congressional investigation was conducted."[6] With heavy opposition from McCarthy and Nelson, the Taft-Ellender-Wagner legislation was battered down year after year. In 1949 the Housing Act passed but subsequent negotiations reduced the numbers of units authorized year by year. Other provisions in the act initiated disastrous neighborhood clearance efforts. These would later become the programs called "urban renewal."

McCarthy's committee also attacked building workers in traditional craft unions in the AFL as incompetents who produced "slack" work and would impede the postwar housing process. McCarthy found in William Levitt an ally who would testify that only federal aid in the form of FHA insurance for "production advances" to large private builders, coupled with the abolition of zoning codes and building codes, and the end of union labor, could solve the postwar housing shortage. The National Association of Manufacturers weighed in on Levitt's side.[7] Senator McCarthy also hired a New York public relations firm, Bell, Jones, and Taylor, to make sure the publicity favored conservative Republican testimony. Their other clients included savings-and-loan associations, the National Association of Home Builders (NAHB), and NAREB.[8]

POSTWAR DEMAND: NO WAY TO FAIL WITH THE FHA

The year 1945 was the sixteenth in a row when new construction did not meet the demand for new housing. The need was intense. People were doubled up with relatives, friends, and strangers. War workers and veterans lived in rooming houses and camped out in cars. Some

tried to convert chicken coops and barns into family housing. Demand
for shelter was expected to grow as waves of demobilized veterans,
wartime savings at the ready, married and formed new households.
Builders laid their plans ambitiously, but even they often underesti-
mated the intensity of demand and its remarkable duration. Backed by
the FHA and the VA, banks gave loans for the construction of ten million new homes between 1946 and 1953, creating a gigantic private
housing industry. By the mid-fifties, annual housing starts topped a
million and a half, stimulating additional demand for furniture, appliances, and suburban schools.[9]

Before the war, one-third of all houses were built by their owners.
Small contractors, who averaged fewer than five houses a year, built
another third. By the late 1950s, about two-thirds of the new houses in
the United States were produced by large builders.[10] Leading the postwar housing efforts were large developer-builders who could handle
the government paperwork, achieve economies of scale, and under-
sell small builders. They totally reorganized the industry. With the
FHA behind them, as well as numerous other government programs
left over from the New Deal and wartime, large builders had the resources to do serious community planning, but only a few, like Philip
Klutznick's American Community Builders (ACB) in Park Forest, Illinois, attempted it. Others, even the biggest firms, still pushed the marketing of lots with houses, not the physical planning of towns. In this
they resembled the creators of earlier streetcar suburbs. When pressed
to name a tract's advantages, a developer might offer "100 percent
American Family Community," "good radio reception," or even "the
regular route of the Good Humor Man," none of which required any
investment.[11] A very large developer might advertise a swimming pool
or perhaps donate land for a church. Invoking the benefits of economies of scale, they built tracts the size of cities and reaped enormous
profits. They left the job of creating the physical infrastructure and
social fabric to the federal, state, and local governments, and the new
homeowners.

LEVITT AND SONS: THE GENERAL MOTORS
OF HOUSING PRODUCTION?

Throughout the twentieth century, makers of houses have tried to
emulate manufacturers of automobiles, but the comparisons are often

Sketches of Cape Cod houses at Levittown. There were six versions of this design, almost identical. Courtesy of Nassau County Museum Collection, Long Island Studies Institute, Hofstra University.

hard to pin down. Identical automobiles can be run off the assembly line in a factory, but houses have to be joined to specific, unique sites. Standardization of sites is difficult and ugly. During the postwar years, large-scale American builders did level hills and fill valleys, but monotonous terrain supporting identical houses was not satisfying to residents. Some developers thought that encouraging buyers to trade in subdivision houses the way they might trade in cars for newer models every year might work, but families were more likely to move to another neighborhood rather than choose a new house in the same tract.

Using a single design could lower the cost of houses. Alfred Levitt said, "As in your car, the parts in a Levitt house are standardized; each part will fit any house of the same model. . . . the Levitt factory . . . is the land on which we assemble our houses."[12] Although they are often credited with this, Levitt and Sons did not originate rapid production of houses in a continuous production process. The mail-order companies from 1900 to 1930 had standardized parts and preassembled bathroom units and kitchen cabinets. In 1939 Fritz Burns in Mar Vista, California, was one of the first to emphasize a continuous production process on the street, plus sweat equity in the finishing.[13] Levitt and Sons pushed in the same direction in a 1942 project for 750 FHA Title VI houses in Oakdale Farms, Norfolk, Virginia, where they refined and systematized over two dozen basic tasks of house building.[14] William Levitt, Alfred's brother, also learned ways to speed construction when working with the Seabees, the Navy's construction arm.

After the war, Levitt and Sons added vertical integration of suppliers to maximize the standardization of the firm's process. All materials from nails to appliances were made to exact specifications and purchased through a subsidiary, the North Shore Supply Company. Materials arrived precut and "combat loaded," so that the first items needed were on top. Levitt and Sons also owned the Grizzly Peak Lumber Company and forests in California, so that they controlled their source of wood. They hired non-union workers who were equipped with new small power tools to perform repetitive operations on house after house. Compared to skilled carpentry, the de-skilled work was boring, but Alfred Levitt thought the money made up for this. A complex system of subcontracting rewarded Levitt operatives who moved up to foreman status.

Interviewed by a reporter for a *Time* magazine cover story in July 1950, William Levitt came across as a forty-three-year-old, hoarse-voiced chain smoker of three packs a day, with "a liking for hyperbole that causes him to describe his height (5 ft. 8 in.) as 'nearly six feet,' and his company as the 'General Motors of the housing industry.' "[15] The Luce publications, *Time, Life, Fortune,* and *Architectural Forum,* promoted every aspect of Levitt's operations, so this is one of very few sarcastic comments to be found in magazines where the Levitt product was regularly extolled. Alfred Levitt, William's brother and the firm's designer, styled their first Cape Cod to recall Sears mail-order houses like "The Nantucket," which mimicked colonial farmhouses, offering a neo-traditional appeal. They built thousands of almost identical 800-square-foot houses, with a living room, kitchen, two bedrooms, one bath, and a driveway but no garage. Minimal variations, such as six feet of picket fence versus six feet of rail fence, were all that distinguished one house from another. Residents as well as visitors might find themselves "lost in the W's." Western, Willowood, Wildwood, Woodgreen, Wisteria, Wheelbarrow, Wildflower, Wedgewood, Wishbone, Wisp, Wing, Watchtower, Ward, Wayside, Weaving, Wavy, Water, and Wander Lanes were all adjacent.

After a year of renting the first batch of houses, the Levitts streamlined the paperwork, stood behind the product with an unwritten one-year warranty, and began to sell Cape Cods for $6,990. The Levitts produced a fairly sound house according to construction assessments of the time, although not an architecturally sophisticated one. Like Fritz Burns, Levitt and Sons also relied on some sweat equity, giving veterans and their wives the chance to convert the attics of their houses into additional bedrooms, build garages or porches, and landscape the yards. Rather than boast that sweat equity lowered prices, Levitt claimed an ideological advantage. "No man who has a house and lot can be a Communist," claimed William Levitt. "He has too much to do."[16] After the Cape Cod, they produced a "ranch" with a carport for $7,990 [Levitt contracts specified that the residents must be of the Caucasian race] although they could employ household help such as maids or yard workers who were not. Kenneth Jackson has noted that by 1960, Levittown had not a single resident who was black. With 82,000 residents it was the largest all-white community in the United States.[17]

The public reaction to the prices was positive—stories of customers standing in line for days appeared in the press. In October 1952, *Fortune* magazine gushed that Levitt offered "The Most House for the Money." Bendix washers, General Electric stoves, and Admiral televisions were installed in the houses. Levitt promoted [joint print advertising: the house builder endorsed the products, and the products were often selling points for the houses.] He believed in creating a brand name; customers would buy a Levitt house rather than a small builder's house, just as they would prefer the A&P to a general store.[18] Levitt also developed a public relations campaign to make sure that every last step in the house-building process was publicized to the maximum, as well as every product used in construction and furnishing. In 1952 *Fortune* praised "Levitt's Progress," also publishing William Levitt's whining complaints about government interference— strict FHA and VA inspections and standards. The inspectors were concerned about Levitt's proposal for asbestos shingles, called "Colorbestos," as a way to lower costs for the exterior sheathing of houses. Despite hundreds of millions of dollars of FHA-insured financing, Levitt said with a straight face: "Utopia in this business would be to get rid of the government, except in its proper function of an insurance agency."[19] The Levitt firm was now the biggest private home builder in the country.

Levitt and Local Government

The Levitts were obsessed with producing seventeen thousand standardized houses, but oddly, they had no master plan for their site and little concern for its balanced development. Between 1947 and 1951

Levitt and Sons built and heavily publicized seven small shopping strips, which the Levitts found highly profitable to lease,[20] as well as nine swimming pools and seven small parks with children's playgrounds and some baseball fields. They benefited from proximity to a large public park at Jones Beach. For public relations purposes, the Levitts added a "town hall" in 1951, despite the fact that Levittown was a large, unincorporated community with no government of its own. For a city of eighty thousand people, these public facilities were extremely minimal.

Levitt and Sons lacked planning expertise. Both Bill and Alfred Levitt had dropped out of college to work with their father, Abraham Levitt, a former lawyer who had started the family firm by asking his sons to join him in building one neo-Tudor house in the Depression. The firm took off, with Bill as salesman and Alfred as draftsman-designer, but no one had formal qualifications in land use planning, civil engineering, or urban design. Despite its urban scale, their Long Island community was built without a master plan, expanded one part at a time, because their land purchases were not always contiguous. Levitt and Sons found it convenient to have someone else pay for the infrastructure of the city they were creating.

In 1951 NYU students and faculty conducted a study of "The Impact of Levittown on Local Government."[21] Despite its nonpartisan tone, the study demonstrates why Levitt and Sons could not handle urban-scale development. The Levitts used federal government guarantees to obtain production advances to purchase potato farms and bankroll their construction of over seventeen thousand homes. They then proceeded to push the cost of building urban infrastructure for seventy to eighty thousand people onto the budgets of local governments. At that time, regulation was minimal and, although it was growing rapidly, Nassau County had no master plan. Levittown, not a political entity itself, was divided between two towns, Hempstead and Oyster Bay. The company related to towns and the county by passing on the responsibilities for public services as fast as possible.

To get construction equipment to the house sites, Levitt and Sons had to build roads, but they dedicated them to the towns so the towns would assume maintenance costs. However, the company failed to integrate their road systems with county and state highways. To provide water, the company constructed wells, pumping systems, and distribution mains. They sold the wells and pumping equipment to the local towns at 50 percent of cost, and dedicated the mains to the towns, so the towns would maintain them. Levitt and Sons did not plan for urban-scale sewage disposal. They used individual cesspools—not even septic tanks—attached to each house, rather than building sewers. Engineers in the Nassau County Department of Public Health protested without success. They knew that effluent from cesspools could pollute the water table, and they foresaw lawns boggy with raw sewage causing outbreaks of disease.[22] Many suburbs of the 1940s and 1950s were built with septic tanks to increase profits. When septic tanks failed, homes became unsalable. The federal government had to provide money for localities to install sewers in the 1960s. Meanwhile, one engineer said in disgust that the use of septic tanks in new subdivisions was like "a person walking down the street with a silk hat on his head and a hole in the seat of his britches."[23]

Similarly, the Levitt firm failed to plan for trash removal. They left this up to private contractors, whose private waste removal services would be paid for by the residents. By 1951, the local haulers were told that facilities in Oyster Bay were overtaxed. A quarry in Hempstead was used as a temporary dumping area, while Hempstead struggled to build a disposal plant. The Levitt firm also ignored the public transportation that such a large new population would need. They did not anticipate the parking spaces Levittown residents' cars would require, overwhelming the local small towns and their main streets. Most expensive were schools needed by tens of thousands of children. Levitt and Sons often boasted that they "set aside" land for schools to both towns, but according to the NYU report, they paid for nothing and built nothing.[24] Towns had to assess the taxpayers in special districts to pay for the land costs as well as school buildings, school operations, and public libraries. State government provided financial aid to avoid a crisis.

Landia

Occasionally the Levitts were asked to give their views on good design practice. William Levitt's response was ambivalent. A *Fortune* reporter noted that although he "believes it is no longer socially desirable to build rental housing—or to live in cities—Bill Levitt rents a twelve-room Manhattan apartment."[25] Abraham Levitt's response was practical. He planted trees and flowers everywhere, dedicating himself to the landscaping of the bare lots scraped by the family bulldozers, ensuring that as the planting matured, the area would gain character. Alfred's response was more thoughtful: "Levittown is the largest community ever built by a single company. . . . we made many mistakes, and we had to solve many unexpected problems."[26]

Alfred professed an enduring interest in the Regional Plan Association, revealed when he designed another community, Landia, with much lower density, for a 675-acre site near an existing railroad line on Long Island. By 1951 Levitt and Sons had acquired the land. Although it was never built, Landia would have had sewers, a railroad station, a continuous belt of parks, a major shopping center, and thirty acres for light industry, all serving a community one-tenth the size of Levittown, 6,500 people in 1,750 houses.

Levitt and Sons split up after Bill said he could no longer make decisions with Alfred. Bill took over. Two more traditional Levittowns were constructed, one in Bucks County, Pennsylvania, outside Philadelphia, near the U.S. Steel plant, starting in 1951, and another in Willingboro, New Jersey, begun in the 1960s, after Abraham had retired. All three Levitts became wealthy men, although William Levitt lacked the steadiness of his father and brother. When they were gone, he was prone to overexpansion.[27] Once the U.S. housing market slowed, he also began to build in France and in Puerto Rico. The Puerto Rico Levittown became a colorful place covered in tropical vegetation, rather unlike the ones in Long Island, Pennsylvania, and New Jersey.

LAKEWOOD, CALIFORNIA: "WE SELL HAPPINESS IN HOMES"

Lakewood developed a little bit more slowly than Levittown, but eventually it was slightly larger in size. The three developers, Ben Weingart, Mark Taper, and Louis Boyar, described it as "a $250,000,000 planned community."[28] In 1949 they bought ten square miles of flat land near Long Beach from the defunct Montana Land Company. Boyar subdivided this into forty individual tracts, most of them 157 acres apiece: "The biggest tracts had a population of 2,400 as soon as the moving vans pulled away from the curb."[29] The entire area was gridded with streets meeting at right angles, lined by lots of 50 by 100 feet, the smallest size permitted in Los Angeles County. It held 17,500 houses and about 80,000 people. Almost all of them were white.

The developers were stingy with recreational facilities, but a county supervisor did persuade the developers to build one swimming pool in a local park and lease an existing golf course on their property to the county. Frame and stucco houses of 1,100 square feet were the standard. They were sold with no appliances. There were sewers, required by the county, and a Waste King electric garbage disposal in every kitchen to minimize the sanitation issues, although disposal by water was wasteful in a semiarid climate. O'Keefe and Merritt gas stoves, Norge refrigerators, and Bendix "Economat" washers could be added to the purchase price at an extra charge of nine dollars per appliance per month.[30] Each house had one small tree, planted by the developers, in the planting strip in front of it.[31] The developers hired William Garnett, the noted aerial photographer, to fly over the land recording their progress. His chilling images of rows of houses sprouting from fields became famous, but not for the reasons the developers anticipated.

Aerial view of Lakewood, Calif. Photograph by William Garnett.

Single-family house
in Lakewood, Calif.
Photograph by author,
2001.

From the start, Lake-
wood included a large,
enclosed, pedestrian shopping mall, the Lakewood
Center Mall, surrounded by 10,580 parking spaces, as well as sixteen
small commercial centers, each containing a dry cleaner, a barber, a
beauty shop, and either a drugstore or a five-and-dime. Most also had a
grocery store. All were within walking distance—a half-mile at most
from the houses.[32] The shopping mall was anchored by a branch of the
May Company, designed by architect Albert C. Martin with four giant
neon M's. Each one sixteen feet high, they faced north, south, east, and
west. Opening in February 1952, the shopping center provided everything eighty thousand new residents needed, and also drew in outside
customers. While Levitt lost residents to other people's malls, Lakewood raked in the cash. Lakewood also became famous in 1954 for
initiating the "Lakewood system," contracting for services with Los
Angeles County rather than organizing and paying for firefighters,
police, and other essential town services after incorporation as an independent city. William Fulton notes that in Southern California,
"dozens of small municipalities were created on the cheap" following
the Lakewood example.[33]

In 1954 Ben Weingart and Louis Boyar were subpoenaed to testify
before Homer Capehart's Senate subcommittee on "irregularities in
their federally backed mortgages and construction loans."[34] D. J.
Waldie relates that the Indiana senator accused Weingart of setting up
two or three hundred dummy corporations to shield his investments.
Weingart invariably answered the charges, "You'll have to ask Mr.
Boyar." The developers had not gotten FHA Title VI funding, ensuring
a 90 percent production advance. Instead, they had proceeded under
the National Housing Act, Section 213, pretending to be the organizers of "mutual homes." They got their employees to front dummy corporations, using a New Deal program planned for rural cooperatives

with a maximum of 501 houses apiece. The "cooperatives" bought land from the developers, making them a profit. Then the "cooperatives" hired the developers to build houses for them, making them another profit. Then the "cooperatives" dissolved. Thus the three principals built the largest suburban community in America. Their manipulation of the complexities of housing legislation was devious but not illegal.

PARK FOREST, THE GI TOWN

Park Forest, Illinois, was a private development that partook of the idealism of the New Deal and the experience of the Resettlement Administration. According to historian Gregory Randall, Philip Klutznick, a federal government official under both Roosevelt and Truman, declared: "We aren't interested in houses alone. We are trying to create a better life for people. In our view, we will have failed if all we do is to produce houses."[35] The son of Polish immigrants, Klutznick grew up in Kansas City, Missouri, and practiced law in Omaha before becoming a special assistant to the U.S. attorney general with expertise on land use and housing law. In wartime, he became a regional coordinator for the Office of Defense Housing, based in Chicago, and then commissioner of the Federal Public Housing Authority under Truman. When he was approached by Nathan Manilow, a major Chicago real estate developer, about heading up a "GI Town," Klutznick said he might be interested if it was a real town and not an overgrown suburban development: "The town must have legal standing in the region and obligate the residents to be responsible for the future of the village."[36] He added that "the planning would require locating housing areas, commercial areas, industrial sites, parks, and other community services. It would require new utilities and roads, a good water supply, and well-designed storm and sanitary drainage systems."[37] Klutznick also wanted to build with union labor.

It took three or four tries for Manilow to persuade Klutznick to head the effort. He and Manilow became the major stockholders in a firm called American Community Builders (ACB). As Gregory Randall has documented, they selected a site of 2,400 (later over 3,100) acres about thirty miles south of Chicago on a railroad line. ACB hired experienced housing architects, Jerrold Loebl and Norman Schloss-

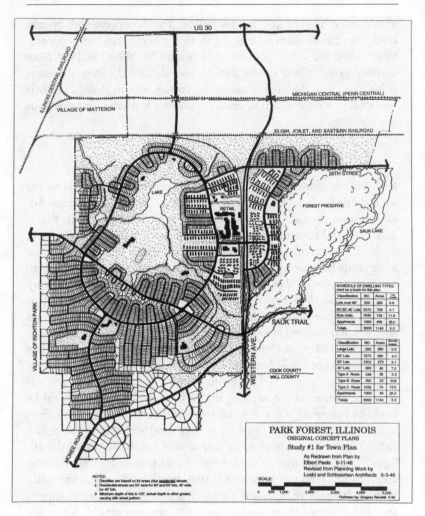

Park Forest, Ill.: original site plan from 1946, shopping mall plan, and revised
site plan from 1952, Elbert Peets, landscape architect and site designer, redrawn
by Gregory C. Randall for *America's Original GI Town: Park Forest, Illinois.*
© 2000, reprinted by permission of the Johns Hopkins University Press.

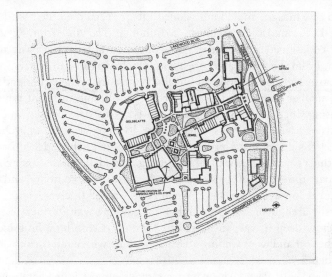

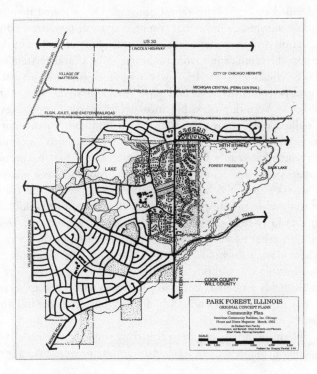

man of Chicago, and commissioned Elbert Peets, the noted Washington, D.C., landscape architect, coauthor of *The American Vitruvius* and codesigner of Greendale, Wisconsin, to lay out the basic town plan. From the first, Park Forest was intended as a "garden city" with a nearby railroad station, sites for industry, a shopping center and several smaller commercial areas, parks, schools, and different types of housing, including apartments, three types of row houses, and six kinds of house lots. Peets worked with Richard Bennett, an architect who left a position as a professor at Yale to join Loebl and Schlossman for this project. They walked the site again and again, discussing how to spare the groves of trees, make the best use of the contours, and deal with the low-lying wetlands. When Peets wanted to create a lake in a marshy area, Bennett reported that "he couldn't wait for the survey to see how deep it was; so he said if I would excuse him, he took his clothes off and went wading all over the thing with a tall stick to check the depth."[38]

Changes to Peets's site plan were made almost immediately when ACB decided to begin with rental housing. This allowed them to escape some unforeseen industrial zoning complications, proceed under FHA Section 608 loan guarantee programs, and get sufficient density to support the retail center from the start. Using Clarence Stein's Baldwin Hills Village as a model, 3,010 two-story townhouses and flats were grouped in courtyards and superblocks, designed in traditional styles. Some were duplexes, but most were in larger groupings. The FHA dallied over approvals. ACB lost a building season, but construction started in late October 1947. In 1948 tenants were moving in, the Klutznick family first among them. At the first barbecue, the developers pressed residents to vote for incorporation as a village and begin to take over the local government. Meanwhile the company began to develop the shopping center with a branch of Goldblatt's as anchor for forty-four smaller stores. Klutznick realized that he had a revolving market of thirty thousand people poised at the moment in life when most household goods were needed. The shopping center was successful, and although Goldblatt's did not survive over time, Marshall Fields and Sears came in. ACB also succeeded in recruiting some industry to the sites near the railroad, but never the full amount planned.

Finally, the company began to construct single-family houses. They had originally planned three or four thousand homes at prices between

Aerial view of Park Forest, Ill., showing multi-family housing with shopping center at upper right. Park Forest Public Library.

$12,500 and $14,000, higher than Levittown or Lakewood. ACB increasingly faced competition from local tract developers who were building more cheaply on the outskirts of their area, attempting to take advantage of ACB's investment in green spaces and a town center. Under pressure to avoid slow home sales, ACB moved downmarket. Peets's elegant planning for small residential neighborhoods with a hierarchy of streets, parks, and pedestrian circulation was discarded in favor of through streets with no connecting greenbelt and fewer landscape buffers. Those streets did have the advantage of making better connections to the surrounding areas, but the pedestrian orientation was sacrificed to the flow of cars. Although Peets's approach to the residential neighborhood was in all of the planning textbooks as a model of good design, it was challenged within Park Forest by those who thought that Levitt and Sons was making more money by building cheaply.[39]

Just as Alfred Levitt was silenced by his bottom-line brother, so

Single-family houses in Park Forest. Park Forest Public Library.

bottom-line issues prevailed at Park Forest. Costs were slashed at every turn: houses were moved closer to the streets to save on piping, planting strips were removed, sidewalks were combined with curbs to save on concrete work and installation, and so on. Nevertheless, the "GI town" was a success, with streets patriotically named for the Illinois Congressional Medal of Honor winners. Over time, the houses were all sold, and the town filled out to a population of 30,000 by 1956.[40] By the late 1950s and early 1960s, ACB began to dissolve, selling various parts of the village that had not been on the market before, including the rental housing. Both partners became wealthy men. In time, Klutznick became the developer of Chicago's Water Tower Place, then Secretary of Commerce in the Carter administration.

THE RESIDENTS' STORY: CLASS, FAMILY, AND CONSUMPTION

Developers liked to say that the acquisition of a single-family house and the process of furnishing and expanding it made blue-collar residents "middle-class." Sociologists such as William Whyte, Bennett Berger, or Herbert Gans, who studied the sitcom suburbs, disagreed. Working-class residents who moved to suburbs were mixed by ethnicity and religion more than before—Italian-American, Polish-American, and Russian-American, Catholic, Protestant, and Jewish—but all white.

Families moved into a culture of consumption and became dependent on cars. Rituals such as backyard barbecues and parents' parties in tot-lots may have seemed novel but were not defining.

Perhaps it is more accurate to say that the sitcom suburbs compli-cated class relationships rather than erasing them. Race and gender were set against class in a particularly painful way. Racial segregation, always part of the suburban experience, usually managed through deed restrictions, was now enforced by government loan policies and local bankers' red-lining. So was gender discrimination in lending. The long-term economic effects of racial and gender exclusion were height-ened by the vast scale of new tracts and by their promotion in mass culture. Fifty years later, households headed by persons of color and women still lagged in their rates of home ownership. In 2000, 73.8 percent of white, non-Hispanic households owned houses, but only 47.2 percent of black and 46.3 percent of Hispanic households did. While 82.4 percent of married-couple families owned houses, only 49.1 percent of female-headed households did.[41]

Compared to the streetcar suburbs, sitcom suburbs in the 1950s offered far less flexibility about multiple units and family types. The three-generation family was split. Older members remained in inner-city neighborhoods as adult children were scattered into new suburbs. There was great pressure on breadwinners—whether white-collar or blue-collar—to keep up their spending. John Drone, the fictional char-acter created by John Keats in his critique *The Crack in the Picture Window,* proclaims that he has three jobs and is making all his pay-ments—house, car, and consumer credit. Tom Rath, the main charac-ter in Sloan Wilson's novel *The Man in the Gray Flannel Suit,* is nagged by his wife because she does not like their house and thinks he needs to earn more money.[42]

Rosie the Riveter, the typical working woman who was pushed out of the paid labor force in the late 1940s, came back in to help with the bills. By 1959 a third of U.S. women were working for pay. In the 1950s Americans consumed three-quarters of all the appliances and gadgets produced in the world. *Life* photographer Nina Leen pho-tographed a housewife with all of the items her family would consume in seven days, a critique, but many shots like this were meant to be taken straight, as evidence of the nation's economic might. Gender was a bad joke. The housewife's role was celebrated in ridiculous ways. A patriotic golden eagle might embellish the linoleum on her kitchen floor. Candidates in the Mrs. America contest got to parade in bathing suits as well as compete in making beds.

Unlike Britain, where television was introduced with public educational and cultural programming, the United States developed competing commercial stations with advertising pounding. Women dressed like chorus girls danced around cars. Moms in high heels and dresses heated frozen dinners in commercials that seemed like extensions of family-oriented, prime-time programming. Thousands of television commercials and print ads used the model house as the setting for all sorts of goods from detergents to diapers, dishwashers to Dodge cars. Their impact was increased by product placement in sitcoms and films. As Karal Ann Marling has observed, houses and television screens seemed to merge in a single message: "The person sitting in the living room window watching the set was a kind of minor-league star as well as a spectator. Look at me! Look at my house and my new color TV! Life in the 1950s imitated art—as seen on TV."[43]

As the fifties wore on, attention given to houses, appliances, and consumer products became more explicitly political, and the themes of the dream house and the cold war were interwoven in the televised 1959 Nixon-Khrushchev "kitchen debate" in Moscow.[44] At this exhibition, the United States displayed a model house, nicknamed "Splitnik," an all-electric kitchen, and dozens of small appliances, as well as canned foods, Pepsi, and cosmetics. Vice-President Nixon boasted to Khrushchev that this exhibit proved the superiority of the way of life of an ordinary American worker. He also claimed that appliances had removed household drudgery for women. Boasting about toasters in Moscow may seem odd, but one must remember the postwar labor unrest experienced in the United States and the importance of suburban life in dividing the working class on race and gender lines. Nixon sounded like a TV commercial, but in the background were echoes of Levitt saying, "No man who owns a house and lot can become a Communist."

CRITIQUES

Recent films such as *Pleasantville, The Truman Show,* and *Blast from the Past* satirize postwar suburbs as overly controlled places characterized by neo-colonial clapboard houses, neat lawns framed by picket fences, and racial exclusion, but in the 1950s the sitcoms were straight and the movies lacked irony. As critic Ella Taylor has observed, "Television became a home appliance that could be used to sell other home appliances to its owners; and as time went on, it also sold, through the episodic series, an image of desirable family life with consumption casually woven into the fabric of its stories."[45] Sitcoms and films thrived, but they were always about model families in new communities where every family had a house, a car, and a television. Television reached all households, even the families who did not get the houses, and because of this, many groups excluded from the sitcom suburbs of the 1950s, and from the public subsidies supporting them, still saw the tract house as an emblem of belonging and upward mobility. Distress over gender roles and concern about FHA practices that created federally sanctioned racial segregation were rarely explored, even by critics. In the postwar era, when Lewis Mumford complained about the proper design of neighborhoods and towns, his attacks targeted social conformity among subdivision families rather than the social and economic exclusion behind the suburban developments. Along with many other intellectuals, he laid himself open to the charge that he was becoming a snob.

Interplay between real estate developers and filmmakers in this era is fascinating. In *Bachelor in Paradise* (1961), a bachelor (Bob Hope) heads for a California tract to write an analysis of its social life, sure he will hate it. By the end of the film he has married the only single woman within miles—a real estate agent—and moved in for good. In *Mr. Blandings Builds His Dream House* (1948), an advertising executive (Cary Grant) tires of New York and moves his family to an exurban, custom-built, neo-colonial house. During the construction process many mistakes are made and Blandings is overcharged for everything.[46] Because Eric Hodgins wrote the original short story for *Fortune* magazine, it is likely that his fiction, and the subsequent film, were meant to play alongside the McCarthy housing hearings, where private developers stressed the impossibility of making postwar housing with unionized skilled workers in the construction trades. Film historian Catherine Jurca argues that *Mr. Blandings,* with its humorous account of one family's search for the dream house, was also the perfect vehicle to reassure Washington that Hollywood was not itself "red." "Through its strategic conflation of writing advertisements, building homes, and making movies, *Mr. Blandings* is able to advertise itself and the project of filmmaking in general as scrupulously loyal to American institutions such as the home and family and also as central to their production."[47]

Hollywood public relations man Paul MacNamara described *Mr. Blandings* as a "promotion man's dream." Corporate tie-ins with companies marketing steel, linens, paint, and carpet brought free print advertising to the film. General Electric rushed a new electric kitchen to the set so it could be used in the film; then it advertised, "Mr. Blandings' Dream house has come true! And it's an all General Electric Dream!"[48] Finally, in the biggest promotion of all, over seventy model Blandings "dream houses" were constructed around the country and raffled off as publicity for the film. For example, in Kansas City, NAREB developer J. C. Nichols demonstrated that he could build the same house for less than the Blandings paid. People lined up and orders poured in.

Meanwhile, Hodgins wrote *Blandings' Way*, a sequel never filmed.

Visitors line up to tour J. C. Nichols's replica of Mr. Blandings's dream house, Country Club District, Kansas City, Mo., 1948. With seventy of these across the country, this was "a promotion man's dream" for the film *Mr. Blandings Builds His Dream House*. Western Historical Manuscript Collection, Kansas City.

The hero gave up commuting and moved his family back to an apartment in midtown Manhattan, where Blandings could walk to his job in an ad agency selling laxatives, dog food, and cheap whiskey. Unfortunately, most suburbanites couldn't afford this option. They were stuck with the sitcom, which cast them as Mr. Homeowner and Mrs. Consumer. Houses kept getting a little larger, and many families tried to move up as they discovered the "mansion subsidy," tax deductions for mortgage interest that rose with the cost and size of the house. Estimated at $100 billion annually, the mansion subsidy remains larger than the annual budget of the Department of Housing and Urban Development.[49] As housing activist Cushing Dolbeare has noted, in the United States, citizens tolerate "the basic inequity of a housing subsidy system that provides open-ended subsidies through the tax system to the affluent while denying them—primarily because of cost considerations—to low-income households that cannot otherwise obtain decent, affordable housing. It should be clear that a better distribution of our housing subsidies could, in fact, realize the goal of decent housing for all in this country."[50]

LEGACIES OF GOVERNMENT-SUBSIDIZED PRIVATE DEVELOPMENT

As urban critic Barry Checkoway notes, back in the 1950s *Fortune* was fond of portraying suburbs as "exploding" over the landscape, the happy result of consumer preferences that created a boom. But, he says, "ordinary consumers had little real choice."[51] Vast American suburbs of the post–World War II era were shaped by legislative processes reflecting the power of the real estate, banking, and construction sectors, and the relative weakness of the planning and design professions. Despite the fact that FHA programs were effectively a developer subsidy, they were presented as assistance to the American consumer. Sprawl became the national housing policy.

In *Modern Housing in America: Policy Struggles in the New Deal Era,* historian Gail Radford defines the 1930s and 1940s as the time when Americans developed a "two-tier" policy to subsidize housing. Cramped multifamily housing for the poor would be constructed by public authorities, and more generous single-family housing for white, male-headed families would be constructed by the private developers with government support.[52] Looking back to midcentury, we can see how this split disadvantaged women and people of color as well as the elderly and people of low incomes. The split also had profound implications for urban design: inadequate financial resources behind one effort and wasted material resources behind the other. And worst of all, it mystified many working-class and middle-class Americans, who saw minimal subsidies for the poor but never understood that their own housing was far more heavily subsidized.

So, despite the greater scope for urban public amenities suggested by New Deal legislation enabling federal involvement in town building and public housing, it was NAREB's influence on the FHA's mortgage insurance for private developments that had the greatest long-term effect on patterns of American urbanization. As real estate historian Marc A. Weiss has written: "This new federal agency, run to a large extent both by and for bankers, builders, and brokers, exercised great political power in pressuring local planners and government officials to conform to its requirements." Between 1934 and 1940, Weiss concludes that "FHA had fully established the land planning and development process and pattern that a decade later captured media attention as 'postwar suburbanization.' "[53] Developers of the sitcom suburbs insisted that mass-producing two- and three-bedroom houses in distant, car-dependent tracts was not just one way, but the only way to house the nation. However badly they were built, however lonely their locations, these new houses and raw neighborhoods could always be upgraded. And this is what the residents did, pouring time and money into creating schools, civic organizations, and town committees to make public improvements and generate a sense of community. Year after year, American women, even more than men, dedicated their energies to these volunteer campaigns.

Unfortunately, citizen activists were working in a difficult context because the language of real estate speculation had become the standard way of discussing housing and town planning. Levittown and Lakewood were highly publicized models of profitable development, and the developers of more carefully planned communities like Park Forest ultimately changed course. By the mid-1950s private developers claimed to represent the authority of "the market," while taxpayers and overworked town governments had to deal with the so-called externalities of environmentally irresponsible development. In the sitcom suburbs, the triple dream for housing was flattened into a stereotype of a traditional house stuffed with appliances and furniture, equipped with two cars, and surrounded by a yard. The ideal of situating that house in a planned neighborhood with pedestrian access to schools, shops, parks, and public transit had all but disappeared. The sitcom suburbs did not offer "the most house for the money" in societal terms, but it would take many decades for Americans to understand that designing solid neighborhoods would be less expensive than subsidizing developers to sell single-family houses.

Chapter Eight

EDGE NODES

O Almighty God, who has given us this earth and has
appointed men to have domination over it; who has
commanded us to make straight the highways, to lift
up the valleys and to make the mountains low, we
ask thy blessing upon these men who do just that.
— REVEREND RAYMOND F. WRENN,
    "Prayer for America's Road Builders"

IN THE 1930S A MOTORIST DRIVING along a dusty, narrow road
in Fairfax County, Virginia, could get a cold drink at Tyson's general store or fill up at a two-pump gas station. Today Route 66
meets the Capital Beltway near Tysons Corner, a suburban place with
more commercial space than downtown Miami.[1] Tysons challenges
all of the old architectural conventions about massive development involving high-rise densities. It appears dense and sparse, upscale and
downmarket at the same time. Dulles Airport is nearby, but Tysons
is more than an untidy airport extension. Inside a knot of freeways
and arterials sit unrelated high-rise and low-rise buildings, a vast as-
semblage of houses, apartments, garages, shopping malls, fast-food
franchises, and corporate headquarters. In its wide parking lots, new
Mercedes sedans gleam next to old clunkers.

Journalist Joel Garreau included Tysons Corner in his 1991 list of
"edge cities," places he defined as "5,000,000 or more square feet of
leasable office space—the workplace of the Information Age," plus
"600,000 square feet or more of leasable retail space," that is, malls.

He also said that an edge city "has more jobs than bedrooms," "is perceived by the population as one place," and "was nothing like a 'city'
as recently as thirty years ago." Garreau claimed to identify over one
hundred American "edge cities." Robert E. Lang expands this with
"edgeless cities," smaller growth nodes. "Edge node" is the more
accurate term and can cover both types.[2] Tysons is one of many edge
nodes in Fairfax County. It was nurtured by Til Hazel, a lawyer turned
developer, who began his career handling litigation concerning the
location of Beltway entrances and exits before he turned this knowledge to use as a real estate investor.[3] Starting with a shopping mall,
Tysons Corner grew to include 60,000 white-collar jobs and 15 million square feet of commercial space on 1,700 acres. It resembles an
older commercial strip with all of the buildings exploded in scale, or a
model with all the building blocks for both suburb and city thrown on
the ground by a two-year-old having a tantrum.

I drove to Tysons Corner at 11:30 a.m. on a summer Saturday and

Tysons Corner Store, 1935, Fairfax County, Virginia. Photograph by
Samuel R. Pearson, Courtesy of the Fairfax County Public Library.

Tysons Corner, as an "edge city," 1989. Photograph by Scott Boatright.
Courtesy of the Fairfax County Public Libary.

parked first at "Fairfax Square." Fairfax Square lacks a square. It is an
office building with expensive ground-floor retail: Gucci's offered a
pair of hot pink snakeskin stiletto heels priced at $1,200. Next door,
Tiffany's displayed diamond bracelets and crystal, while Hermès,
Paris, stocked fabulous scarves and ties. Upstairs were eight stories of
advertising agencies, public relations firms, law offices, and investment
banks. To one side sat a Crown filling station and the red plastic
mansard roof and golden arches of McDonald's. How could Gucci's
and McDonald's coexist? It is hard to imagine a customer who would
indulge in trademark leather luggage and then enjoy a Big Mac.

On the far side of Leesburg Pike, across from Gucci, Tiffany, and
Hermès, sits a shopping mall called Tysons Corner Center. Since the
Leesburg Pike carries six to eight lanes of fast-moving traffic and the
mall lacks an obvious pedestrian entrance, I decided to negotiate
the street in my car rather than on foot. This is a problem planners call
the "drive to lunch syndrome," typical of edge nodes where nothing is

planned in advance and all the development takes place in isolated "pods." I drove through the dreary decks of parking hiding the mall from the minimal sidewalk. Finally I reached a large shopping mall with the usual chain offerings, and wondered how Tysons Corner Center could generate over 50,000 automobile trips per day.[4] This edge node has swallowed many of the former jobs and commercial activities of downtown Washington, D.C., as well as other small towns and older suburbs, with the result that Tysons Corner's malls appear to be the only places left for people to go.

Near the malls a Ritz-Carleton hotel looms twenty-odd stories high with a Chippendale pediment of the kind made famous by architect Philip Johnson in New York. It towers over car dealers' showrooms and a mall centered on a knockoff of a Frank Lloyd Wright store in San Francisco. Corporate headquarters sheathed in mirror glass, stone, or stucco form a backdrop for the malls. Executives usher clients in suits and ties into the buildings. Clerical workers flood out at noon for a quick fast-food lunch. Below one office tower, I watched forty men standing in the full sun in an asphalt parking lot marked "Enterprise Corporation," where trainers in red T-shirts were leading a round of aggressive martial arts stances and karate kicks. It appeared that they were drilling new security guards. Tysons Corner offers jobs for all skill levels, from flipping burgers and opening the gate at a ten-story-high apartment community to trading stocks and selling diamond bracelets, but nothing looks local. On the scattered, irregular skyline, Bank of America, Wachovia, Smith Barney, Bechtel, Booz-Allen, and Hamilton parade in large neon letters.

In 1995 Bank of America issued a famous report on sprawl in California. The bank pronounced: "Urban job centers have decentralized to the suburbs. New housing tracts have moved even deeper into agriculturally and environmentally sensitive areas. Private auto use continues to rise. This acceleration of sprawl has surfaced enormous social, environmental, and economic costs, which until now have been hidden, ignored, or quietly borne by society." Their analysts concluded: "The burden of these costs is becoming very clear. Businesses suffer from higher costs, a loss in worker productivity, and underutilized investments in older communities. . . . We can no longer afford the luxury of sprawl."[5] Perhaps Bank of America forgot to tell their branch office not to locate in Tysons Corner.

A mile away down a curving two-lane road, the landscape still looked like small-town Virginia. A family was holding a yard sale in front of a red brick bungalow. A realtor's SOLD sign swung over the front lawn. A little bit farther down the road stands the Shiloh Baptist Church, a small white clapboard structure with a stained glass window, surrounded by old oaks and maples, next to a meadow of waist-high grass and goldenrod. In the meadow a patch of gravel and cedar mulch studded with a dozen tiny juniper bushes supported a white neoclassical sign with pencil-thin columns: "Wilshyre of McLean, A Reserve Community," with "Single Family Homes, From the Upper $800's." And in tiny, almost microscopic print, at the very bottom, a peaked-roof house with an equals sign proclaimed "Equal Opportunity Housing." Many townhouses and high-rise apartments, looking like rental projects, lined the roads nearby. Clearly the developers saw a market for tract mansions priced at over $800,000, but I was surprised they saw it so near to Tysons.

For all its size, Tysons Corner is a suburb that has evolved from automotive building types rather than from the residential building types connected to the picturesque enclaves of the mid-nineteenth century. Its connection to leafy natural landscapes is a negative one. In 1997 the *Washington Post* reported that Fairfax County had lost 40 percent of its tree cover, mostly since the mid-1970s with the arrival of Tysons Corner and several other edge nodes. Writers Glenn Frankel and Steven Fehr interviewed Til Hazel and told him that twenty-eight acres a day were disappearing because of new construction. "So what?" he replied. "The land is a resource for people to use and the issue is whether you use it well. . . . Is the goal to save green space so the other guy can look at it?"[6] When asked about the process of developing rural land, Hazel, a veteran of decades of legal wrangling over land use, said, "It's a war. How else would you describe it?"[7]

ORIGINS OF THE EDGE NODES:
ROADSIDE STRIPS OF THE 1920S

At times, consumers' decisions to purchase automobiles have been invoked as an easy explanation for the transformation of American suburbs from carefully planned picturesque enclaves to the centerless sitcom suburbs, and then to the harsh asphalt of an edge node like Tysons Corner. The activities of automobile manufacturers, commercial real estate developers, and the federal government have been far more important in determining patterns of transportation than consumer choice. The automobile has been affordable for many working people since 1916, when Henry Ford lowered the price of a Model T runabout to $345, but what automobile manufacturers wanted was to eliminate all other transportation choices.[8] The greatest spurt in American families' automobile ownership took place in the 1920s, the decade when automobile manufacturers began strategizing about federal subsidies for roads and developers began reshaping buildings to accommodate consumers in automobiles. Gas stations, supermarkets, shopping strips, motels, small restaurants, and billboards started to line the way out of town.[9] As building types changed, beginning with the gas station and the supermarket, street grids of regular blocks in organized city and small-town neighborhoods were extended with roadside strip development (or ribbon development) serving the auto-

Automobile strip construction with flamboyant gas station and tourist cabins, Shannon County, Missouri, 1942. Photograph by John Vachon, Library of Congress, LC-USF34-064299.

Fast-food restaurant, Route 1, Guilford, Conn. Author photo, 2002.

mobile. The same building types found on the strips and "hot dog trails" of the 1920s grew into the edge nodes of the 1980s, although they went through some dramatic transformations.

The first of the buildings on the strip was the gas station. The earliest filling stations evolved from livery stables that supplied gasoline through a hose and a funnel. (Aspiring women drivers were warned against the mess.) Pumps got more sophisticated, as did the filling stations.[10] Gas stations and car washes settled into predictable forms, as oil companies organized franchises and promoted streamline moderne stations designed for easy visibility. The oil companies were an active part of all political lobbies promoting the production of automobiles and roads.

The lessons of the service stations were taken up by entrepreneurs selling food. In the 1930s Ralphs Grocery Company, established in downtown Los Angeles in 1873, invested in large self-service stores equipped with checkouts, sited in convenient locations for home-bound automobile commuters. L.A. became so crowded with competing supermarkets that by 1939 only about 40 percent of them were yielding good profits, but the suburban supermarket surrounded by parking remained popular.[11] The biggest chains held on and the smaller entrepreneurs folded, a pattern that would be repeated many times in the growth of the strip.

In addition to gas stations and supermarkets, roadside strips contained auto showrooms, diners, miniature golf courses, motels, and drive-in movie theaters by the late 1930s.[12] A few chain stores, such as Sears, also moved out to the strips. Nationally, only a small percentage of Americans lived in suburbs before 1940, so most retail stores were still in city centers or small-town Main Streets, but across the United States people were patenting ideas for roadside commerce. Richard and Maurice McDonald, brothers from New Hampshire, worked as set builders at Columbia studios in Hollywood. They moved to Pasadena in 1937, and then to San Bernardino in 1940 to run drive-in restaurants. In 1948 they fired their short-order cooks, bus boys, dishwashers, and car hops because they had invented the "Speedee Service System," a plan for serving mass-produced hamburgers on paper plates, the cheapest lunch around. Richard McDonald's design for their roadside stand featured golden arches holding up a slanting roof.[13] Fast-food operations like Carl's Jr., Taco Bell, and Jack in the Box followed the McDonald's example. Ray Kroc began to franchise McDonald's widely, locating new sites by flying over recently suburbanizing areas in a Cessna. Soon the food franchises were pushing older food drive-ins and diners out of business, just as the gas station franchises had disposed of the livery stables and small gas stations.

By the mid-1950s real estate promoters of the commercial strip were attaching it to the centerless residential suburb. Both strips and tracts expanded under the impact of federal subsidies to developers, but since these subsidies were indirect, it was hard for many citizens or local officials to know what was happening. The sitcom suburbs offered the cheapest housing available in the postwar years. However inconvenient, however remote from railroad stations or bus routes, families coped with them because they had few other choices. In the late 1940s and early 1950s, not everyone did own a car. Men sometimes carpooled to work. Women walked to shops if they could, or begged a ride from a neighbor. Because of dispersed houses, the demand for cars rose, including the demand for second cars and the market for used cars.

Dispersion of jobs also began to increase the demand for automobiles. The suburbs of the late 1940s functioned as "bedroom" communities for dense downtowns supplied with suburban trains, bus routes, and subways, places like New York and Chicago. At the same time they housed both white-collar and blue-collar workers with jobs in many diverse suburban locations, including the aircraft plants near Levittown on Long Island and near Lakewood, California. Some suburban factories had been located close to railroads since the 1890s, often with workers' housing nearby, but by the 1950s manufacturers were increasingly choosing suburban locations for new plants because they were accessible by truck. Employers' locational choices encouraged workers' reliance on automobiles, and many little commercial strips grew outside of suburban plant gates, complete with gas stations, fast food, and supermarkets.

SUBSIDIZING THE STRIP: 1954 LEGISLATION
FOR ACCELERATED DEPRECIATION

After millions of families purchased model houses in residential suburbs during the late 1940s and early 1950s, Americans began to wonder if the United States could sustain the postwar building boom. Although huge sitcom suburbs like Lakewood, California, and Park Forest, Illinois, had included shopping malls, most developers built FHA subdivisions consisting entirely of houses. For the real estate industry, commercial space looked like the next step. In the 1954 Internal Revenue Code, a Republican Congress changed forty-year, straight-line depreciation for buildings to permit "accelerated depreciation" of greenfield income-producing property in seven years. By enabling owners to depreciate or write off the value of a building in such a short time, the law created a gigantic hidden subsidy for the developers of cheap new commercial buildings located on strips. Accelerated depreciation not only encouraged poor construction, it also discouraged adequate maintenance. After the original owners had depreciated a commercial property, it was possible to pass it on to another owner who could depreciate it again, on a slightly less generous basis. After time, the result was abandonment. This provision also de-skilled the construction workforce, since only the crudest and cheapest buildings were in great demand.

A decade later, architect Peter Blake, the editor of *Architectural Forum,* fulminated about the results in a muckraking book called

God's Own Junkyard: "This book is not written in anger. It is written in fury," he intoned.[14] Under "accelerated depreciation," Blake explained, a building "can be depreciated faster in its early years than in its later years." As a result, "a syndicate that has built a big office building can 'write off' most of the cost of this building in the first seven or eight years after completion—so that it becomes most advantageous to the syndicate to sell the building . . . and let the next owner start the same 'accelerated depreciation' process all over again." Was this a good idea? As an architect, Blake was all for keeping construction workers employed, but he thought accelerated depreciation destroyed the building industry altogether: "This gimmick was introduced as an anti-recession move, by the Eisenhower Administration in 1954, to stimulate speculative construction. It certainly worked. But from the point of view of architectural quality, the gimmick proved disastrous, for it wiped out the one remaining incentive to a good building: pride of ownership. All of a sudden, an owner was rewarded for selling out fast!"[15]

In the wake of the tax bonanzas for new commercial projects, roadside strips boomed. Private developers responded to the lack of planned centers, public space, and public facilities in suburbs by building malls, office parks, and industrial parks as well as fast-food restaurants and motels. Developers received huge tax write-offs for "every type of income-producing structure," including malls, gas stations, supermarkets, motels, fast-food restaurants, offices, rental apartments, and shopping centers. Existing mom-and-pop operations such as small motels, diners, and retail shops did not benefit because the construction had to be new to qualify for the write-off. Most of the little businesses gave way to Holiday Inns and McDonald's as chain operations and franchises took advantage of the tax bonuses. A commentator in *Fortune* magazine explained that the number of motel rooms jumped 50 percent in four years, in "a riotous atmosphere reminiscent of a gold rush."[16] One journalist reported that Harry J. Sonneborn, Ray Kroc's partner in franchising McDonald's, told a group of Wall Street investors: "We are not basically in the food business. We are in the real estate business. The only reason we sell fifteen cent hamburgers is because they are the greatest producer of revenue from which our tenants can pay us our rent."[17] As with home building in the 1940s, government subsidies led to the restructuring of the entire commercial real

estate sector. Larger and more standardized operations began to dominate a new kind of landscape.

Historian Thomas Hanchett notes, "Throughout the mid-1950s,
developers had sought locations *within* growing suburban areas. Now
shopping centers began appearing in the cornfields *beyond* the edge of
existing development."[18] These sites were usually at the far edge of
existing suburbs or in unincorporated areas because many developers
wanted the freedom to invest in the cheapest land they could find
to create a "growth node" or a "tomorrowland."[19] In these remote
places, there was little or no land use planning or traffic planning
beyond what the commercial developers organized to get customers to
their sites. Developers often designed projects where the expected traffic counts exceeded existing road capacity. They cared nothing about
the appearance of the roadside and often used billboards to show
customers the way. With the 1965 Highway Beautification Act, environmentalists attempted to restrict billboards to areas zoned for commercial or industrial use. The outdoor advertising lobby gutted the
legislation. Every "tomorrowland" was an "anticipatory" commercial
zone, whether or not it was zoned for commercial use.[20]

Hanchett notes that as greenfield commercial development boomed,
the lucrative tax write-off of accelerated depreciation cost the federal
government about $750 to $850 million per year in the late 1960s,
and over a billion per year in the 1970s. The *Wall Street Journal*
hailed "Profits in Losses."[21] Businesses that were profitable could
show a tax loss, and even businesses that weren't profitable could look
pretty good after accelerated depreciation, provided the overall enterprise was large enough to be making money elsewhere. Commercial
real estate became a tax shelter, and venture capitalists were attracted
to it, accelerating the turnover of cheap buildings. Each new round of
accelerated depreciation led to another set of profitable losses. After
several rounds, structures were abandoned in favor of new buildings
in more distant sites. Nothing could have been more damaging to
older businesses in both big cities and small towns. As the boom accelerated, the federal government encouraged suburban developers to
cannibalize their own cities. The Tax Reform Act of 1986 and a reces-
sion in the late 1980s ended a thirty-year spree, but not before a glut
of commercial real estate had been produced which lasted well into
the 1990s.[22]

SUBSIDIZING THE ROAD GANG: 1956 LEGISLATION
FOR INTERSTATE HIGHWAYS

A massive program of government road building also began in the mid-1950s, orchestrated by both official and unofficial lobbyists for automobile interests who had worked toward these ends for several decades. The Department of Agriculture had begun road building in 1916 to help farmers get products to market. With farmers' wives declaring, "You can't go to town in a bathtub," the purchase of a car had also assumed social importance, and in some farm households even preceded investment in indoor plumbing.[23] According to automobile historian James Flink, by the late 1920s many automobile manufacturers felt they had saturated the market for cars and trucks among farmers and rural Americans. They wanted to expand in an urbanizing society, and they believed that automotive expansion depended on suppressing alternative modes of urban transit, such as the trolley, and opening up cities and suburbs to cars and trucks with the construction of freeway networks. In 1932 Alfred Sloan formed the National Highway Users Conference (NHUC), which came to include some three thousand groups dominated by General Motors. In 1937 the Automobile Manufacturers Association (AMA) turned one of its divisions into another lobbying group, the Automobile Safety Foundation (ASF). There was also an American Association of State Highway Officials (AASHO). In 1942 many joined a more secretive group called the "Road Gang," 240 representatives of "automobile manufacturers and dealers, automobile clubs, oil companies, truckers and the Teamsters Union, highway engineers, and state highway administrators."[24]

The Road Gang met weekly in Washington, D.C. and lobbied for the 1944 Federal Highway Act, winning 60 percent federal funding for local roads. Meanwhile, General Motors, Firestone Tires, Mack Truck, and Standard Oil of California, among others, were active in buying out one hundred electric trolley lines in order to replace them with buses. In 1947 they lost a major antitrust suit in federal court, but the penalties assessed against them were slight. The corporations involved were fined $5,000 apiece and the executives were fined $1.[25] Because trolley line owners had worked the land speculation game through political bosses in the cities where they were located, many observers were not sorry to see them go. The national lobbying groups for automobile and trucking interests who replaced the local trolley syndicates were equally arrogant, but their campaigns focused on federal subsidies rather than local political patronage.

The Road Gang had flourished in wartime, even though about 80 percent of war materials were moved by rail.[26] Beginning in 1939, the chief of the Bureau of Public Roads in the Department of Agriculture, Thomas H. MacDonald, promoted a plan for a national system with 30,000 miles of divided highways. Using the rhetoric of national defense, the auto lobby pushed for this project, looking for increased federal funding. Although a new highway program was politically very contentious, President Eisenhower appointed an advisory committee of executives linked to General Motors, Bechtel engineering, the trucking lobby, and the Teamsters Union (to which truckers belonged) to negotiate the various special interests involved. In 1956 Eisenhower signed the Interstate Highway Act providing for 42,500 miles of a "National System of Interstate and Defense Highways" across the country at an estimated cost of $27 billion. Architectural critic Lewis Mumford observed that the kindest thing you could say about the voters who had elected the Congress that passed the legislation was that they had no idea what they were doing.[27] Journalist Helen Leavitt thought that Congress had been bought and bullied. In her brilliant book *Superhighway—Superhoax,* she noted that there was no real concern for national defense, since overpasses designed for fourteen-foot vertical clearance were too low to permit the passage of many Army, Navy, and Air Force weapons loaded on transporters, including Atlas missiles. The highway builders had never even consulted the Defense Department.[28]

By 1958 cost estimates for the Interstate system were $41 billion and rising. Since construction was to be administered by states with 90 percent federal financing, the locations of highways would be determined by state highway engineers in charge of the largest federal pork barrel Americans had ever seen. In the process of creating routes into cities and towns, highway engineers destroyed many older neighborhoods, especially those inhabited by people of color. They were accused of driving suburban "white men's roads through black men's bedrooms," but they didn't care.[29] The locations of new suburban highway interchanges also had great significance for local commercial real estate, given the 1954 tax laws.

Historian Mark Rose notes that highway engineers were overconfident about "solving problems through technical expertise; and they had neither the skills nor the inclination to deal with leaders speaking for neighborhoods, flower gardens, parks, natural beauty, or nongrowth." The road building was brutal and speculation was rampant. Rose called it "federal funding for localistic and largely impermeable commercial and professional subcultures."[30] The engineers had the worst possible attitudes about gender as well as race, mocking women protesters as "little old ladies in tennis shoes" while celebrating highway openings with local beauty queens in evening dresses with ribbons reading "Miss Concrete" and "Miss Black Top."[31] The engineers were also insensitive to national politicians' critiques while bonding with the members of local growth machines. In every state, road gangs enriched automobile, truck, oil, construction, and real estate interests by providing infrastructure worth billions of dollars to open up new suburban land for speculation and development.

The federal support by the FHWA for the highwaymen and the automobile industry in 1956 resembled the pattern of public funding developed by the FHA for the housing industry in 1934. Just as the American tract house was separated from the neighborhood, so the car was separated from the road. Under FHA, the federal government encouraged private developers to build the house and sell it as if it were a consumer good like a chair or a table, leaving the costs of a sound residential neighborhood (such as sewers and schools) to be borne by local taxpayers. Under the Interstate Highway Act, government encouraged private companies to sell new cars, buses, and trucks, leaving the cost of building essential highways to the states and the nation. The federal government set physical standards and provided massive, direct funding to states for the roads, unlike the arrangement for the housing, but the result was similar. Taxpayers shouldered the costs.

In both cases, affluent citizens—people who owned houses and cars—got the benefits of federal subsidies, rather than poorer citizens without shelter or transportation. In vain did transit planners note that the government's concern was to move people rather than vehicles. In both cases, big businesses—real estate developers and banks, automobile manufacturers and trucking firms—got direct benefits. In both cases, the business interests who favored the production of individual houses (rather than apartments) and private cars (rather than trains, trolleys, or subways) were pigheaded. They did not concede that public housing or public transportation had an important place in the United States. Instead, both real estate and automobile lobbyists howled about government "competition" with private enterprise, while refusing to admit that they were heavily subsidized themselves. In 1998 journalist Jane Holtz Kay reported that American drivers paid less than half the real costs of driving a car.[32] Worst of all, when road builders blasted their way through existing neighborhoods, especially neighborhoods inhabited by people of color, in order to build Interstate highways leading into cities from suburbs, they depleted affordable housing. The road builders destroyed cities physically and socially during the same period that commercial real estate interests were encouraged to abandon cities economically in order to take advantage of greenfield incentives.

"PLANNED SPRAWL" AND THE RISE OF THE MALL

The greatest beneficiaries of federal highway programs and commercial real estate subsidies were the developers of shopping malls. Well-designed, small shopping areas had been part of earlier elite picturesque enclaves, such as Lake Forest, Illinois, Roland Park, Maryland, and the Country Club Plaza in Kansas City. Small strip shopping areas had also emerged on many suburban arterials in the 1920s. By the 1940s architects such as Victor Gruen were promoting "shopping towns" with anchor stores and smaller stores surrounded by parking.[33] Gruen was a Viennese émigré who worked on luxury boutiques in Manhattan before developing a firm in Southern California. Gruen designed the first fully enclosed mall at Southdale, near Minneapolis, in 1956, and prospered as a specialist in retail malls.[34]

Malls in the late forties and early fifties were risky. Suburban customers still believed in making major purchases in the central business districts of cities and towns, where they expected to find the greatest selection of merchandise and the most competitive prices. After the tax laws of 1954, this changed. Shopping mall developers were among the biggest beneficiaries of accelerated depreciation, and they most often located projects where the older strips met the new interchanges of major highways. With the new tax write-offs, over 98 percent of malls made money for their investors.[35] Together, the tax breaks and the new roads explain the orgy of commercial real estate built in automo-

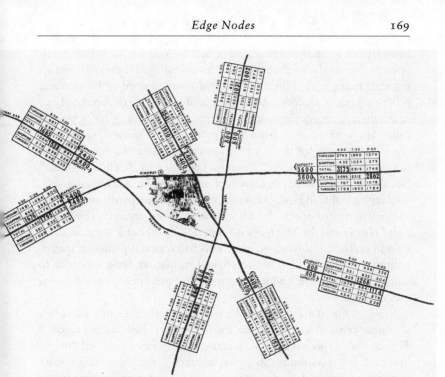

Victor Gruen, diagram for Garden State Plaza Shopping Center, Paramus, N.J., showing traffic counts for highways and arterials, some overloaded by expected new traffic. Victor Gruen Papers, Manuscript Division, Library of Congress.

tive configurations after the mid-1950s. According to Hanchett, tax incentives helped spur the construction of many more shopping centers than would otherwise have been started.[36] Frequently state and local governments also subsidized malls with "economic development" grants, infrastructure such as local access roads, and abatements of local taxes.[37] The culture of land use planning became very corrupt in many places, with both elected officials and paid staff in local governments receiving handouts from speculators, builders, and bankers in exchange for tens of millions in subsidies.

In a landmark study of the late 1970s, *Planned Sprawl,* sociologist Mark Gottdiener looked at the largest township in Suffolk County,

Long Island, to analyze the planning behind roadside suburban development. He challenged observers who called the landscape chaotic, showing that physical disorder resulted from planned and systematic profit-seeking by builders, developers, and banks. He documented one case where a developer sought and received rezoning for a project called Dollarhaven Mall from local politicians. In general, Gottdiener noted many ways for developers to promote deals: "buying blocks of tickets to party functions," "purchasing a service from a business" (such as a local newspaper, construction firm, or car dealership associated with a political boss, his associates, or a councilman), and making campaign contributions.[38] Other writers railed against *The Great Land Hustle* and the *Mortgage on America*.[39] Although some academics and politicians advocated more effective regional planning, metropolitan government, and environmental regulation, little was done to halt the federal, state, and local subsidies for growth channeled to real estate developers.

Between the mid-1950s and the late 1970s about 22,000 suburban shopping centers were built. By the late 1990s there were 43,000.[40] They included thousands of strip malls, euphemistically called "neighborhood or community shopping centers," with one large store such as a supermarket, drugstore, or low-cost department store and a line of little stores facing parking. There were hundreds of "regional malls" like the Connecticut Post Mall in Milford, Connecticut. Regional malls were sited on at least thirty acres, usually enclosed, with multiple shops and at least one big anchor store including 100,000 square feet of leasable space. And there were the superregional malls, totaling over 1,400,000 square feet of leasable space. At one place in New Jersey, citizens renamed their municipality "Cherry Hill" after the mall developed by James Rouse in 1961. Other localities were not so delighted. Malls eroded the economic base of older downtown department stores as well as stores on Main Streets in small towns and older suburbs, leaving empty storefronts. They privatized and commercialized public space. As historian Lizabeth Cohen has documented, mall owners were often anxious to restrict public access, and one of the ways of achieving this was to make access by public transit minimal, or to organize bus routes to reinforce market segmentation and racial segregation by race and class. Cohen suggests that malls also feminized public space: "they enhanced women's claim on the

Regional mall with manufactured housing in trailer park at left and
wetlands at top. Connecticut Post Mall, Milford, Conn., 1998.
Alex S. MacLean, Landslides.

suburban landscape but also empowered them more as consumers
than producers."[41]

By 2000, Americans had built almost twice as much retail space per
citizen as any other country in the world: over nineteen square feet per
person.[42] Most of it was in malls. A superregional such as the South
Coast Mall in Orange County, California, claimed to do more retail
business every day than all of downtown San Francisco.[43] The Mall of
America (MOA) in Bloomington, Minnesota, is even more gigantic. A
project of the Ghermezian brothers, with Melvin Simon and Associates
as developer and managing partner, it opened in 1992. The largest
superregional mall in the United States, in 2002 MOA included four
anchor department stores and over 520 stores, 51 restaurants, 8 night-
clubs, 14 theater screens, and theme park attractions. Its Camp Snoopy
offers twenty-eight rides on seven acres, a virtual NASCAR speedway,
a bowling alley, and 1.2-million-gallon aquarium with three thousand
marine animals, including sharks and stingrays. With a gross building

Amusement parks were added to shopping malls to draw customers, just as playgrounds were added to fast-food outlets. Camp Snoopy, Mall of America, Bloomington, Minn. Courtesy of Mall of America.

area of 4.2 million square feet and leasable space of 2.5 million square feet, it draws between six hundred thousand and nine hundred thousand visitors weekly. Attractions include hair-coloring demonstrations, children's fashion shows, cheerleader tryouts, mall walks for seniors, and a show of red, white, and blue flowers called "Great American Backyard." At 42.5 million visitors per year, the Mall of America claims to top Disney World, Graceland, and the Grand Canyon as the most popular tourist destination in the United States.[44]

FROM THE MALL TO THE EDGE NODE

Edge nodes expanded with the rise of malls, especially the super-regionals with their surrounding seas of parking. In edge nodes, site plans are scaled to the truck or car, never to the pedestrian. Edge nodes have assumed different forms in various parts of the country since the 1970s, but many of them are in unincorporated areas rather than politically bounded towns. Many have a maze of overlapping jurisdictions such as county, town, and special service districts. Most nodes are "boomers" like Tysons Corner, exploding out of strip commercial areas on older arterials near freeway interchanges, where loose zoning and automotive uses have prevailed since the 1920s, and a new mall brought development to the area. Garreau uses the term "pig in the python" to describe the way some boomers are formed as big nodes within a linear strip.[45] Edge nodes can also be "uptown," that is, on the site of an older downtown, perhaps one that has been razed by urban redevelopment, with land then sold on favorable terms to new private investors. Such is the case in Stamford, Connecticut, where an industrial city making Yale locks gave way to a mall and corporate offices.[46] A third kind of edge node is "greenfield," located in open, undeveloped land, usually near a freeway exit.

The privately planned new towns and Title VII communities founded in the 1960s provide an exception to Garreau's typology. Urban planner Ann Forsyth notes that all were "highly designed— and designed with parking seen as 'landbank' for future expansion."[47] The developers, planners, architects, and landscape architects who worked on these projects saw themselves as providing an alternative to the sprawling suburbs of the 1950s. Columbia, Maryland, was developed by James Rouse beginning in 1963. With about fourteen thousand acres, Columbia held eighty-eight thousand residents in 2000. About one-fifth were African-American because Rouse had emphasized achieving racial integration. The Woodlands, outside of Houston, Texas, was developed by George Mitchell, beginning in 1964. He hired Ian McHarg to develop an ecological focus for the planning of 15,000 acres (now 27,305 acres). The Woodlands reached 55,649 inhabitants by 2000. The Irvine Company began to develop a new town in 1960 and hired William Pereira as master planner for more than ninety-three thousand acres in Southern California. The city of Irvine holds one hundred and thirty thousand people. These three planned developments included regional retail as well as neighborhood retail centers serving both single-family houses and apartments. All three managed to create long-term job development, including office parks, and by 1991 they appeared on Joel Garreau's list of edge cities, although they derived from consistent attempts to plan and develop large new suburban communities.

For the most part, edge nodes are uncomfortable and ugly places. Building is cheap; depreciation is accelerated; obsolescence is rapid. Money might be spent on a corporate headquarters when a corporation intends to stay, but developers of speculative office parks design for rapid turnover. There is little site design beyond inexpensive buildings with big signs and parking lots, although private security services and building maintenance services are often provided to tenants. Developers of industrial parks also build minimal buildings. Clustered around malls, offices, and industry are office services, such as lawyers, accountants, and printing, and other services, such as fast food, chain motels, cineplexes, and freeway churches. When geographer Peter Muller documented the growth of King of Prussia, Pennsylvania, in 1976, his diagram showed the Pennsylvania Turnpike, Interstate 76, and U.S. 202 wrapping a series of pods, with a mall, office parks, industrial parks, hotels, fast food, a freeway church, and a music fair.[48] It lacked the pedestrian structure of a traditional downtown, where sidewalks allowed pedestrians to walk from office to restaurant or from church to shopping. Despite Muller's optimism about the upscale

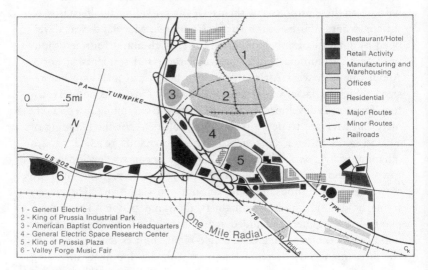

Site plan of edge node at King of Prussia, Pa., 1976, from Peter O. Muller, *The Outer City: Geographical Consequences of the Urbanization of the Suburbs*. Reprinted with permission of the Association of American Geographers.

King of Prussia mall providing "prestige" addresses for adjoining businesses, there was little public space. His diagram showed an edge node that could grow but could not improve with time. Each new single-use pod was surrounded by its own sea of parking.

The older building types that had been on the strips of the 1920s were replaced by newer facilities as the nodes grew, but they did not produce places with a pedestrian presence. Fast-food franchises disrupted sidewalks with drive-throughs that encouraged people to eat on the road. They also displaced public playgrounds with private ones to attract children and parents to fast food. Chain hotels and motels supplanted older hotels and tourist courts. Cineplexes, multiple-screen theaters housed in big, warehouselike buildings without sidewalks, replaced art deco single-screen Main Street theaters, whose slogan had been "the show starts on the sidewalk." Freeway churches drew large congregations to locations near offramps, surrounded by seas of parking, replacing churches on downtown corners. Over time, many evangelical freeway churches added sports facilities, fitness centers, and food courts to their sanctuaries. They were designed to look more like malls than churches.[49]

By the 1990s planner Robert Cervero noted that most edge nodes were being built at densities too low for the effective provision of public transport, yet high enough to cause traffic gridlock. Each new pod added to an edge node might be designed for internal traffic circulation, but the parcels tended to agglomerate with no consistent land use planning or traffic circulation beyond the property line.[50] "Suburbia may be paved with good intentions, but mainly it is paved," said architect Douglas Kelbaugh.[51] Introducing new urban design guidelines is uphill work; renovation of existing spaces is even harder.

BIG BOXES, CATEGORY KILLERS, AND OUTLET MALLS

In the 1990s big-box discount stores of fifty thousand to two hundred thousand square feet began to undercut the older shopping malls that had been at the heart of the edge nodes. The largest big-box stores like Wal-Mart sell almost everything—drugs, hardware, linens, furniture, stationery, toys, clothing, electronics, plants, and eyeglasses. Their supercenters also include a full supermarket. Wal-Mart had over nine hundred thousand employees in 1999, which makes it the largest private employer in America, surpassing General Motors. Wal-Mart has claimed that 93 million Americans shop there every week. It also operates in many other countries, exporting American-style big-box retailing.[52] Category killers—slightly smaller big-box discount stores of twenty-five thousand to one hundred thousand square feet—attempt to dominate (or kill) a particular sales category. Toys "R" Us specializes in toys, Staples in office supplies, Home Depot in building supplies and hardware.

In the face of the big boxes' aggressive expansion, local drugstores, stationery stores, clothing stores, and hardware stores have disappeared by the tens of thousands, changing the shape of older suburbs and small towns.[53] In the ten years between 1983 and 1993, the state of Iowa lost 7,326 small retail businesses. Making the case against sprawl, activist Al Norman contended, "There's one thing you can't buy in a Wal-Mart. That's small town quality of life. And once you lose it, you can't get it back at any price."[54] Through the 1990s the big boxes "killed" older malls, chain supermarkets, chain drugstores, and small department stores, as well as little markets, pharmacies, and clothing stores. The scale of roadside commercial development became overwhelming. Less and less was local. Warehouselike buildings were dictated by management rules about "facilities" of twenty-five thousand to two hundred thousand square feet, with no interior columns, no windows, and parking for thousands of cars.[55] Most of these buildings had no relationship in siting or style to the character of the towns where they were located, although occasionally local planners were able to persuade chains to insert their operations into older structures.

Big boxes were tied to national or international chains, part of an expanding global economy often requiring port and airport access as well as access by truck. Ports such as Long Beach, near Los Angeles, were restructured to accommodate vast containers filled with manufactured goods headed to American discount stores from foreign farms and factories. Airports expanded their cargo areas. Highways were jammed with trucks hauling fifty-three-foot-long containers to speed four billion tons of "just-in-time" merchandise to retail outlets every year.[56] The trucking firms demanded wider arterials and bigger intersections. Trucks shook the foundations of older buildings when they tore into towns.

A few attempts have been made to disguise the bloated architectural scale of big boxes and outlet malls. Developers may present them as villages by decorating one facade of the warehouse or by putting a veneer of Victorian trim on the central public circulation, leaving the rear for the trucks. Sometimes old-fashioned items designed at the human scale, such as sailboats or train coaches, have been added to an outlet mall's design. Their purpose is to serve as "memory points," landmarks to keep thousands of customers from getting lost in rows of warehouses. More common is a lineup of two or three big boxes as a "power center" with no access designed for pedestrians at all. The trucks find this best. One big-box retailer, Target, has emphasized aesthetics in its advertising, hiring noted architects and industrial designers to create its lamps and tea kettles and bring order to store interiors. Unfortunately, they have not yet campaigned for better exterior and site design to modify the scale of the big boxes and parking lots.

Defenders of the big boxes and outlet malls argue that they attract customers. Wal-Mart underwear is cheap, and so is Home Depot's

A big-box store pretending to be a village. Christmas Tree Stores, Orange, Conn., 1998. Alex S. MacLean, Landslides.

An outlet mall pretending to be a New England Victorian village,
Clinton Crossing, Clinton, Conn., 1999.
Alex S. MacLean, Landslides.

plastic paneling, and so are McDonald's hamburgers.[57] Outlets do beat
smaller stores' prices, but quality is often low. Even if quality is the
same for mass-produced products, such as flashlight batteries, the customer is missing the local experience the old neighborhood stores used
to provide. The customer's time and the customer's automobile replace
a neighborhood store's clerk and personal service. Once in the big box,
self-service is usually the rule, as customers fill carts and lug purchases.
Labor costs are low, compared with traditional department stores,
hardware stores, or restaurants, because often workers are part-time
and working at the minimum wage without benefits. Many big-box
employers discourage unionization. However, Wal-Mart workers who
claimed they were frequently forced to put in overtime without pay
organized class-action suits across the country in 2002.[58]

Many of the giants are now under close scrutiny for their effects on
American towns. Companies may argue that they compete to serve
"the market," but federal subsidies for roads and commercial overbuilding have supported the rise of the giants and contributed to the
demise of thousands of small local businesses. It is hard to find a small
town or older suburb that has not been disrupted. Not only local
restaurants but also family farms and small ranches which used to pro-

vide vegetables and meat have been displaced from the American land-scape by the rise of gigantic global businesses purveying fast food. But not every transaction in the edge nodes is about making a profit on inexpensive goods and services. In a heavily franchised landscape, many calculations cycle back to real estate, and the rise of mass invest-ments in Real Estate Investment Trusts (REITs). The Teachers In-surance and Annuity Association (TIAA) handles pension funds for professors and teachers across the United States. While researching malls I was disconcerted to discover that my own retirement savings helped to build the Mall of America.

LEGACIES OF ACCELERATED DEPRECIATION

Although it has become the most visible of American suburban land-scapes, the edge node has few architectural defenders. Even developers despair: "Shopping centers built only in the 1960s are already being abandoned. Their abandonment brings down the values of nearby neighborhoods. Wal-Marts built five years ago are already being aban-doned for superstores. We have built a world of junk, a degraded envi-ronment. It may be profitable for a short-term, but its long-term economic prognosis is bleak."[59] Those who do speak in favor of edge nodes, like Joel Garreau, tend to idealize them as a temporary, rough "frontier" of economic growth. He admits most nodes are "as ugly as poison ivy."[60]

No one has yet done a definitive economic study of how much edge nodes have been subsidized by federal tax concessions and local gov-ernment subsidies. Because of federal, state, and local giveaways, gov-ernment has encouraged very large businesses to cannibalize smaller businesses, wiping out many Main Streets and older suburban com-mercial areas, but few Americans understand how their tax dollars have supported this destructive process. The end result has been a mall glut. About four thousand dead malls were empty or abandoned in the United States in 2002.[61] More failures are expected. Older big boxes and outlet malls have also been abandoned. Some developers and designers are working on plans for adding housing to retail in dying malls in order to redevelop older complexes. Meanwhile, the edge node has replaced Main Street, and both shoppers and workers are stuck in traffic.

Few Americans can describe the physical form or financial underpinnings of edge nodes like Tysons Corner or King of Prussia. Even scholars and design professionals are often unaware how complex, hidden subsidies have boosted their growth. Jobs and commerce have moved to edge nodes, but few people want to live in them. The presence of housing in edge nodes is often the result of spot builders filling in leftover sites with "affordable" housing units. Nearby freeways make many of these units undesirable. Occasionally expensive apartments for households without children are added near upscale mall areas, such as the Houston Galleria or the new Southdale Mall in Edina, near Minneapolis, but most affluent families prefer to live elsewhere. Ugly environments, cheap gas, and subsidized freeways mean that workers commute to residences far outside the edge nodes, scattering into less dense areas, creating one more suburban pattern, the rural fringes.

Chapter Nine

RURAL FRINGES

So what is this land spawned by the car?
— JANE HOLTZ KAY, *Asphalt Nation*

S INCE THE 1980S, NEW DEVELOPMENT on the rural fringes of
edge nodes has expanded to cover more square miles than central
cities, older suburbs, and edge nodes combined.[1] Residents of the
rural fringes are often employed in edge nodes like Schaumburg, Illinois, twenty-five miles northwest of the Chicago Loop, close to O'Hare
Airport, home to the Woodfield Mall, the world's largest in the 1970s.
By 2000 Schaumburg contained 75,386 residents, 73,000 jobs, and
more than thirty million square feet of office, commercial, and industrial development, including two major malls, sixty-five shopping centers, and Motorola's corporate headquarters.[2] Although Schaumburg
included subdivisions and apartments as well as shopping, one person
told a reporter, "The only way you can see other people from Schaumburg is through their car windows, as they drive home from work."[3]
The senior planner in town confessed that his job got more difficult
when Schaumburg became a verb used by people in other places, as in
"We don't want to Schaumburgize our town."[4] Responding to complaints about placelessness, developers created "Streets of Woodfield,"
a rehabilitation that turned the enclosed Woodfield Mall inside out,
creating retail frontage on streets. Planning officials in Schaumburg
also developed "Town Square," a shopping center that also included a
library and town offices, in a district called "Olde Schaumburg Cen-
tre,"[5] but nothing stopped workers from taking to the road to find
more pastoral places to live.

By the mid-1980s residential development was shooting forty miles north and west of Schaumburg toward semirural McHenry County, sixty-five miles from the Loop. The small town of Crystal Lake grew from 14,000 in the early 1970s to over 35,000 in 2000.[6] For a time, the town ran schools on split shifts. McHenry County built more roads. The town raised property taxes to cope with rising demands for infrastructure, police, fire, and school services.[7] Between 1987 and 1995, a quarter of the farms in McHenry County were sold for development.[8] Halfway between Schaumburg and Crystal Lake, environmentalists report that "residents of new, large-lot subdivisions on once rural land" have become "worried about growth, opposing condominiums, apartments, theaters, restaurants, and shopping malls near their homes."[9] The hope of living amid greenfields has faded as residents have had to attend planning and zoning meetings night after night to protest new development and excessive traffic.

Rapid fringe development across the United States has removed both farmland and timberland. Speculators have held land, then sold to developers who have built where and when they wished, causing leapfrogging or scatteration. Clearing of land has reduced wildlife habitat. Runoff from construction and from impervious surfaces has damaged streams and lakes. Excessive use of septic tanks and garden pesticides has caused water pollution. Roads have become congested, and more and more vehicles have polluted the air.[10] Planner Tom Daniels has called the rural fringe "America's land-use battleground," where "developers, long-term landowners, quick-buck land speculators, politicians, and realtors are matched against other long-term landowners, politicians, environmentalists, and newcomers who want to keep their new communities attractive and fiscally manageable."[11]

Attempts to stop development on the rural fringe between 1970 and 2000 did not always halt change. Paradoxically, citizens' campaigns in some cases accelerated sprawl, because the LULUs (locally unwanted land uses) and other kinds of excessive development were sent to adjoining towns farther out into greenfields. Using large lot sizes to limit residential development could have the same effect. A zoning law requiring five acres per house would encourage developers wanting to build less-expensive housing to move out to the next town, a practice known as leapfrogging, unless there were regional plans or state plans that specified an urban growth boundary (UGB) or other infrastruc-

New subdivision in former fields outside traditional small town,
St. Albans, Vt., June 1995. Alex S. MacLean, Landslides.

ture requirements to limit development. Many cites and states did not
have these in place. Even states without large cities, such as Vermont,
have been affected by fringe development so vast it has overpowered
small town centers and rural landscapes.[12]

ATTRACTIONS OF THE RURAL FRINGE

The United States has always had runaway suburbs, but never in such
diverse and dispersed locations. Compared with the 1820s, when the
borderland was close to a city center, or the early 1900s, when the
interurban lines defined linear corridors extending from centers, fringe
development between the 1970s to 2000 was much more dispersed
around metropolitan regions and beyond them. The edge of the city
was everywhere and nowhere. Geographer Pierce Lewis called this
condition "the galactic metropolis" in 1980.[13] Journalist John Herbers's *The New Heartland* expanded upon many of Lewis's definitions
in 1986, suggesting that fringe development could be seen as a rejec-

tion of both the industrial city and the crowded suburb. Fringe development appeared just outside metropolitan counties. It could also be found outside of many small cities and towns, including college towns, state capitals, and county seats. People also relocated in places far removed from large cities, "along rivers, coastlines, and reservoirs; near recreation and retirement areas; on marginal farmland; along country roads; on remote land that is barren except for its physical beauty."[14] While Herbers thought this growth was largely invisible in the 1980s, by the 1990s fringe development had become all too visible.

Pull or Push?

People were both pulled and pushed to the fringes. Outside every edge node, as well as every small city, the sounds of new construction on former farmland filled the air. Part of the attraction was a fashion for country styles—farmhouses, barns, old painted furniture, quilts, and wood stoves were hot consumer items. The *New York Times* launched a column titled "Havens" that extolled the scale of "narrow streets, mature trees, picket fences, a mix of architectural styles and beguiling shops . . . a grocery store within walking distance."[15] Many families took a small town's charm for granted when they bought a distant house, only to find that the town's physical character was soon compromised by excessive new development. Some analysts, including Herbers, also said that the rush to the fringe reflected white middle-class flight from urban areas with increasing numbers of recent immigrants and people of color.[16] Fringe development surely reflected the desire to escape central cities with declining infrastructure, pollution, and poor schools, as well as ugly, automobile-scale edge nodes, in favor of places with old-fashioned, pedestrian-scale Main Streets, where residents could take pride in small-town character.

The preference for unspoiled rural or small-town landscapes was always part of American suburban life. But in the 1960s and 1970s, jobs moved to edge nodes and builders completed distant parts of Interstate freeway systems enabling long commutes to rural places. Most states also dedicated about 20 percent of their annual budgets to road building, bringing many remote areas within reach.[17] In the 1980s and 1990s, the rise of digital technologies used by all classes for "telecommuting" took people to the fringe. Aging members of the baby boom generation born after World War II also began to settle in fringe areas, where some hoped to enjoy an inexpensive retirement.

Long-Haul Commuters

Some young couples were pushed to the rural fringe because land was cheapest. These were the only houses some families could afford, so moving way out seemed the only route to home ownership. The trade-off was a commute of one to two hours each way. After the spectacular rise of the computer industry in the Silicon Valley in the 1980s and 1990s, housing prices soared around San Jose. When median housing prices in the suburb of San Carlos hovered around $680,000, Tracy, California, an agricultural area about sixty miles east, offered a median house price of $225,000 to those willing to commute. Journalist Patricia Leigh Brown interviewed Yolisma Garcia, a program systems manager for Sun Microsystems, who remarked, "You don't question it, you just do it." She owned a four-bedroom house with a pool. Many long-haul commuters believed they were young and strong enough to stand it. After a year or two, burnout was common. Another man complained to Brown, "I spent 2,048 hours working . . . 1,100 hours commuting . . . 608 with my family. I spent twice as much time driving as with my kids."[18] If the dream was peaceful family life, the reality was the road.

"The only good choice for most suburbanites is to drive, and to drive a lot," lament the authors of *Once There Were Greenfields*.[19] Americans have over 131 million passenger vehicles, almost twice as many cars and trucks as children.[20] Between the 1970s and 2000, automobile trip length has increased and the number of trips per person has increased, as well as the number of trips per household and the number of people driving to work alone. Transportation planners report "astonishing growth": "vehicle miles traveled grew by 40 percent in only seven years, between 1983 and 1990."[21] They are still rising and there has been a decline in other modes of travel and in average vehicle occupancy. As a result, roads have become gridlocked, and critics such as Jane Holtz Kay have assailed the "asphalt nation" where Americans waste eight billion hours a year stuck in traffic.[22] She notes that households spend more on their cars than on income tax.[23]

Telecommuters

While some households have been pushed to the fringe by the high cost of housing close to jobs, others have been pulled to fringe settings by the desire for open space or a slower pace, coupled with a chance to work at home. Telecommuting—working at home with an electronic connection to one's co-workers or clients—has made it easier for everyone from top executives to clerical staff to remain in remote locations. All economic classes have become part of a telecommuting pattern that also exploits fax, e-mail, and cell phones. In 2000, 19.6 million workers were telecommuting regularly (at least one day per week), and the numbers were rising.[24] An advertisement by a business services firm called guru.com showed a mom, small baby, and cat around a cluttered kitchen table where the mom was telecommuting. It was captioned "Lunch with Co-Workers." A full-page advertisement by Verizon showed a pleasant old-fashioned Cape Cod colonial surrounded by lawn and mature trees, with the headline "Thanks to High Speed Internet Access, Centrex [and] Voice Mail, You Just Opened Another Satellite Office."[25]

Verizon's slogan "How to get life done" is a nervous mantra. While the search for peaceful domestic life in quiet country settings has been constant since the 1820s, the most recent rush from the city has been marked by odd moments of frenzy, as paid work spilled into family life in new and anxious ways. The home as "electronic cottage" might become a kind of twenty-four-hour sweatshop, with one or two adults trying to accomplish a full day's work with the computer. Psychological studies have established that prolonged hours of interaction with the Internet have tended to make people feel distant from their social circles, distant from their families, depressed, and isolated.[26] Sociologists have also noted that the struggle to allocate the "second shift" of cooking, cleaning, and child care after a full day on the paid job tends to wear out many marriages.[27] Telecommuting might reduce schedule conflicts for employed parents who need to be in two places (home and work) at the same time, but it presents a potential spatial conflict. Earning and nurturing might collide inside the family house twenty-four hours a day, seven days a week. A monograph by Laura C. Johnson documented the process, situated it in the historical context of homework by women, and noted that many women she interviewed thought there should be better planning for child care and neighborhood workplaces for telecommuters.[28]

In the 1990s high-income telecommuters were often managers who might spend some days in the head office, but some were "lone

"Lunch with Co-Workers," detail from guru.com advertisement, *New York Times Magazine*, April 9, 2000. Mom telecommutes at kitchen table and lunches with baby and cat. Photograph by Julian Broad, courtesy of DDB Worldwide Communications Group, Inc.

eagles," highly specialized professionals such as screenwriters or consultants with no locational constraints. Other employees are telecommuting because it saves their employers the cost of permanent office space. Some employers practice "hoteling" or "hot-desking," requiring workers to share desks on alternate days at headquarters or at specially built "telecenters," usually located in edge nodes. Some public officials have recommended telecommuting as a solution to the lack of public transportation and the delays of overcrowded freeways. In 2000, Connecticut's Department of Transportation issued an optimistic video, *Telecommuting: The Road to Success,* to encourage both employers and employees to seek this option.[29]

When low- or moderate-income clerical workers became telecommuters, they often squeezed a desk into a kitchen or bedroom. Advice books like Debra Dinnocenzo's *101 Tips for Telecommuters* suggested that telecommuting could become extremely stressful, since children crowded parents working at home and neighbors pestered them. She

advised serious at-home workers to arrange child care. Men understood this. Women sometimes tried to do two things at once or work
late at night when children were asleep. Dinnocenzo offered a chapter
entitled "If You Mix Childcare and Work (God Help You!)." She also
recommended "Be Your Own OSHA Inspector," and pointed out
grossly unsafe and uncomfortable working conditions that would be
illegal if found on an employer's premises.[30] Since OSHA does cover
at-home workers, enforcement issues are sure to become more important as telecommuting grows.

RELUCTANT SUBURBS, HOT TOWNS, AND VALHALLAS

The rural fringe includes existing small towns overwhelmed by new
construction as well as farmland cut up for houses. Fringe counties
may include many modest "reluctant suburbs," a few affluent "hot
towns," and an occasional superrich "Valhalla." Older towns surrounded by new tract houses were first called "reluctant suburbs" in
the 1960s by sociologist William M. Dobriner. His analysis is still
valid. He used this term to describe "Old Harbor," his fictional name
for a town on the Connecticut coast outside of New Haven opened up
to development by the building of Interstate 95. In Old Harbor the
influx of new residents meant that people could no longer find a place
to park on Main Street. There were not enough pews in the churches
or desks in the schools. The villagers tore down parts of the old town
to create parking lots. They built new schools, "added policemen and
fire engines and . . . widened the critical streets."[31] Multiply this process by a few thousand towns and the financial logic of the fringe
appears. Existing residents must tax themselves heavily to pay for new
growth or see essential services deteriorate. By 2000 this pattern had
been repeated many times in reluctant suburbs, where rapid growth
often brought fiscal insolvency. Local officials could recite the cost of
each mile of sewer or water pipe, each middle school classroom, each
mile of town road graded to serve new development. Taxpayers knew
these numbers too.

Dobriner's sociological study also addressed the difference between
the old-time residents, whose families went back many generations in
the town, and the new commuters. The newcomers said: "We like Old
Harbor although the way it's building up it will be like a city in no

time. Well . . . we won't be around here forever." Dobriner concluded, "For the villagers, Old Harbor is their community and they have a fierce sense of possession about it. It is a property that they share. And like any valuable property it is cared for and cherished. It must not be profanely or rudely used." On the other hand, he saw new residents treating the place as "another commodity . . . a product that can be rationally consumed." Yet somehow, villagers and newcomers struggled to reach a truce: "They need each other, the villager to sell and the suburbanite to buy."[32]

Urbanist Peter Wolf has termed more affluent places where "lone eagles" settle "hot towns."[33] In very rural Cornwall, in Litchfield County, Connecticut, a risk arbitrageur put in an ISDN line so he could make real-time trades on Wall Street from his spot in the woods. Next door was Michael Pollan, a writer who filed his stories by e-mail attachments. Pollan observed, "As traders and architects, accountants and software developers take to the hills around here, you may not be able to see our offices from the road (and that road may not need to be widened), but we do leave our telltale marks on the land all the same." While Cornwall stayed quiet, Litchfield, Connecticut, the old county seat, began to look like a hot town. Pollan reported "the old pharmacy with its zinc soda fountain has given way to a coffee bar where you can pay $3.75 for an iced latte."[34] Litchfield also attracted wine bars, gourmet restaurants, and stores selling cashmere sweaters in thirty-six colors. They drove out the mom-and-pop grocery, the diner, and the agricultural agent. Local discount stores sold more office supplies. Roads were widened. New malls were developed on the arterials leading into the town center. Traffic increased. Big houses appeared in the woods and in farmers' fields.

A step up from the hot towns are what writer Joel Kotkin calls "Valhallas," existing communities with attractive natural landscapes and traditional village architecture, such as Camden, Maine, Nantucket, Massachusetts, and Jackson Hole, Wyoming. Digital technologies make it possible for new residents to transform these pleasant places, once known as resorts, into very exclusive enclaves.[35] Often they can only be reached quickly by air, perhaps by private jet. Some residents are lone eagles, but more are dot-com millionaires who claim to want small-town life, outdoor recreation, and the pleasures of beautiful views for themselves and their children. Inevitably, the arrival of exceptionally wealthy residents brings rapid change. As Valhallas sprout large new mansions or ranches, local residents find they can no longer afford housing. When upscale restaurants and luxury emporia open, they drive out local cafes, drugstores, and hardware stores. Existing jobs disappear, but the new residents want to hire servants and groundskeepers.

HOUSING PATTERNS IN THE FRINGES

Fringe housing patterns have included many options such as old farmhouses, inexpensive communities of trailers or manufactured housing units, retirement communities, and tract houses, as well as more ostentatious tract mansions. Trailers account for 10 to 20 percent of new housing units because of their affordability, and unregulated fringe counties have become a common place to find them. Retirement communities have also increased in number since the 1960s, many of them offering a variety of health service options to residents. Single-family houses also changed in response to demographic trends that appeared at the same time as distances to the fringe increased.

Sometime early in the twentieth century, starting with the mail-order suburb, Americans began to idealize the house and separate it from its neighborhood. In the 1950s many families were thrilled to have a new house, never mind that dad, mom, and three children might be crowded into a structure with an average size of 800 square feet, two bedrooms, one bath, sited on a 5,000-square-foot lot. From the 1970s through 2000, smaller households became the norm, including single parents, childless couples, single people, retirees, and couples with fewer children. The smaller households bought new houses almost three times larger than the 1950s houses. In 1999 the average size for a new house was 2,250 square feet, sited on a 12,910-square-foot lot.[36] The smaller the household, the more houses were needed to contain the population. The bigger the houses and yards, the longer the distances became. The amount of land used to house Americans expanded much faster than population growth would have suggested.

Fringe lifestyles also required new spaces that caused the house to expand. On the fringe, both adults and teenagers needed cars to drive in different directions to work and school. These cars required garages, and a family with two or three or even four cars usually chose to build those garages into the house, creating a very lumpy profile. A single parking space requires about 200 square feet, bigger than an average bedroom; two cars need 400 square feet. A four-car garage may be a structure as large as a whole Levittown house in 1947. This type of dwelling might be called a "snout house," with a big garage stuck out in front, shortening the driveway and blocking the lawn. If an older house was enlarged very noticeably, so that the addition towered over the original structure, it became, in planners' jargon, a "house on steroids."

Providing separate wings, complete with bedrooms, bathrooms, and living areas, for parents and children, especially teenagers, increased the size still further. And then there was the home office. One or two generous home offices could easily add 300–600 square feet to a middle-class house. For the home office to function as a place to receive visitors, it had to be positioned somewhere near an outside entrance, a side or front door. Some designers pushed it close to the sidewalk. Others made "flex-houses" with a possible home office on the first floor convertible to a master suite with closets and bath. Some developers preferred to situate at least one home office as an accessory apartment—often located over the garage—which could also be rented or used for guests or servants. All of these options added bulk.

With increases in the size of tract houses, critics began to speak of "tract mansions," "McMansions," or "monster houses."[37] The prevalence of tract mansions and the desire to have houses wired produced a wave of "teardowns," as older houses were demolished to provide sites for huge homes in pleasant settings or established neighborhoods.[38] During the affluent late 1990s, teardowns occurred in many parts of the country, despite the efforts of preservationists who complained that the demolitions eroded neighborhood character because the new tract mansions were almost always out of scale.

In the hot towns and Valhallas, architect-designed residences also reached sizes rarely thought practical since the Gilded Age of the late nineteenth century, when Tuxedo Park, New York, emerged as an example of conspicuous consumption. Some called the new houses "starter castles," as newly rich media billionaires, movie stars, computer moguls, real estate executives, and financial partners commissioned twenty-thousand-square-foot houses with private movie theaters and every possible lavish accessory. Horse barns, corrals, polo fields, swimming pools, and tennis courts might surround these structures. Houses were designed in many nostalgic, neo-traditional styles. Adirondack log "cottages" were often favored in the West, neoclassical and shingle styles in the East. Occasionally mansions from the Great Gatsby era of the 1920s were given a facelift, but more often the structures were new.

FRINGE FAMILY LIFE: THE TAXI PARENT
AND THE FRANCHISE WORKER

By 2000, close to 60 percent of mothers of children under the age of one were in the paid labor force.[39] The expansion of the fringe coincided with the entrance of large numbers of women into paid work. The combined income provided by two workers helped to pay the mortgage, but without a stay-at-home mom of the kind celebrated in older suburbs, life for children on the fringe could be isolated and disconnected. Parents who moved to the fringe expressed a desire for views, clean air, and connection to nature for the children, but semirural areas did not usually provide extensive supports for employed mothers. Women continued to manage most of the nurturing of men, children, and the elderly as a "second shift."

In the mid-1980s many working women thought that suburban housing patterns might be redeemed by the addition of day care, elderly care, and accessory apartments to provide more flexibility in single-family neighborhoods. The predominance of new family types, including the two-worker family and the single-parent family, suggested that these changes were necessary. Change did happen in Europe, with city complexes like the Frauen-Werk-Stadt of Vienna, a huge project designed by women for women, with the understanding that women citizens pay taxes and should get their fair share of the housing and services. American reformers traveled to Europe and wondered why it was so hard to imagine housing complexes with high-quality day care in America, much less build them.[40] The built environment of American suburbs did change to reflect new gender roles, but not in egalitarian ways.

Women already living in suburban settings were encouraged to take paid jobs in the edge nodes in the 1970s, 1980s, and 1990s, including clerical work and sales jobs in malls as well as professional and executive positions. In some cases, couples working in different areas chose a housing location on the fringe where each partner could drive to a different suburban job. To deal with fringe locations, American women doubled their miles driven between 1984 and 2000, making many more trips to serve other family members than men did.[41] Marketers coined a new term, "taxi parent," to sell goods to the family trapped in the car. The taxi parents had children with multiple activities: "two soccer games a week and two track meets a week (they start at 5 and some are an hour away), soccer practice one night a week and track practice all five weekdays." Or they had several children with distant destinations: "12-year-old Gavin to baseball and bowling," "10-year-old Danielle to theater class," "8-year-old Shelly . . . usually late for guitar class."[42] These extracurricular activities were familiar to parents in sitcom suburbs, but on the rural fringes, distances increased. Taxi parents bought containers for storing and serving hot or cold foods and beverages in their cars. They added televisions and CD players, plus minilockers for sports gear, back-seat organizers, and trash containers.

Affluent families also often hired poor women of color as nannies and maids, some commuting out to affluent fringes from lower-income neighborhoods.[43] If domestic workers had no cars, corporate cleaning franchises, such as Merry Maids and Maids International, drove them. Many of these operations paid the minimum wage while charging residents about $25 per hour for domestic service. Families of all classes also patronized fast-food franchises, which also employed part-time, minimum-wage workers without benefits. Some also used franchise day-care operations. For poor women, especially poor women of color, access to decent, affordable shelter for themselves and their children in the fringe was limited, as well as access to solid jobs and affordable, quality child care. These had long been described as problems for women in the city, but the suburbs and the fringes did not improve most women's situations. The conflict between class and gender was exacerbated by distance. Only upper-class and upper-middle-class women of the rural fringe enjoyed large houses and paid help with their parenting and housework.

LEGACIES OF THE FRINGE — COMPLAINTS ABOUT SPRAWL

With each added mile from the old central city, the rural fringe becomes less tenable physically, ecologically, and socially. Bitter conflict has occurred in many once-rural places, as long-term fringe residents have divided into two camps. Some want to fight to protect their farmlands, woodlands, and towns from what they call "suburban sprawl." Others decide to sell out. Some hope to use the profits to find another, unspoiled place to go. Working in the tradition of William Garnett, who had photographed Lakewood, California, in the 1950s, photographers attacked excessive growth in the 1970s, documenting the material culture of sprawling tract houses and malls in Western landscapes. Robert Adams shot *denver* and *What We Bought: The New World* as a critique of lower-middle-class housing and mindless consumerism between 1970 and 1974. Lewis Baltz, who photographed the more upscale resort of Park City, Utah, also followed the sale of lots and houses in a rural landscape. By 1975 both were included in a group of photographers, many of them drawn to fringe development in the West, in an exhibition called "New Topographics."[44]

Meanwhile, economists were searching for ways to quantify the difficulties faced by small towns on the fringe in paying for infrastructure such as roads, sewers, and schools to accommodate new residents. The most famous report, *The Costs of Sprawl,* was issued in 1974, and *The Costs of Sprawl—Revisited* appeared in 1998.[45] Sprawl was hard to define, but most definitions involved low-density, single-purpose residential or commercial construction in locations distant from existing public services and infrastructure, as well as ugly, over-scale, automobile-oriented developments that damaged air and water quality. Wherever big developers went, their commercial and residential projects were out of scale with the traditional small towns that had inspired the rush to the fringe.

National organizations such as the Sierra Club and the Natural Resources Defense Council led the fight against sprawl in the 1980s, analyzing environmentally unsustainable patterns of development and encouraging local chapters to take up activist "sprawl-busting" campaigns. Environmental activists and planners began to provide guidelines for managing or slowing growth, called "slow growth." Architects joined the fray, contributing designs for energy-efficient buildings, sometimes called green buildings, and for "pedestrian pockets," mixed-use enclaves designed to combine residences, stores, and jobs, increase walkability, and reduce traffic. Journalists publicized many of these designs and began to cover more citizens' protests around planning controversies. Both Democrats and Republicans found the sprawl issue important in local and state elections.

Prominent in the environmentalist slow-growth literature was discussion of the urban growth boundary (UGB). The state of Oregon passed the Oregon Land Use Act in 1973 requiring thirty-six counties and 236 municipalities to agree on urban growth boundaries with state review. Although intended to protect farmland and forests, the law had the effect of creating a much more evenly dense fabric in Portland, surrounded by a greenbelt. After two or three decades, several other states, including Florida, Maryland, New Jersey, Vermont, and Washington, were working along similar lines. Many of these efforts were centered on regional planning, attempts to slow scattered growth, bound it, and shape it. Florida established concurrency programs requiring that adequate sewers, water, and roads must be in place before new growth could occur. Maryland directed development to particular areas designated for new growth. At the state level, Vermont reviewed all projects over a certain size, and also all projects above a certain elevation, in order to protect the mountains.[46]

While planners were optimistic that growth boundaries and regional planning could regulate density, many environmentalists and community activists worried that "smart growth" would permit business as usual for large developers once new rules were worked out. They favored more stringent economic measures to check development subsidies. As a countermove, conservative groups borrowed the language of environmental reform. Just as feminists interested in parental leave and child care had seen "family values" become the rhetorical terrain of the right in the 1980s, so environmentalists heard "no-growth" and "slow growth" spun to the right in the late 1990s. Real estate and construction groups such as the Urban Land Institute (ULI) and the National Association of Home Builders (NAHB) began promoting the "business benefits" of growth management or "smart growth."[47] Even the conservative Heritage Foundation published *A Guide to Smart Growth,* albeit one that attempted to refute environmentalists' arguments rather than endorse them.[48] In 2001, the arrival of George W. Bush as president, and his appointment of conservative Republicans, such as Secretary of the Interior Gale Norton, to his cabinet, were followed by statements that high energy use was preferable to conservation. The NAHB reported: "Republican control of the executive branch may make things easier for housing on the regulatory front. A lot of builders had been rather apprehensive about the prospects for a federal bureaucracy led by Al Gore."[49]

Rural fringes continue to grow, while local governments attempt to gain some control. Although a number of states have authorized growth boundaries or are actively attempting to develop regional planning, most federal interventions continue to support dispersed residential development. FHA's mission is advertised as help for American consumers, not developer subsidy: "FHA can put you 4500 dollars closer to the American dream . . . being part of a neighborhood and owning a home. It's a mission we've pursued since 1934, and one that has improved the lives of 30 million families."[50] Decisions about the size and location of new development are most often made by private corporations that build hundreds of houses and millions of square feet of offices or retail space, unconstrained by regional planning. Without planning, new edge nodes develop. Some sprout telecenters instead of corporate headquarters. Some include outlet malls or power centers instead of retail malls. Many new nodes take business from edge nodes built ten or twenty or thirty years ago, such as Schaumburg or Tysons Corner. Rural fringe residential areas continue to spread out from new nodes.

Whether they act out of financial constraints or are attracted to the semirural life, Americans continue to choose to live in locations remote from existing neighborhoods and public transit. They know they are going to drive, and drive a lot. The walkable neighborhood and public transit—both of which require substantial public investment—may never appear in thousands of diverse fringe locations, but developers of commercial real estate do seek to expand into growing places. The representatives of chain stores, fast-food franchises, and strip malls are often just behind the recent fringe settlers, scouting suitable sites from low-flying planes. They watch where housing development is happening; they run the numbers. Then these developers bring proposals for new big-box stores as well as new subdivisions to charming little semirural townships for approval. In April 2000 Americans told reporters for the Pew Center for Civic Journalism that sprawl, "the complex of problems such as growth, traffic, poorly maintained roads, inadequate sewer and water infrastructure, and crowded schools," was the most important local issue in the United States.[51] College-educated Americans were the most concerned. White Americans identified this issue more often than people of color. Black Americans thought that crime and poverty were more important. Sprawl remained rather vaguely defined, and the causal relationships between sprawl, persistent poverty, crime, and growing inequality were poorly understood.

Part Three

THE NEXT SUBURBS

Chapter Ten

NOSTALGIA AND FUTURISM

So, fellow Pilgrims, are we progressing on the road to
Eutopia, or lost in the Slough of Despond?
—ARMANDO CARBONELL, in *Smart Growth:*
Form and Consequences

I N 2003 AMERICANS have had almost two centuries of experience
with suburban boosters and their growth machines. Living farther
and farther from older city centers, Americans spend an increasing proportion of their income on home mortgages and car payments,
and purchase freezers, washers, computers, and barbecues as if
there will never be a shortage of oil, electricity, water, or air. American movies and television convey the vision of suburban prosperity
to other nations. American corporations promote consumption
around the world, building highways, shopping malls, and single-
family houses. At home, underneath the apparent prosperity lies anxi-
ety. Can the United States sustain growth at the rate of 1.5 million
new housing units a year? Is there something inherently shaky about
the whole edifice of credit, consumption, and public subsidies for private development?

As environmentalists wrestle with the economic implications of
sprawl, architects are tackling its physical symptoms. Many believe
better designs can result in better suburbs for the twenty-first century.
The "new urbanists" argue for a return to a slower way of life. They
elaborate a cozy past, where old-fashioned family life is honored in
neo-traditional houses gathered into beautifully landscaped enclaves.

The futurist "smart house" advocates prefer a fast-paced world where new digital technologies might bring families freedom from chores and boredom. The "green" architects idealize a connection to nature and design housing to limit the consumption of nonrenewable resources. Designers who grapple with shelter do not always know much history. The nostalgic neo-traditional developments, the science-fiction houses, and the sustainable experiments have all been tried. At the end of the nineteenth century, Ebenezer Howard, founder of the Garden Cities movement, proclaimed a return to the architectural forms of the pre-industrial village, and Edward Bellamy, founder of the Nationalist movement, envisioned a world run on electricity and mass com-munication. Energy conservation was a focus of research during the Depression and World War II. These precedents are rarely cited, but when architects talk about new projects that might be historicist, wired, or green, they often hold a nostalgic, idealized view of affluent families and the picturesque enclaves and borderlands of the American past. Many designers also weaken their visions by trying to fit their projects into "the market" as defined by current real estate develop-ment priorities. New forms for model houses never solve major urban problems, but they may be sold as if they can. New real estate develop-ments may demonstrate local solutions to physical problems, but in themselves, they cannot change the national economic and political conditions that underlie sprawl.

BACK TO THE PICTURESQUE ENCLAVE

"No more housing subdivisions! No more shopping centers! No more office parks! No more highways! Neighborhoods or nothing!" is the cry of Andrés Duany and Elizabeth Plater-Zyberk, architects who have created imaginative plans for entire neo-traditional enclaves.[1] The developers who first hired them in the 1980s studied marketing surveys and pitched their projects to middle-class families. While some consumers wanted a house with perfect architectural details, others wanted more sociability and community. And still others wanted to stop worrying about unforeseen development spoiling their views. The designers claimed to have the answer: a new suburban neighborhood with a master plan, tight building codes, narrow streets, attractive public places, and dedicated open spaces, such as parks, beaches, and golf courses.

Seaside, Florida, and the Rise of New Urbanism
Architects interested in historic building patterns have rediscovered the picturesque enclave with its shared parkland—places like Riverside, Illinois, and Palos Verdes, California. One of the most influential new projects of the early 1980s was Seaside, Florida, by developer Robert Davis. Davis had spent vacation time as a child on the fine white beaches of the Florida Panhandle near Alabama with his grandfather, J. S. Smolian. He inherited about eighty acres of land located across from the sand on Route 30-A. As a successful Miami developer, Davis hired architects Elizabeth Plater-Zyberk and Andrés Duany's firm, DPZ, to design a model community for the Seaside property. In a remote location reachable only by car, they developed a master plan for a small, pedestrian-oriented resort of neo-traditional vernacular houses set in indigenous landscaping. The project was specifically designed to recapture a pre-automobile way of life. The developer wanted a place for "extended porch-sitting, leisurely strolling and sharing time with those you care most about, in a way that urban existence rarely allows."[2]

By 2001, over three hundred cottages lined narrow brick streets

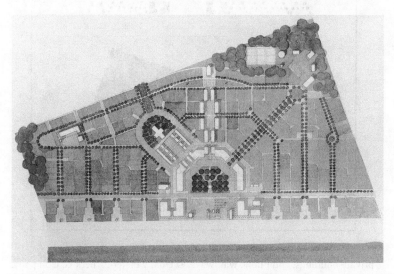

Plan for Seaside, Fla., 1981, showing beach, access pavilions, and town center.
© Duany Plater-Zyberk & Company, Architects and Town Planners.

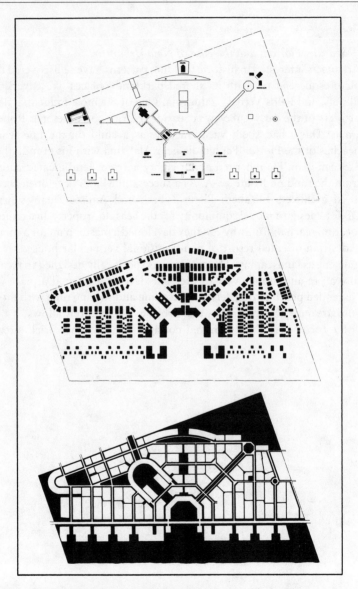

Diagrams of Seaside, showing (from top) public buildings,
private buildings, and public walkways. © Duany Plater-Zyberk & Company,
Architects and Town Planners.

leading to beach pavilions providing access to the Gulf of Mexico. Neat oyster-shell paths, common parks, and planting strips encouraged walking and bicycling by both adults and children. The DPZ firm developed both a town code and a building code to reconnect designers of houses with the Northwest Florida vernacular building traditions of bungalows and dog-trots. They encouraged wood-frame cottages with deep overhangs, ample porches, windows located for cross-ventilation, and ceiling fans. The combination of porch-sitting and walking fostered by the design helped to re-create the ambiance of a small Southern beach resort of eighty to a hundred years ago, in the era of the horse and buggy. The automobile had pushed families off porches into the relative quiet of the backyard in the 1920s. Air-conditioning and television had drawn them indoors in the 1950s.[3] Seaside promised to draw people back outdoors for casual conversations between family and friends on porch and sidewalk. Seaside also promised environmentally sound landscaping: "The absence of lawns, except in a few public places, does more than spare us the noise of lawnmowers. No lawns means no fertilizer and pesticides to keep them up, and vastly reduces the water usage for irrigation. Native

Seaside, Fla. Small wooden houses in Florida panhandle vernacular, oyster-shell path, indigenous vegetation. Author photo, 2001.

plant species, which predominate here, require no irrigation once they are established."[4]

Architects from all over the world were attracted to Seaside by the chance to design ornament, experiment with colors, and socialize in a convivial setting. Rules stimulated playful formal solutions: all the picket fences on a street had to be different. Next to the Central Square (contoured as an amphitheater) stood a tiny Greek Revival post office, an upscale food market, and several mixed-use buildings with apartments above shops. Across the street, adjoining the beach, was "Per-Spi-Cas-Ity," an outdoor market of small wooden stalls with a "Cinderella Circle" of brightly painted wooden Adirondack chairs.

Because the lots in Seaside were small, the density high, and the architectural constraints very strict, many Florida developers thought Robert Davis would lose a lot of money developing a town center on his small, flat piece of property. They did not believe conventional four-story, beachfront condominiums along the Gulf could be seen as less attractive than small houses a few blocks from the water, located on streets with beach access through community pavilions. Davis proved that building a town center for Seaside made a difference. In 1982 the best lot in Seaside cost $12,000. In March 2001, "Dreamsicle," a 700-square-foot house with 170 square feet of additional porches, located on Rosewalk at the edge of town, was on the market for $475,000 (unfurnished). "Breakaway," a 2,115-square-foot house on Pensacola Street, with a 524-square-foot guest house called "Romance" was priced at $1.1 million (furnished). Waterfront lots cost about $1.7 to 2 million.[5]

Everyone who bought in Seaside had to pay yearly assessments to a Neighborhood Association controlling street and common area maintenance as well as beach access. In addition, most residents joined the Seaside Swim and Tennis Club to have access to swimming pools, tennis courts, and croquet. Owners were identified with painted signs on their houses listing the names of houses, parents, children, and pets, plus their hometown. At 517 Forrest Street, for example, was "Mom's Off Duty" with Rick and Ramelle Forman of Madison, Wisconsin, plus their daughter, Alison, and Freddie, their cat. The personal touch hid a complex system for renting houses and their accessory apartments to tourists as if they were hotel rooms through the Seaside Cottage Rental Agency. Tourism picked up in 1998 after Seaside was chosen as the film location for *The Truman Show*. Actor Jim Carrey starred as Truman Burbank, a young man who has spent his whole life on live television and doesn't realize that his entire "town" is just the set for a reality-TV show. Producers substituted lawns for Seaside's indigenous landscaping to make the place look more conventional. The film implied a critique of Seaside as an overly controlled, cute place, but the location fee helped to pay for the construction of a charter school in 1996 for children in grades six through eight.

Seaside recalled the success of Llewellyn Park, New Jersey, in the 1850s. In both places, common land attracted wealthy residents to a picturesque development in a remarkable landscape. In both places, lifestyle pioneers mingled with millionaires. One was a suburb reached by railroad and the other a community of second homes accessible only by car, but both made their designers famous and led to dozens of imitations. Media attention positioned Seaside as a model for suburban housing in the United States, although architects and planners debated the quality of DPZ's efforts. Some critiqued Seaside as nostalgic, while defenders noted that modernist designers such as Deborah Berke, Steven Holl, Rodolfo Machado, and Jorge Silvetti had all designed buildings in Seaside. Some critiqued Seaside as elitist. Defenders noted the modest size of the houses, if not their prices. Others said Seaside couldn't be a model for how to house Americans, since it was an expensive resort with only three hundred houses and few full-time residents. Defenders replied that rising prices in Seaside persuaded developers that there was money to be made by building walkable neighborhoods around an attractive town center.

In 1993 Duany and Plater-Zyberk joined forces with some West Coast architects to form a loose association called the Congress for the New Urbanism (CNU). Californian Peter Calthorpe was known for his strong interest in energy conservation and public transit. He and Douglas Kelbaugh argued for "pedestrian pockets" or "transit-oriented development" (TOD). Their work also emphasized mixing housing with commercial space and creating walkable neighborhoods.[6] Others who joined them came from a mix of backgrounds, including solar homes. While all of the CNU architects were in favor of infill (new construction sited within existing neighborhoods), many of their first projects turned out to be affluent greenfield efforts on the suburban fringe. Developers found it easier to assemble raw land and architects

Celebration, Osceola County, Fla. Houses in eclectic pre-1940 styles,
concrete sidewalk with planting strip. Author photo, 2001.

Celebration, showing the center with retail and housing facing
the waterfront of the new lake. Author photograph, 2001.

found it easier to rezone and recode in unincorporated areas. As the
size of projects grew, it was difficult to find a developer wealthy
enough to build a very substantial town center or any regional authority able to build light-rail transit. However, CNU's leaders received a
lot of press attention for the projects that did get built and they

became more credible as both urban and regional planners. By 1996, they were at work on a thoughtful, substantial charter defining new urbanism as "a complex system of policies and design principles that operate at multiple scales," including regions, neighborhoods, and streets.[7] By 2000, the largest firms associated with the movement had hundreds of projects completed, including redevelopments of public housing and old malls, as well as new residential communities.

"Disney's Town of Celebration": Theme Park Meets Enclave

The wit, charm, and modest scale of Seaside, as well as the energy and transit-oriented tone of the charter of the Congress for the New Urbanism were underscored when a much larger development called "Celebration" was established by The Walt Disney Company near Orlando, Florida, in 1994. Unlike Seaside, Celebration was not an incorporated town, although it was advertised as "Disney's Town of Celebration." Thirty years earlier, Walt Disney had purchased 28,000 acres in Osceola County, a citrus and cattle-ranching area in the Florida interior. Disney hoped to build an expanded version of his Southern California theme park, own the surrounding hotels, and build a model town called EPCOT (Experimental Prototype Community of Tomorrow) for 20,000 workers. EPCOT never became a housing development— today it is a theme park. The other ventures thrived. By 1990 Orlando was one of the fastest-growing areas in the United States, home to Walt Disney World Resort and a host of other theme parks focused on everything from sea creatures to the Bible. In 1991 Joel Garreau identified four edge cities there, including one that had taken over the old downtown, so the entire urban region looked a bit like Tysons Corner with scattered office and commercial developments as well as theme parks next to gridlocked freeways.[8] When Orlando's roads literally couldn't handle one more theme park, Disney ventured into real estate development.

Disney's Michael Eisner commissioned Jacquelin Robertson (of Cooper, Robertson and Partners, a New York urban design firm) and Robert A. M. Stern Architects (a New York architecture firm) to draw up a master plan. They proposed a residential area housing 20,000 people on about 4,900 acres in an unincorporated part of Osceola County, a site split off from the Reedy Creek Improvement District (the physical planning entity that included the Disney amusement parks and hotels). The Celebration Company, a subsidiary of The Walt Disney Company, was a developer with deep pockets. Disney poured $2.5 billion into transforming an unpromising wetland into a large and handsome town center—dredging an artificial lake, building roads, parks, and bridges as well as downtown shops. Others built a hotel and schools. An eighteen-hole golf course designed by Robert Trent Jones, Sr., and Robert Trent Jones, Jr., ran through the middle of the site, recalling developer Hugh E. Prather's dictum "The American businessman wants his golf."[9] The links were banded by "Estate Homes" ($600,000 and up). Lesser neighborhoods were handsomely landscaped with parks and playgrounds to serve "Village Homes" ($350,000), "Cottage Homes" ($250,000), townhomes ($250,000), and apartments. Styles included "Classical, Victorian, Colonial Revival, Coastal, Mediterranean, and French." At the edge of the site, next to the freeway, stood "Celebration Health," a 260,000-square-foot "wellness center" (a hospital run by Florida Health, part of the Church of Seventh Day Adventists), and "Celebration Place," a 109-acre office park.[10] Noted architects designed all of the public buildings, but they were not from the younger generation of new urbanists. Robert A. M. Stern's buildings stressed context. Others were more exuberant "signature" buildings in personal styles, including Aldo Rossi's office park. Some worked beautifully, such as Caesar Pelli's art deco theater, sited where its exuberant shapes were reflected in the new lake. Others fell flat, perhaps attempting irony, including Philip Johnson's town hall, with a forest of tall, thin columns and a gigantic door.

I visited Celebration in March 2001. After an hour and a half stuck on crowded freeways within Orlando, I spotted the white three-rail fence that wrapped the exterior of the development, an imitation of the rural fences used on the old horse farms and ranches of central Florida. Once inside, I drove to the Celebration Hotel. Two 1950s Cadillacs permanently parked in the forecourt echoed the theme of Florida plantation culture. In a lobby overlooking the lake, cypress root lamps illuminated ceiling fans, wicker furniture, and large bird cages. Additional props included framed photographs of the horse-and-buggy world of the citrus and cattle towns in central Florida in the 1920s. At the reception desk two women wearing identical white silk blouses and pearls greeted guests. An antique fishing rod and a couple of old brown leather suitcases—the kind often featured in

Ralph Lauren ads—were positioned by the desk as if their owner had just arrived. Decor in the hotel room was nostalgic. In case I hadn't decided what to think, memo pads next to the phone read "Celebration Hotel, 'Delightfully Charming.' "

I headed to the dining room past more historical photos. One showed ten African-Americans clearing land with tractors. Next to my table was an image of an African-American crew picking oranges. The old Florida plantation theme was full-blown when I spotted a view of orange groves with two white overseers on horseback. Although Florida is a multiracial state, the only African-American I saw at the Celebration Hotel that night was standing outside next to the antique Cadillacs, parking cars.

The next morning I walked over to the Celebration sales center, housed in a building designed by Charles Moore. I examined the large, well-lit scale model of Celebration, inquired how large the entire Celebration site was, and asked about future development, pointing to areas labeled "future residential" or "future multi-family," but I never got a satisfactory answer. Although advertised on billboards as "Disney's Town of Celebration" and on a website saying "Welcome to Celebration, Florida," Celebration is not a town with political boundaries but a real estate development in Osceola County. My question about boundaries was not trivial. When I noticed a sign stating that only "cast members" were allowed to handle the lights on the site model, I realized the real estate sales people held the same job title—cast member—as workers in Disney's amusement parks. Cast members cared for the streets early every morning in Celebration, just as they did in the theme parks, and the streets were spotless.

I walked around the neighborhoods closest to the center of the project and the lake, passing small parks planted with flowering trees and traditional beds of flowers, like well-tended English public parks. This was not indigenous landscaping, so it felt artificial in central Florida, but I liked the parks and playgrounds and lingered on the perfect sidewalks. The eclectic houses—federal, Victorian, Greek revival, Spanish colonial revival—were well kept and the cars were out of sight, in garages accessed from alleys behind the streets. There were large porches and flourishing private gardens. It was a sunny day, and I was the only person in sight. Although designed to represent the passage of time through various architectural styles, everything in Celebration was new, so I felt as if I had wandered onto the set of a Technicolor movie. I was convinced that I had returned to an affluent moment in the 1920s, before the crash, to experience a community of middle-class single-family houses, just the way Herbert Hoover envisioned it.

I returned to the sales office, where I asked if I could visit a model house. All of Celebration carries the corporate logo of a large tree shading a small pony-tailed girl on a bicycle riding past a picket fence, trailed by her dog: CELEBRATION. FLORIDA. EST 1994. In the neighborhoods closest to the center, the houses were all sold. The salesperson pointed to a map with the locations of new model houses. "Can I walk?" I asked. "You don't have a car?" she replied in astonishment. I did have a car, but I had to walk all the way back to the hotel to get it, and then drive a mile to the open houses.

Writer Alex Marshall has observed that Celebration's designers have tried to "re-create an urban neighborhood without creating the transportation network that spawned such neighborhoods. . . . So what you get is a peculiar thing, an automobile-oriented subdivision dressed up to look like a small pre-car centered town."[11] There is another ambiguity as well. The presence of the office park suggests that Celebration is going to become an edge node. Indeed, when I checked public records, I found that in 2002 The Celebration Company filed a "Master Development Plan" with Osceola County that showed "Celebration West" across Interstate 4 from "Celebration East." The plan detailed four phases of development through 2020 and included 6,777,033 square feet of retail, commercial, and industrial development. Some residential areas included possible densities as high as forty dwellings to the acre. The height limit on the master plan for Celebration West is twenty-six stories.[12] If this future development occurs, the residential area, including the high-priced golf-course "Estate Homes," will be an adjunct. If many future residents live at very high densities several miles away from the pedestrian center, amid new commercial and industrial projects of Phases 2, 3, and 4, "Celebration" will no longer feel like the upscale picturesque enclaves of the 1920s it now resembles. Only Phase 1 was visible on Celebration's first plans and models, so some buyers may be in for a shock if it turns out that the expensive picturesque enclave was simply the anchor for a new edge node.

The promotional literature for Celebration that I saw suggested

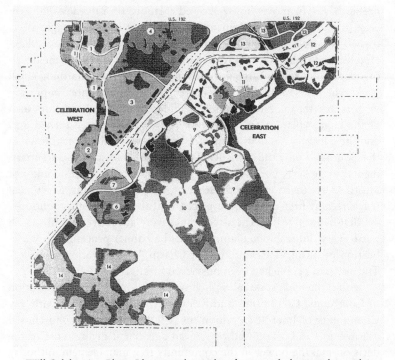

Will Celebration Phase I become the anchor for a much denser edge node?
Detail of Map H, from "Master Development Plan" for Celebration,
revised June 26, 2002. The highly publicized Phase I (1994–2004), located
just above the words "Celebration East," includes town center, residential
areas, golf course, office park, and hospital. Possible future development
includes: 1, 5, 14, residential and/or office, and/or hotel; 2, 7, mixed use; 3,
office and/or retail, and/or hotel; 4, attraction and/or hotel, and/or office; 6,
public and/or educational; 8, 9, 10, 11, 12, residental; 13, office and/or retail,
office and/or hotel, office and/or hospital. The "attraction" includes 1,780,000
square feet of industrial zoning. Courtesy of the Osceola County Permitting
and Development Department.

that Disney's salespeople, like many in the real estate world, always
straddled the line between life and entertainment, reality and fantasy:
"The destination your soul has been searching for," promised one ad.
Another crooned: "There was once a place where neighbors greeted
neighbors in the quiet of the summer twilight. Where children chased

fireflies. . . . The movie house showed cartoons on Saturday. The grocery store delivered. . . . Remember that place? It held a magic all its own. The special magic of an American hometown." The magic flickered like the stream of light from a movie projector. Parts of the development were excellent: the art deco movie house, the charming small parks, the pleasant waterfront. The expansive central area impressed visitors, but the experience of it was undercut by staged interiors such as the banal "plantation" hotel (not run by Disney, as it turned out) and the corny 1940s malt shop. Celebration was unlike a real town in that it housed only the affluent. "Downtown" had schools and apartments, to be sure, but most Disney theme park employees could not afford to live there, even in the least expensive apartments. Most local teachers and firefighters were priced out also. Too many boutiques sold Disney souvenirs. The streetscapes were attractive, but in March 2001 every old-fashioned lamppost held a banner proclaiming "Celebration of Taste," "Celebration of Charm," "Celebration of Style." The notepad people had been busy outdoors.

Behind the real estate sales pitch was a hundred-page "Declaration of Covenants, Conditions, and Restrictions" (CC&R's). As with any Community of Interest Development (CID), a person who purchased a house in Celebration had to sign an agreement giving most of the decision-making power in the community to a management authority representing the developer. The agreement limited what residents could do with their property—no colored curtains, for example. There were restrictions on what they could plant in their yards, where they could park their cars, and how soon they could resell their houses.

When journalists descended on Celebration in its first few years, most were determined to report that it was not "the happiest place on earth." Some builders used crews of illegal immigrants to build houses and many did not deliver a satisfactory "product."[13] Some students and parents were disappointed by the much-advertised model school, leading to lawsuits.[14] Encephalitis-bearing mosquitoes put a cramp on porch-sitting, while residents who planned to play golf found the tee times taken by Japanese tourists.[15] If anyone wanted to protest, the "Town Hall" designed by Philip Johnson housed only the real estate managers hired by The Celebration Company, not elected local government officials, although eventually property owners would have more say.

After a few years, debates about illusion and reality at both Seaside and Celebration wound down. If Seaside could be described as a resort where the theme was Southern rural architecture, Celebration was a community where the theme was pre-1940s Southern small-town living. Yet despite the gibes, both Robert Davis and The Walt Disney Company invested in substantial, attractive public realms intended to shame get-rich-quick developers of edge nodes, malls, and fringe subdivisions. Their message was simple: we sell more houses because we design better public places. As far as the architects were concerned, these developers were exceptional clients, clients to be courted.[16] As far as the developers were concerned, sales prices would validate their investment in neo-traditional design. Their careful attention to the public realm, especially its pedestrian scale, was welcome, but inevitably other developers copied what they liked from these model enclaves without imitating the most expensive investments in site design and architecture.

Gated Enclaves

Neither Seaside nor Celebration had a gate with a guard at the entrance, although both were closely supervised by private real estate developers. The *Charter of the New Urbanism* took a principled position against gated communities, but many critics of new urbanism felt that the design of expensive new suburban areas resembling old-fashioned elite enclaves encouraged exclusivity, whether or not the enclaves had gates. Gates had been part of the appeal in exclusive communities such as Tuxedo Park, and a century later, developers working on projects for almost all income levels found that gates enhanced the sense of security many buyers sought in the sprawling suburban landscape. Evan MacKenzie in *Privatopia* and Ed Blakely and Mary Gail Snyder in *Fortress America* have documented the rapid rise of gated communities in the 1990s.[17] When anthropologist Setha Low interviewed residents in several gated communities, many expressed fear about unsafe neighborhoods, overdevelopment, and uncertain resale values. In order to gain a measure of stability, those who chose to locate in gated communities—perhaps 16 million people by 2002— submitted to arbitrary rules and restrictions, while they enjoyed club-like amenities and private policing of their grounds.[18] Among the gated communities that catered to particular interests were those with golf courses or private beaches. In 2002, new gated communities were also being designed for evangelical churches. Many churches had expanded to offer around-the-clock activities to members including social services, sports, and fast food, as well as religious worship. Journalist Patricia Leigh Brown reported on a visit to the Community Church of Joy in suburban Phoenix in 2002, where the congregation was planning to add a housing development with a full-time chaplain. This congregation would also include a water park, "part of an Olympic-size aquatic center . . . [on] a Christian theme, with laser shows depicting Jonah and the whale and David and Goliath." Another specialist in religious history called this "Christian cocooning."[19]

LOST IN THE BORDERLAND: LONELY "SMART" HOUSES

While new urbanist designers have tried to re-create old-fashioned pedestrian towns, with face-to-face community, designers of wired houses have tried to create a futuristic solutions by relying on virtual community. In the early 1990s, most new residences on the rural fringe included one or more computers hooked up to the Internet. People might work at home, shop on the Internet (e-tailing), and enjoy computer games. Some designers then began to use more comprehensive digital technology to address the physical split between paid employment and home. Others looked at ways to lighten nurturing work. In the most complex futuristic house designs, telecommuting might coexist with family life, while housework, child care, and elderly care might be assisted by robots and virtual reality.

The idea of using technology to eliminate housework goes back to Catharine Beecher's "close packing of conveniences." It has been elaborated with every succeeding generation. In 1893, at the Chicago World's Fair, a chef was pictured cooking with lightning bolts, demonstrating the arrival of electricity. By the 1930s General Electric had a slogan, "Electricity is her Servant," and was displaying a "magic home" at fairs. Westinghouse built a "Home of Tomorrow" in Ohio; Libby-Owens-Ford promoted a "Day After Tomorrow" kitchen.[20] In the 1950s robots polished floors in the American "Splitnik" house displayed in Moscow, the setting for Nixon and Khrushchev's kitchen debate. Throughout it all, in real life women's hours of household and child-rearing work increased rather than decreased. Expectations were higher. Families owned more clothes and wanted them cleaner. They had bigger houses. Many of the appliances people acquired were simply gimmicks.[21]

Meanwhile, novelists and filmmakers seized the potential for humor. Jay Williams and Raymond Abrashkin, authors of *Danny Dunn and the Automatic House,* invented The Scuttler, a robotic device that could bounce around a baby or roast a chicken in response to voice commands. Jessica Steen's 1999 film *Smart House* told the story of a house called PAT (Personal Applied Technology). PAT is a traditional-looking house with dormers, shingles, and overstuffed furniture, in addition to interactive digital systems. Home to a lonely widower and his two children, PAT is able to analyze their dietary needs, cook and serve their favorite meals, and clean up spills. PAT can also provide LCD (liquid crystal display) landscape views, generate virtual playmates for the children, and pick out their clothing. The son must recognize that PAT (represented in virtual reality as a 1950s housewife) is unable to give a hug, in order to see why his lonely dad has fallen in love with the house's designer, a real woman. The plot concludes with a reconstituted traditional family inside a perfect digital house. Locked into all the "smart house" wiring is a wistful vision of happy family life unchanged since 1900.

Millennium Houses

In 1998 two sisters, architects Gisue Hariri and Mojgan Hariri, designed a digital "house for the next millennium" for *House Beautiful.* On a two-acre suburban lot, the Digital-House was

Sketch of "The Scuttler," a robot, by Owen Kampen, from Jay Williams and Raymond Abrashkin, *Danny Dunn and the Automatic House* (New York: Archway/Pocket Books, 1965.) By permission of William H. Abrashkin and Barbara Williams.

sized at 3,200 square feet. The computer renderings showed the house set on a lawn surrounded by woods so that other houses or neighborhood activities were invisible. Using a structural steel frame, the designers developed a core with active matrix liquid crystal display (AMLCD) walls.[22] To the structural core the designers proposed to attach factory-made modules for bedrooms, work areas, and living space. These rooms could be delivered by truck, as if they were "appliances that can be added and exchanged to reflect new domestic situations."[23] The plans indicated three separate floors, each with a bedroom, bathroom, and work space for what the Hariris described as a family, consisting of "three independent beings free from preconceived notions of gender roles, domination and sexual preference."[24] There was a living room (also labeled media room), a kitchen with a virtual chef, and a dining room. While much of the project seemed practical, the designers noted that the bedrooms would be equipped with a "Dream-Recording device, so one could review one's dreams on the liquid wall of the room at any time."[25]

Rear facade of the Digital-House, with joggers.
From "The Digital-House, Unwired Landscape/Physical Fitness,"
by Hariri and Hariri—Architects, New York, 1998.

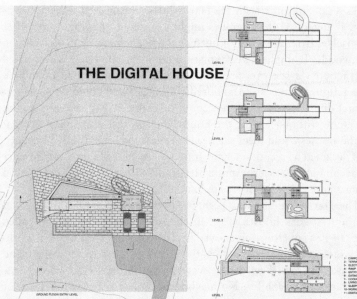

Plans for four-level house with multiple workspaces.
From "The Digital-House."

Kitchen with virtual chef. From "The Digital-House."

As a polemical project, the Hariris' design captured a lot of attention. It suggested that families might use new technologies to buffer themselves from the work of nurturing while remaining in seclusion in the woods. It implied that isolation could be modified with virtual interaction via the ever-present AMLCD screens, instead of human interaction. Friends from hundreds of miles away could "visit" for a virtual dinner party. Children could be connected to schools around the globe without leaving the house. This project also suggested that digital houses could meet the needs of mass manufacturers, because it was designed as a container for rooms to be plugged into, a container to accommodate consumption. It straddled the distinction between "smart houses" and "smart appliances."

The Hariris' house was perhaps the most frequently discussed of all the live/work houses in a Museum of Modern Art exhibit called *The Un-Private House* assembled by Terence Riley.[26] Many of the others were remarkably chilly, characterized by vast LCD screens and expanses of glass. Few people were shown in most of the architects' drawings in the exhibit. No neighborhood context was designed, or even desired. In some ways, this entire group of hi-tech houses recalled the efforts of the Case Study program, run by *Art and Architecture* magazine to develop modern houses after World War II. Most of the Case Study designers tested the aesthetic and technical possibilities of steel and glass, while retaining the program of the traditional family house. Only a couple of these designs recognized alternative family scenarios or the need for a neighborhood.[27] As in the *House Beautiful* series and the Un-Private House show, neighborhood was not a priority.

House_n: The MIT Home of the Future
Another ambitious attempt to design a digital house began in the 1990s at MIT as a multidisciplinary research project. It was funded by major corporations including Compaq, Procter and Gamble, Bentley Systems, Inc., Owens Corning, NET Silicon, Superior Essex, International Paper, Invensys, and Olivetti. The website for "House_n" (the *n* is an infinite variable) includes phrases such as "interactive user interface environments," "customized mass-consumption," and "electronically mediated."[28] Project director and architect Kent Larson discusses energy-producing walls (using passive solar technologies) and all-

seeing counter systems: "All horizontal surfaces in the home may eventually incorporate object sensors." He views this as leading to "continuous and unattended inventory of objects in the home." The inventory will allow for "automated reordering of commodities, appliances that interact with objects and connect to the manufacturer's website for optimized control, low-cost robotics systems designed to interact with tagged objects, digitally mediated medicine dispensing, and automated routing of goods from factory to warehouse to kitchen cabinet."[29]

In short, House_n is being designed to run its inhabitants' lives because every horizontal surface will read the bar codes attached to every product in the house, just the way an automated supermarket checkout can identify the goods, tally the cost, and make change in 2002. The house will act on this information in far-reaching ways. The website promises "appliances we can communicate with [at] both a functional and emotional level." For example, "The refrigerator is going to be able to make an inventory of the food . . . using the new RFID tags, access internet and buy the missing items for you." The website also promises a washing machine that can sort clothes. And finally, the designers come up with the most intrusive scheme of all: "Your toilet is going to be able to monitor your health. It is going to analyze the urine, measure your weight and blood pressure." At the same time, "All appliances will communicate with one another sharing useful information."[30] Potential purchasers or investors may wonder if the house will put an overweight homeowner on a diet.

Residents will be expected to talk to House_n: "As chip capacity increases, we are going to be able to incorporate voice recognition. . . ."[31] Somehow, this seems like the plot for a zany movie. Here's the opening: I come home from work and toss my briefcase on the floor, where a robot zooms over to pick it up and carry it to my study. I order a hanger from the closet to come get my coat. Then I call out, "Poached salmon, dill sauce, new potatoes, spinach salad, apple pie," and sit down to watch the cooking proceed. My children (or grandchildren?) will gather round the table. "Mom, was there really a time when you and Dad had to drive all the way to a supermarket, take things off the shelf, haul a sack of groceries, and cook the food yourself?"

But this narrative may be too literal. If the house is in charge, and talking to suppliers, perhaps residents won't be able to give orders: "Software developments are increasingly enabling systems to 'think for themselves.' Artificial intelligence is now reaching the stage where systems can be programmed to predict situations and outcomes based on previous experience, and take the action accordingly." Any good cook will wonder about the quality of food that has been prepared by automation. Surely family interaction in the kitchen will be missed, but perhaps cookbook author Mark Bittman will be on contract to the stove manufacturer, and interaction will be with a virtual chef, as promised in the Hariri project.

The House_n designers adore virtual reality: "In combination with sensors which detect our movement and devices which convey the sensation of touch to our bodies, software programs can rapidly generate computer images and reactions which give us the experience of being in another, 'Virtual Reality.' " Perhaps the family won't even be eating. They can have a virtual dinner experience, and then House_n will not have any dirty dishes or pots and pans. Some might wish to go straight to a pill with all the vitamins included. Anna Bowman Dodd's sarcastic science fiction novel from 1887, *Republic of the Future*, depicted mass-produced food delivered from Chicago to New York via electronic "culinary conduits." She wrote with savage humor: "When the last pie was made into the first pellet, women's true freedom began."[32]

Of course, parents may not be coming home from work. The House_n designers predict that digital technologies will affect personal communication, shopping, news, banking, education, medical care, entertainment, political participation, and the maintenance of autonomy in old age. "Increasingly, these activities will take place directly in the home. As our notion of banks, bookstores, universities, communities, and cities change in response to new technologies, the home will take on extraordinary new importance."[33] Realtors are the ones who usually insist on calling a house a "home." The MIT project followed this convention, designing a house to privatize the neighborhood on behalf of simplifying residents' lives.

The House_n team is building a "Living Laboratory," a model house next to MIT, where volunteers will live in the prototype for anything from one week to four months. They are currently inviting corporate research as well as academic proposals.[34] They have an interest in "trans-generational environments," that is, care for children or the elderly handled digitally. For anyone wondering about privacy issues or ethical considerations with human subjects, the implications are worrying. Kent Larson notes that "arrays of sensors embedded in the environment and miniature wearable computers will simplify the task of obtaining data about the activities of people. . . . By monitoring what people typically do, it then becomes possible to predict what they might do next, enabling imaginative new products with comfortable, natural, and easy to use interfaces that bridge the digital and physical domains." Larson, the project director, concludes that "eventually, sophisticated systems will be self-programming, with the environment melding ever more intimately with the individual over time."[35] Is that "melding" or "meddling"? House_n would satisfy most of the security requirements for house arrest without direct police presence.[36]

Neo-traditional Digital Houses

In the 1980s and 1990s fringe areas sprouted both traditional houses and futuristic houses, and by 2000, many Americans thought they could combine historicist exteriors with wired interiors. In the 1970s and 1980s postmodern architects rediscovered eclectic styles of architecture. They began to explore traditional wood-framing systems and classical proportions. The neo-traditional house at first offered a different ambiance, an old-fashioned, cozy imitation of colonial or Victorian America, complete with acreage and perhaps even a horse or two, something like the houses idealized by Andrew Jackson Downing and Catharine Beecher. While some chose federal and Greek revival styles, others favored Victorian eclecticism, bringing back an interest in Gothic revival and shingle styles. Porches returned, especially in projects that took up the vernacular styles of Victorian resorts. The craftsman bungalow reappeared. There was also interest in regional vernacular house forms that suited local climates.

As Seaside and Celebration became popular, Americans found it easier to locate an architect willing and able to design a single new house to fit in the physical context of an older neighborhood. When the neo-traditional house gained popularity among architects, it helped to reconnect architects with builders, who had always favored traditional styles, but its potential charm was usually compromised by the ever-present car.[37] Most neo-traditional houses were sited for the automobile, not for a town. Forms from the eighteenth century such as hip roofs, twelve-over-twelve windows, and paneled doors coexisted with three-car garages, huge driveways, dangling power lines, and improbable sites far from other houses. Volumes were also reshaped on the interior. Ceilings might be manipulated to offer double-height spaces. Perfectly proportioned parlors and dining rooms gave way to interconnected great rooms and kitchens, living/dining areas, home offices, or television/video screening rooms. Indeed, the floor plan of a neo-traditional house was often quite like the plan of the Hariris' digital house, with a media room and three home offices. It was also likely to be sited in a large-lot fringe suburb and require a long commute.

Residents of neo-traditional houses at times seemed as if they would like to step into the frame of a Normal Rockwell painting or step onstage in a production of *The Music Man*. Their lawns were perfect, American flags were fluttering, and everyone was ready for a Fourth of July parade with the high school band. But like the residents of digital houses, they had computers, cell phones, and hectic schedules. They did not follow the gender patterns of the early twentieth century, when most families depended on stay-at-home wives. The digital houses and the neo-traditional houses might look different, but the occupants' life patterns might be similar. When a software engineer was asked by a radio interviewer how digital technologies had changed the United States, she replied cheerfully that everyone lived more as a software engineer did ten years ago: people interacted with computers all the time, on crazy schedules that did not separate working from living. Some of the wired people might live in futuristic-looking digital houses, where LCD screens might change the decor every day, and some might live in neo-traditional houses with antique furniture. Both the futuristic live-work houses and the digitized neo-traditional houses were shown in popular shelter magazines. Editors did not think it schizophrenic to alternate them—pods of both kinds of houses could be produced—and most people would want computers. Architect-futurists argued that the United States would continue to be wired and telecommuting would spread.[38]

Houses to Customize Mass Consumption

This aesthetic split reinforced the idea that the only really important issue was to maintain consumption. Consumption was assumed to be a universal goal by the designers of House_*n*. Architects might claim a larger role in the design of the built environment if they could succeed in personalizing mass consumption within the mass-produced house. Many ideas about "customizing" were first launched one hundred years ago when the mail-order house industry started to build momentum. Sears, Roebuck and Co. and the other mail-order house companies who offered precut houses would ship them with additions or subtractions according to a customer's choices. Many offered a range of plumbing, heating, and hardware choices, as well as prefabricated cabinets and built-in furniture. Herbert Hoover looked at ways to increase consumption in the 1920s, when he worked with Better Homes in America, Inc., and William and Alfred Levitt were heirs to this tradition, as builders who promoted diverse manufacturers' products, including washing machines and televisions. Perhaps the silliest cross-promotion was developed by General Motors. In the 1956 advertising film *Design for Dreaming,* they showed a magical Frigidaire kitchen that permitted a housewife to go to a GM Motorama car show and find more time for driving.[39]

What is most dystopian about all of the digital houses designed for customized consumption is the implication that the entire landscape could be covered with new houses lacking any social or economic neighborhood context. Designers minimize the need for family or neighborhood interaction if they plan for digital surveillance as a route to ordering mass-produced commodities as well as handling work and civic life. If many external activities, such as paid work, exercise, shopping, seeking entertainment, and voting, are able to be done in-house through the various electronic communications systems, reasons for going outside decrease. The residents become isolated, although the house continues to function as a container for mass-produced goods and electronic media. In a landscape bristling with tens of thousands of digital houses and cell towers, where the ground is laced with hundreds of thousands of miles of fiber-optic cable, neighborhoods may not exist. Car journeys involving traffic problems may disappear, although the roads will be clogged with delivery vans.

BACK TO NATURE: SUSTAINABLE HOUSES

In addition to the neo-traditional enclave and the wired house, architects designed sustainable "green" houses to limit the use of nonre-

newable resources in suburbs. Green houses pointed up the larger
issues of sustainability—cutting wasteful consumption of land, energy,
and water—but at the scale of the house, they didn't always achieve
those ends. Solar technology was not new. The first solar water heater
was patented by a Maryland inventor in the 1890s, and during the
Depression and World War II, when oil and gas for heating were in
short supply, many designers believed the solar house would predominate after the war.[40] Dr. Maria Telkes, a scientist at MIT, worked with
architect Eleanor Raymond to create a successful prototype in the late
1940s that was celebrated in *Life, Fortune,* and the *Saturday Evening
Post,* as well as numerous technical publications. The Telkes-Raymond
house was built without an auxiliary heating system and by 1949,
their prototype could handle three-quarters of the heating load in the
cold and overcast climate of Boston.[41] Government agencies took it
up. Other solar houses were also given publicity, including one by
architect George Keck in Illinois. Mechanical engineer George Lof
designed a solar hot-air heating system in Colorado.[42]

All of these breakthroughs failed to attract building industry
support during the 1940s and 1950s. As Levittown, Lakewood, and
Park Forest demonstrated, developers of large tracts wanted to build
cheaply, even to the point of ignoring essential sewers in Levittown.
Developers resisted any suggestion that a site plan could orient houses
to the south for solar gain, because it would be too complicated to
organize. They resisted any FHA suggestion that insulation was important, with or without solar heating, because the expense would cut
their profits. The homeowners paid the fuel bills, so the developers did
not care about the long-term cost of energy.

In the late 1940s, coal and oil were relatively inexpensive, and
American utilities had been campaigning since the 1920s to increase
electrical demand. General Electric saw high demand for electricity as a
double source of profits—from sales of generating equipment and from
sales of appliances. They had campaigned in the 1930s to get FHA to
cover the cost of electric appliances on the mortgage of a house in electrical modernization projects. First, large built-in appliances such as
washers and televisions were included, and eventually FHA included
items as small as vacuum cleaners.[43] GE's "It's a promise!" advertising
campaigns assured wartime consumers that postwar life would bring
home ownership with many appliances. As one child of the fifties

remembered, "Excitement infected the entire block when someone got a new refrigerator with a built-in freezer, an automatic washing machine, or a television set with a bigger screen. . . . for our parents, who had lived through the Depression, the ever-expanding economy seemed like a miraculous cornucopia; they took nothing for granted, and approached each major purchase with a sense of awe."[44] What was not obvious to consumers was how little choice they had about the contents of the cornucopia or the energy bills the appliances incurred.

By the early 1950s the tract house as a conventional box was commonplace. Any regional vernacular styles which included adaptations to climate, such as louvers and cross-ventilation, were downplayed in favor of national Cape Cod or ranch-house designs. Solar was consigned to the archives, to be rediscovered decades later. Instead, air-conditioning became a consumer favorite, especially central air-conditioning, which was advertised heavily. Air-conditioning was said to improve family life by keeping housewives and children cheerful rather than irritable, assuring a good night's sleep, and making it easier for a woman to get dressed in a girdle and stockings![45] Promoted for elegance and resale value, centrally air-conditioned homes did well on the market and increased the demand for electricity substantially. The next big spurt of demand was boosted by campaigns for the "all-electric" house in the late 1950s and 1960s. The all-electric house involved replacing oil furnaces with electric heating—expensive and wasteful—because the utilities wished to balance their summer cooling loads with winter demand. Environmental historian Adam Rome has documented how utilities manipulated rates, attempted cross-promotion sweetheart deals with builders, and in some cases offered up-front cash payments to builders for installing electric heat instead of traditional furnaces. Ultimately, Congress held hearings on the promotional practices of public utilities in 1968, but most of the worst practices were not outlawed until 1978.[46]

The solar designs were brilliant in the 1940s and they got better with time, even though developers were not interested at midcentury. By the 1970s environmentalists were promoting solar architecture again, and by the 1990s solar houses had returned, often with roofs and walls of photovoltaic cells. Solar houses could be tied to digital technologies to achieve the most efficient angling of solar collectors. Houses themselves could be designed to rotate through the day. Digital solar houses could monitor and control the temperature of air or water most economically. Windows and doors could also be digitally controlled for best ventilation. Houses could store power in excess of current requirements or pass it on to other uses.

The sustainable house also came to mean more in the 1990s, as definitions of "green" architecture expanded. It could be designed to avoid huge starter-castle dimensions, although well-known "green" architects such as William McDonough were praised for huge projects such as his 11,000-square-foot house in Virginia Beach made of "sustainably harvested wood."[47] The sustainable house could also be made of various kinds of recycled materials. It could be made of nontoxic materials, eliminating items such as carpet glue, formaldehyde-soaked insulation, or "CCA" (chromated copper arsenate) wood. It could be heavily insulated and use low-energy-conducting windows. It could minimize water use with low-water appliances. It could be surrounded with a natural yard rather than a lawn requiring heavy pesticide use. The yard could be landscaped to minimize harmful runoff and to provide habitat for wildlife.[48] Green enclaves were highly publicized, such as Village Homes in Davis, California, a modest community started in the 1970s, or Dewees Island, South Carolina, a more recent development for the ultrawealthy.[49]

Some design innovations, such as the water-conserving toilet, made it into the commercial mainstream in the 1980s, but many other devices remained marginal until the 1990s when pressure from new environmental organizations began to change the sense of what was possible. In 1990 Green Seal was incorporated as a nonprofit group to "promote products and services that cause less toxic pollution and waste, conserve resources and habitats, and minimize global warming and ozone depletion."[50] In 1993 McDonough and chemist Michael Braungart developed the Hannover Principles to guide sustainable design, stressing safe objects of long-term value, elimination of the concept of waste, and reliance on natural energy flows.[51] A number of building industry groups and manufacturers formed the U.S. Green Building Council "to promote buildings that are environmentally responsible, profitable, and healthy places to live and work."[52] The group has a rating system for "green" buildings. "Green" has become a very broad umbrella, with many different groups hoping to stand under it. Green Seal resembles the antisprawl campaigns, and the

Green Building Council echoes the "smart growth" rhetoric adopted by real estate and developer lobbyists such as the National Association of Home Builders and the Urban Land Institute. Green Building and Smart Growth are important, but all of these groups thrive on new construction.

There is growing realization that the problems of excessive fringe suburban development require more than better design. Indeed, the story of the solar house echoes that of the electric car American inventors had designed, built, and sold early in the century. It was innovative, but large manufacturers chose to promote other products and fuels. In 2003 it is too late to correct past mistakes with better new products alone. Even a program for one hundred million solar houses or one hundred and thirty million electric cars could not make the United States sustainable. To turn patterns of excessive consumption into patterns of wise use that can be sustained forever would require severe limits on land use, energy use, and new construction. All such limits have to be enacted despite the opposition of lobbyists for real estate and product development, who have spent decades priming government and banks to work with them to promote new growth.

Looking at the contributions of architects who create historicist enclaves, digital houses, and green architecture, citizens can see substantial demonstrations of better ways to plan and build. Many architects are eloquent as they address the issues. Many are talented and hardworking. But new designs alone cannot redeem a throwaway culture organized around obsolescence and the continual consumption of undeveloped land and new products. Housing is tied to the political economy. Better architecture cannot, in itself, change the larger patterns of social and economic exploitation developed by growth machines which profit from round after round of fringe development. If the United States is to become a more sustainable and more equitable place, older suburbs have to be saved rather than abandoned on the way to new projects.

Chapter Eleven

THE IMPORTANCE
OF OLDER SUBURBS

We can overcome division only by refusing to
be divided.
— RAYMOND WILLIAMS, *The Country
and the City*

THROUGH THE EARLY years of borderlands and elite enclaves,
the busy decades of streetcar buildouts and mail-order houses,
and the last half-century of sitcom suburbs, edge nodes, and
rural fringes, suburbs have rewarded some occupants and disappointed others. Home ownership is higher than it has ever been in the
history of the United States, especially for white, male-headed households, but many people of color and female-headed households remain
renters. Because public incentives encourage private developers to
build for affluent buyers in rural fringes, some families in older suburbs have lost hope of living in orderly, sustainable neighborhoods.
Others have begun to create important programs to sustain and repair
older suburbs.

Reconstruction efforts challenge the simplistic view that all new
growth is good because older buildings are obsolete. There is increasing evidence that in the United States excessive greenfield development
has widened the divide between rich and poor. *Sprawl City: Race, Politics, and Planning in Atlanta* by Robert D. Bullard, Glenn S. Johnson,
and Angel O. Torres documents how poor households, and African-
Americans in particular, have been disadvantaged by the growth of
wealthy white suburbs, the lack of public transportation, and the lack

of affordable housing. *Metropolitics* by Myron Orfield demonstrates how aging inner-ring suburbs in Minnesota and elsewhere have been neglected while state and regional funds go to subsidize affluent fringe growth.[1] Observers on the national front argue the same case. Regional planner Robert Yaro has estimated that the federal government engages in the equivalent of a Marshall Plan every year by spending $100 billion to support growth in distant suburbs instead of using it to maintain existing infrastructure such as schools and public transit.[2] Planner Tom Daniels has listed dozens of federal programs that favor growth over preservation, including home mortgage subsidies. He estimated that in the 1980s, when the United States had to bail out failed savings-and-loans which the Reagan administration had deregulated (authorizing them to buy junk bonds and make "shaky real estate loans" in edge cities), the cost to American taxpayers was $500 billion.[3] While the total federal subsidy to suburban real estate developers and property owners over the past seventy years is still being calculated, there is no doubt that is far higher than most Americans comprehend because of the hidden way it has been disbursed.

GROWTH CONTROVERSIES

The National Association of Realtors (NAR) argues that massive public support for private growth is justified and should continue. The most contentious issue is the "mansion subsidy," established and defended by the realtors' lobby since the early twentieth century, which currently costs the federal government over $100 billion per year, or more than the entire budget of the Department of Housing and Urban Development.[4] Federal tax regulations state that owners of houses are entitled to federal income tax deductions for points, mortgage interest, and property taxes on a primary residence, and these tax breaks increase with the size of the mortgage. The same arrangement is possible on a second house, though the combined eligible mortgage principal is capped at $1 million. While proponents call this tax break a boon to the "middle class," almost half of the tax benefits go to the top 5 percent of taxpayers with incomes over $100,000 per year, the people with the most expensive houses.[5] Since 1997 homeowners have also been able to take a $500,000 profit on the sale of a house before paying capital gains tax. The NAR has argued that eliminating the mortgage subsidy would cause home prices to fall by 15 percent, home sales to fall (although one would expect more people to be buying), and mortgage defaults to soar.[6] The National Association of Home Builders (NAHB), another powerful lobby, insists that growth is in the public interest, creates construction jobs, and serves "the market" of potential buyers.[7] The Urban Land Institute (ULI), another powerful group, which includes fifteen thousand professionals in real estate development, tends to support growth as well.[8] NAR is the direct successor of the National Association of Real Estate Boards (NAREB), whose influence shaped federal and local policy on land use from the 1920s on, while NAHB and ULI are NAR spin-offs. The NAR, with close to eight hundred thousand members, is the nation's largest business trade association. Its Realtors Political Action Committee (RPAC) boasts of being listed as number eleven on *Fortune* magazine's list of the most powerful Washington lobbies, wielding millions of dollars in campaign contributions for local, state, and national elections.[9]

Pro-development forces have argued since the 1920s that building new houses creates jobs and spurs economic growth. They suggest that new construction in affluent suburban areas allows older shelter to "trickle down" to poor families and immigrants, thus meeting the need for "affordable" housing. Unfortunately these units are often located in older, declining neighborhoods without good schools and services. Funding fringe neighborhoods and affluent families through growth incentives and mansion subsidies offers no guarantee of decent housing for poor and working families. Every year, federal and state governments spend billions on growth, while politicians argue that sound public transportation, public schools, heath insurance, child care, and paid parental leave are too expensive for extensive federal support.

"If we don't like sprawl, why do we go on sprawling?" asks Donella Meadows, Dartmouth professor of environmental studies.[10] The political critique of growth machines developed in the 1970s by sociologist Harvey Molotch was expanded in the 1990s by progressive environmentalists who argued that growth machines and the wasteful consumption patterns they promote are central to advanced capitalism in the United States. Major political and economic changes would be necessary to halt them.[11] Some advocates of change have suggested eliminating all federal, state, and local subsidies to fringe development and redirecting those funds to older neighborhoods. Others have argued for "accountable development" with requirements for "living wage" jobs for local workers and public benefits (child care centers, affordable housing, and parks) on projects that receive government subsidies. Some localities have developed "claw-back" provisions in contracts with private developers that give "the city the right to demand the return of its subsidies if the developer fails to deliver on its promises."[12] A few have argued for reparations to people of color and residents of inner-city neighborhoods whose access to resources has been restricted compared to whites and residents of outer suburbs.[13]

Despite the financial analyses of planners such as Yaro and Daniels, many architects and planners remain ambivalent about growth. Although they are willing to speak quite harshly about the highway lobby, most have been unwilling to critique the real estate industry or the framework of public subsidies for private development. Of course architects and town planners want to be optimistic about obtaining work, and for many that means new construction. While "smart growth" received extensive publicity, and citizens could download "sprawl-busting" advice from many websites, most smart growth advocates also stressed new construction rather than rehabilitation. Planners and architects articulated increasingly complex visions of "the promised land," "the brighter dream," "solving sprawl," "the new urbanism," "the transect," "the regional city," and "the new American metropolis," without enough emphasis on preserving and rebuilding existing suburbs.[14] To preserve older suburbs and small towns, the entire structure of tax subsidies for fringe growth would have to be redirected.

SOCIAL AND ECONOMIC PRESSURES FOR REBUILDING SUBURBS

Demographers have offered the most compelling evidence that the preservation of older suburbs and small towns is necessary and urgent. The American population is expected to increase 50 percent by 2050. Demographers project this very substantial figure on the basis of "disparate fertility rates, longer life expectancies, and shifting immigration flows."[15] If these projections are correct, in the next half-century the United States will need affordable housing in decent neighborhoods for one hundred and thirty million more people, including rising numbers of young Hispanic families, the elderly, and new immigrants.

Two alternatives emerge. Private developers welcome these demographic predictions because they believe that population growth offers them a reason to build fifty million more car-dependent tract houses, some of them in gated communities, served by highways, malls, and big-box stores. They claim that this level of demand requires expansion into greenfield locations without existing infrastructure.

The alternative is metropolitan planning to strengthen the built environment of older suburban places, utilize existing infrastructure and schools, improve transit, and strive for a locational balance between housing and jobs. There is no way Americans can create tens of millions of units of affordable housing without preserving existing places and supporting their ability to serve current residents as well as to absorb infill housing. To repair each layer of old growth in metropolitan areas, each of the seven historic patterns must be analyzed for its potential. Subsidies been distributed unevenly over the decades, so economic equity is long overdue.[16] Where there are places with existing houses, existing public infrastructure, and existing community networks (forged over years of propinquity), there are strong social reasons to rehabilitate as well.

Federal or state programs have begun to provide large-scale financial incentives for preserving all seven layers of the suburban city. The United States tends to tolerate a patchwork of overlapping jurisdictions (such as transit or water authorities) as well as a multitude of independent towns and cities within larger metropolitan regions. Some metropolitan areas include hundreds or even thousands of governmental entities.[17] The federal Intermodal Surface Transportation Efficiency Act (ISTEA) programs require metropolitan authorities to coordinate transit planning in exchange for funding. These offer signs of change. There are also diverse nonprofit organizations such as public housing agencies, nonprofit developers, environmental organizations, and economic development groups sponsoring projects that revive older suburbs as well as small-town centers. Myron Orfield supports regional alliances of nonprofit organizations, such as the CenterEdge coalition of Hartford and New Haven, Connecticut, to promote social and environmental change with economic development for residents of older suburbs and inner cities.[18] These alliances help nonprofits gain the strength to develop innovative projects.

PRESERVING HISTORIC LAYERS IN SUBURBIA

Hundreds of books and articles discuss the tools for "smart growth" available to suburbs. They all advocate regional land use planning, but most of them do not include much analysis of how suburbs have developed over time. Historical analysis of different layers of suburban neighborhood development can contribute to preservation by defining the distinctive qualities of different places. While planners may be willing to tackle the poorest and most difficult parts of suburbs, some new urbanist architects tend to promote the cliché of a prosperous "small town" friendly to pedestrians. The result can feel more like Main Street in Disneyland than suburban U.S.A., which has several distinctive layers. Most American suburbs contain more than one of the physical patterns discussed in previous chapters. A picturesque enclave reached by railroad—even one in run-down condition—looks very different from a streetcar suburb, even an affluent one, because each was organized around a particular type of transit. A self-built suburb of the 1920s may resemble a sitcom suburb of the 1940s where owners have expanded their houses over time, but the lot sizes will probably be smaller and less regular. Identifying the old patterns means asking, "What time is this place?"[19] The unique qualities of suburban places are wedded to topography, social history, economic history, and vernacular architecture. Knowledge of how their historic cultural landscapes have evolved can often help to establish priorities for current interventions.

Historic borderland areas are scarce, because they have often disappeared under pressure for development. Yet every now and then an older farm or a small harbor with a few fishing boats has survived as in Guilford, Connecticut. These should be identified as cultural resources in even the busiest suburbs. Borderland areas that have survived also include small resorts, once reached by steamboat from big cities. These may include small hotels and little cottages with a rural feeling. Sometimes the borderland appears as a camp meeting ground for religious revivals outside a city. A few of these remain and can be preserved. Sometimes an amusement park has survived, perhaps at the end of a streetcar line. Often these amusement parks are decaying areas in poor communities, but knowing their relationship to the history of suburbia can help to spark their preservation as popular landmarks.

Historic picturesque enclaves have survived quite well, especially the richest ones where preservationists are vigilant, such as Short Hills, New Jersey. Some older enclaves have fallen on hard times. Interstate Highways were sometimes sited in ways that damaged them. I-95 sliced an edge off Rochelle Park, in New Rochelle, New York, for example. Even lofty Llewellyn Park in New Jersey was bisected by a road. More can be done to recognize the design heritage such places represent and make it accessible to a wider public. However, these are often still places of the elite. A cap on the mortgage subsidy would slow mansionization and teardowns. Public funds are appropriate for older picturesque enclaves when gates are down, and public access to private parks and other preserved landscapes can be developed.

The aging streetcar buildouts come in many forms. A few were middle-class and remain so. A few have been gentrified. More are meticulously preserved testaments to working-class thrift and sacrifice. Many have become extremely shabby, full of graffiti, barred windows, and other signs of decay. Many include industrial buildings. All were built at a density to support transit, and some may need transit restored. Green spaces, schools, and social services often need to be strengthened or added. Tax incentives for new homeowners or programs like the Location Efficient Mortgage (LEF) which enables homeowners near public transit to borrow more, may work here.[20] Tax rebates for long-term owners may be justified since some of these neighborhoods have borne far more than their fair share of the regional property tax burden in recent decades. Some neighborhoods need programs to deal with abandonment by landlords who left after depreciating rental housing or commercial buildings. These sites may need demolition but ultimately can become new infill housing, small parks, or community gardens. Sites of failed public housing also often fall victim to abandonment or arson. Public housing programs such as HOPE VI address the redesign of older public housing projects in ways that physically reintegrate streetcar neighborhoods. If HOPE VI projects include economic development, they are more efficient. If units are designed for single-parent families and the elderly, as well as traditional families, they are usually a better fit.

Mail-order suburbs, self-built suburbs, and sitcom suburbs may be in better shape than the streetcar suburbs, because they were constructed more recently, but many have been troubled by the deterioration of schools and the lack of parks or other neighborhood amenities. These problems were caused by bad initial planning and residential overbuilding. In some of these neighborhoods, informal conversions to two-family status may have occurred. Legalizing accessory apartments can improve an area's flexibility to house seniors and smaller families. Conversion to more energy-efficient dwellings may extend the life of existing houses. Some sitcom suburbs are dense enough to support neighborhood stores and local bus lines. Sustaining good schools in these areas is a logical priority.

Edge nodes demonstrate the urgent need for regional planning to restrict speculation and direct growth. They cry out for growth boundaries, tough infrastructure assessments, and concurrency requirements (transit, infrastructure) to discourage haphazard greenfield development. State legislation in Maryland and Florida has required towns and regions to limit growth in areas with insufficient infrastructure. Some states, such as Oregon, show the positive results of regional planning. It is heartening that over thirty years, voters have repeatedly resisted developers' efforts to remove Portland's urban growth boundary. Each time it has been challenged, voters supported it, and in 2002 the support was resounding.[21]

The physical scale of edge nodes is usually objectionable. New construction should be subjected to design review to enforce architectural guidelines for malls, big-box stores, office parks, and industrial parks, in terms of size, siting, and materials. New parking lots should conform to requirements to increase shade and reduce impervious surfaces. Since many malls are failing in 2003, developers everywhere are attempting to convert dead or dying malls to mixed use (sometimes called "lifestyle villages") by adding housing. Such renovation projects often produce housing for high-end buyers or renters rather than affordable units. Despite the vast subsidies that mall owners have enjoyed over several decades, owners may request more public money to support new private ventures. Instead, local governments might look for ways to reuse old malls to promote public uses currently lacking in edge nodes, such as child care, schools, community colleges, and recreation, or turn to nonprofit developers to build affordable housing for a better jobs-housing balance. Transit is key to long-term survival of new uses.

On the rural fringe, a growth boundary is one tool some communi-

ties are using to halt development. Development impact fees are
another. Requiring dedicated public open space in new subdivisions,
connected to a spine of existing open space, is a third. Rural fringes
require farmland and forest protection to retain their attractive cultural landscapes. Residents may find local land trusts helpful, as well
as the transfer or purchase of development rights. Planning for rural
town centers should emphasize the retention and enhancement of
pedestrian scale. Historic districts can be created with design review
boards to protect older parts of town. "Circuit riders" from state
preservation offices can assist local planning staff. Often zoning codes,
building codes, and lending requirements have hindered preservation
and renovation efforts. Local building codes appropriate for rural historic structures should be developed as alternatives to boilerplate
building codes formed around new construction, which often reflect
manufacturers' lobbies for electrical, mechanical, and plumbing products. Instituting more federal and state tax credits for the preservation
and reuse of older buildings offers financial help. Capping the property tax break here also slows mansionization and teardowns. All of
these tools are partial; each is more effective when applied in combination with the others.

PRESERVATION WITH ECONOMIC DEVELOPMENT

In the best examples of practice, policies developed at the scale of the
town are carried over into the scale of the building, so that building
and neighborhood are unified. Preservation of one large historic structure can stimulate ideas for appropriate new construction in the area,
or new construction can help to weave together the gaps in order
to repair an older neighborhood. Both are part of suburban reconstruction. Although there have been hundreds of notable attempts to
preserve and repair historic suburbs, most have received much less
governmental support and media attention than large greenfield projects. Two outstanding examples of successful reconstruction reveal the
wide social benefits of saving places, whether a community is rich or
poor. These examples also suggest the importance of economic justice
as a guiding principle in the renovation efforts. Organizing projects to
support low- and moderate-income residents can be challenging, yet
the results offer a strong contrast to the more upscale developments

discussed in the previous chapter. Strong local leadership by activists and professionals is necessary. Even small renovation projects can be very complex.

The Burnham Building, Irvington, New York

Irvington is a Hudson River suburb north of New York City. It was founded as Dearman in 1851 by land speculators who made unauthorized use of A. J. Downing's residential sketches, provoking him to write his famous essay, "Our Country Villages." Over time, Irvington developed as an affluent borderland retreat, with large estates surrounding a small waterfront grid town including a commuter railroad station, some industrial buildings, and workers' housing. The Burnham Building was a 30,000-square-foot factory established in the 1880s to make greenhouses and conservatories for estates and botanical gardens. The factory was closed in 1988. Although it sat in a prime location across from the railroad station, the structure quickly became derelict. When Irvington's library needed to expand, the library board purchased the building (listed on the National Register of Historic Places) for $750,000 after citizens approved the project in 1992. Mary Morrisett, president of the library board, then began a private fundraising campaign that eventually reached two thousand five hundred local households who together donated an additional $1.4 million to the renovation. The library wanted to occupy the ground floor. Upper floors were designated for twenty-two units of affordable housing. When the first developer on the project had difficulty raising funds, the Village of Irvington asked Jonathan F. P. Rose, head of Affordable Housing Development Corporation (AHDC) in Katonah, New York, to pursue funding. He was successful in putting together a $7 million package. AHDC brought in the nonprofit Greyston Foundation to own and manage the nonprofit housing, and construction began in 1998.

Tenant selection was based on strict income limits. The residents chosen included six households from a countywide Section 8 waiting list. Another sixteen households rated the highest on a point system favoring Irvington residents who were older, disabled, or single parents, or people working for the town such as municipal or school district employees, volunteer firefighters or ambulance corps members, and municipal board or committee volunteers. Ten times more people

The Burnham Building, Irvington, N.Y., a renovated suburban factory located across from the railroad station. The building now includes the Irvington Public Libary and twenty-two units of affordable housing designed by Stephen Tilly, architect. Author photograph, 2002.

applied than could be accepted. A reporter for the *New York Times* noted that this project set a standard for Westchester County, "one of the wealthiest in the nation, where many communities have gone out of their way to avoid building housing for all but the rich."[22] The bad news is that nine more projects like this one would be necessary to meet the need for affordable housing in one fairly affluent town.

The Natural Resources Defense Council included the project in a book on smart growth, praising historic preservation of an abandoned structure. The developers were cited for creating an innovative mixed-use project near public transit, for anchoring the revitalization of the Main Street and the waterfront, for stimulating a new waterfront park, and for green building. They recycled and refurbished the structure's historic doors and windows, adding triple glazing and heavy insulation for energy conservation. A new solar-heated and solar-cooled community room was constructed for the residents. Impervious surfaces were replaced to reduce runoff to the Hudson River.[23] Shade trees were added.

This project was small but complicated. The team worked for years to put it together, using every possible private and public funding source they could tap, relying on a combination of donations, public spending, grants, and loans. The final result demonstrates exceptional skills deployed in support of common sense. No town wants an eyesore across from its water views and public transit, yet the developers had to run counter to many old regulations and lending practices to finish this project. Speaking about affordable housing, Jonathan F. P. Rose, the developer, noted that restructuring of federal and state housing programs would be necessary to make more mixed-use projects like this one flourish: "First, federal credit enhancement for new projects should go only to those that are within walking distance of mass transit. Second, we should have a point system: if the project is mixed use, it gets more points; if it has day care, it gets more points; if it supports a job–housing balance, it gets more points. We need a system that promotes the kind of world we want."[24]

Concord Village, Indianapolis, Indiana

The federal program HOPE VI (Home Ownership for People Everywhere) was established in the early 1990s to replace older public housing projects with new, mixed-income low-rise housing. Many HOPE VI projects have been built around the country, but one of the most interesting added local economic development for neighborhood residents. In Indianapolis, Concord Village/Eagle Creek, administered by Eugene Jones as the executive director of the Indianapolis Housing Agency, was a joint project of two architecture firms, Clyde Woods of Indianapolis and Tise, Hurwitz, and Diamond of Boston.[25] As part of a broad strategy for economic development, architects Clyde Woods and Stephen Tise and planner Gayle Epp, together with architect Stephen Tise, Jr., organized the 220-unit project so that it could be built house by house. They connected the new construction to an older African-American streetcar suburb. Instead of contracting the whole project to a large builder, they taught and enabled very small builders to create new one- and two-family units to fit in with the existing neighborhood.

In the Haughville neighborhood of Indianapolis, built around the turn of the century, the architects demolished two distressed public housing developments that included many vacant and burned-out multifamily units sitting in a sea of asphalt. After extensive workshops

C   DUPLEX 2/2   TYPE 'A'   B   SINGLE FAMILY 3 BR   A   SINGLE FAMILY 3 BR   TYPE 'A'   B   SINGLE FAMILY 4 BR   TYPE 'A'   G   SINGLE FAMILY 3 BR   TYPE 'C'   D   SINGLE FAMILY 3 BR   TYPE 'B'

Hope VI housing at Concord Village, Indianapolis. The federal project included 220 single-family and duplex units designed by Clyde Woods of Indianapolis and Tise, Hurwitz, and Diamond of Boston, and it was organized so that small local contractors could do the building house by house.

to consult with local residents, they redeveloped the sites to strengthen an older neighborhood by extending the local street grid and complementing the scale, style, and variety of existing homes. The new project of 170 single-family and duplex units faced narrow streets with new buildings similar to the existing local pattern of Craftsman bungalows with front porches. Fifty additional new scattered-site units also helped to weave new housing into the older neighborhood. They also built a day-care center for seventy children and designed new playing fields and open space for the entire area.

For the architects involved, like principals Stephen Tise and Clyde E. Woods, and especially the project architects Daniel J. Glenn, Russell Lewis, and Olon Dotsun, it meant tough, unglamorous work. Helping local contractors take part in a large, federal project by mentoring them as they expanded their skills and experience, these architects empowered low-income neighborhood residents in ways that most HOPE VI projects never attempted. Daniel Glenn explained why he worked so hard to do housing from the producers' point of view as well as that of the residents. He had studied how to provide shelter in developing countries at MIT and believed in grassroots economic development. All of these architects recognized the multiple dimensions of housing as a part of economic production as well as reproduction. They understood the importance of connecting both spatially and socially to an existing community.[26] As in the Irvington case, this project proceeded slowly. It went against the usual framework for public housing, where a large contractor would be awarded the contract to build all 220 units. Restructuring federal programs to include more local economic development would be necessary to make innovative projects like this one the standard rather than the exception.

ADDING PUBLIC HISTORY TO NEIGHBORHOOD PRESERVATION

The process of repairing older suburbs can involve public history and public art as well as the work of environmental activists, politicians, architects, and planners. Interpretation of the history of suburbs is a powerful tool to support reconstruction. Public history can convey the long ideological battle between the suburbs as places of aspiration and hard work and suburbs as places of segregation, stratification, special interests, and profiteering. In every part of the United States, local activists have protested the construction of Wal-Marts and freeways. Environmentalists have fought to save green space and preservationists have protected older buildings. Local history can help to define a positive sense of place in older suburbs by identifying important local victories and establishing landmarks, such as a crusading local newspaper or a volunteer nursery school. It can show the need for more democratic approaches to community development by revealing how hard residents have worked to create a sense of solidarity when places were new and raw.

Conserving the physical character of older suburban places can begin with local history as a way to engage citizens with the political process necessary to support physical planning and rebuilding. Groups like the Power of Place, an organization I founded in Los Angeles, Place Matters in New York, and New Land Marks in Philadelphia have developed many techniques to recapture residents' neighborhood memories, interpret them in public places, and make the most of the physical traces left from other eras.[27] In older suburbs, residents often remember how their grandparents struggled to build a small house. They recall how their mother or aunt worked night after night with other parents to help to establish a decent high school. They remember their father serving as a volunteer firefighter in a new suburban outpost. When family history is shared with a larger public, newcomers hear complex economic stories linking private and public life.

Residents, old and new, can also use local economic history to understand who has been involved in the transformation of the suburban landscape over many decades. They may become curious about which contractors built the local tracts. Who graded and paved the highways? Who owned the earliest strip shopping centers and malls? Finally, residents may want to know how their annual tax dollars are applied to the suburban landscape. Which elected officials support unlimited local growth and the programs of the real estate industry? Which ones support environmental reform?

Even exemplary suburban reconstruction projects such as the two just discussed could benefit from historic interpretation added to community participation. In Irvington, for example, the local public library is a public place inside a renovated factory, so memory of the factory workers' era is implicit. It could be more developed. Interpretation of the greenhouse business carried on in the building might involve adding historical exhibits or new public art on the exterior of the library or the sidewalk. One bronze plaque is not enough. The train station, the wharf, the waterfront public parks, and the Main Street in Irvington are also places where artists and designers might be able to tell the stories of the town and its people in the public realm. Railroad workers and riverboat operators helped build Irvington, as well as wealthy landowners and their servants. Their stories would add to those of the greenhouse workers for anyone interested in interpreting the town's history.

In Indianapolis, the new child-care center and playing fields at Concord Village provide some public space for residents to gather, but this community also could benefit from a more public interpretation of its history. Railroad tracks bound the site on one side, and older industrial sites are nearby. How did this neighborhood look at the turn of the century? What were its industries and job specializations? Where did the streetcars run? Who built the oldest houses? Where did workers go for recreation? Houses, streets, and landmarks such as social clubs and churches provide visible evidence of neighborhood's history.

In revitalized suburbs, as in inner cities, it is important for residents to go beyond architectural history to decode the social and economic history of the place. A complicated story of aspiration, conflict, and disappointment is far more interesting than the bland tale of business success usually told about a prosperous developer. Contestation is the real story of suburbia. Battles over land underlie the developers and builders' process of production as well as the residents' struggle for a decent house, a connection to nature, and a sense of community. In unplanned suburbs, citizens' efforts to secure paved streets or schools may be the big battles. Even in planned suburbs, the struggles to achieve racial integration, to preserve open space, and to protect historic buildings can take on heroic proportions. The Park Forest Public Library, under the leadership of archivist Jane Nicoll, has created a digital archive covering the development history of the town and its progress toward racial integration. Oral history interviews offer rich materials for both scholars and the general public. Town plans and sales brochures document the development along with photographs and local newspapers. In the town itself, a preserved suburban townhouse lets visitors experience the typical early housing in Park Forest and the furniture designs of the 1950s. It also recalls the choice of the developers to convert some townhouses to schools in the transition period before real schools could be built.[28]

FROM PUBLIC HISTORY TO PUBLIC ACCOUNTABILITY

Americans have cherished suburbia in many of its forms, but many people feel puzzled and frustrated by the tracts, malls, and freeways found in edge nodes and rural fringes. A new generation hopes to start over. The problem is that many people believe that starting over means exerting total design control over elite enclaves or placing isolated houses in undeveloped rural land. For all the talk of smart growth, what might it mean to be smart? Suburbia is the hinge, the connection between past and future, between old inequalities and new possibilities. In all kinds of existing suburbs, inequalities of gender, class, and race have been embedded in material form. So have unwise environmental choices. To preserve, renovate, and infill the suburban neighborhoods of the past can make the suburban city more egalitarian and sustainable.

Throughout almost two hundred years of suburban development, advocates of social idealism and good design have warred with those in quest of private profit. The picturesque enclaves designed by Frederick Law Olmsted, the campaigns for multifamily housing by Clarence Stein and Catherine Bauer, the landscaped Greenbelt towns and subur-

ban plans of Elbert Peets, and the energy-efficient houses of Eleanor
Raymond and Dr. Maria Telkes all offered precedents for good design.
In each case, the trajectory of wise development intersected with the
priorities of entrepreneurs who did things another way. In contrast to
the innovative designers, Samuel Gross and Sears, Roebuck, pushed
mundane lots and houses with dramatic sales pitches. The success of
banal subdivisions and overdecorated mail-order houses spurred cyni-
cism.

The excesses of the curbstoners led J. C. Nichols to campaign effectively for public support for private real estate development on an
unprecedented scale. Nichols and his associates in NAREB took on
some well-intentioned supporters, such as President Herbert Hoover, a
former engineer who saw standardization as the route to mass production. Later developers like William Levitt had unsavory political allies,
such as red-baiting Senator Joseph McCarthy. The developers' success
in the years between 1920 and 1960 rested on the use of government
loans and roads to help them exploit undeveloped land and unlimited
energy to maximize the mass consumption of single-family houses.
Without national planning for careful land use or the strategic provision of infrastructure, there was little public gain in exchange for all of
the government support, direct and indirect, that went into millions of
houses, plus the malls, office parks, and industrial parks that followed
them to suburban locations.

Forty years later, Americans can see the economic and environmental consequences of the longest splurge in private housing the world
has ever known. Rural fringes of tract mansions alternate with trash-
strewn streetcar suburbs. Freeways are widened for traffic that never
stops while national supports for day care and schools are said to be
"too expensive." In 2003 the growth lobby is stronger, better organized, and more powerful than ever. Professionals and activists who
attempt to direct federal, state, and local subsidies toward the less affluent, provide public transit, and require more environmental ac-
countability are supported by citizens but opposed by real estate and
highway interests at every turn.

Activist groups who understand the history of suburban development need to be extremely clear in articulating the issues. One popular
textbook defines successful urban planning as "public action that will
produce a sustained and widespread private market reaction."[29] The

belief that planners should invest taxpayers' dollars to produce a climate for private profit-making has been the view of the local growth machines and the national real estate–banking–building–automotive lobby, since the 1920s. It should be challenged by those who believe that the role of public spending is to benefit the community as a whole.

Government officials have not always taken on this role. Requiring high walls to segregate residential neighborhoods in the 1940s, making rules to deny people of color and women mortgages in the 1950s, and guaranteeing huge tax write-offs to developers of minimal strip malls between the 1950s and 1980s have been some of the less attractive tactics of federal government in the past. These misguided efforts have been discredited, but often private interests are still believed when they argue for public funding to support private growth. Countering the budget drain caused by public subsidies to private development, elected officials such as Governor James McGreevey of New Jersey have spoken bluntly: "Let me say to those who profit from the strip malls and McMansions, if you reap the benefits, you must now take responsibility for the costs." Noting that New Jersey was the most congested state in the nation, losing fifty acres a day to sprawl, McGreevey challenged legislators with his "State of the State" address in 2003 when he declared a "war on sprawl."[30]

Antisprawl activists ask hard questions about suburban landscapes, questions with a political and social edge. Can taxation be made more equitable, in order to send subsidies to the people most in need of shelter, rather than subsidize those with the largest houses and mortgages, as the United States now does? Can neighborhoods be integrated economically and racially? Can the building process itself support local residents and their search for meaningful jobs, rather than large-scale developers? Can nonprofits take a larger role in development? Can Americans build affordable housing for every metropolitan household? Can housing be tailored to support the elderly? Can suburbs better fit the changing shape of the American household and women's involvement in paid work as well as parenting? Can the suburban city offer more consistent access to unspoiled nature? Can it be made environmentally sustainable? Will it run out of water and energy? Will citizens choke on air pollution?

Looking at seven suburban landscapes from the past with a critical eye, Americans may begin to build more wisely. Citizens of every age, household type, and income bracket need communities organized for the rhythm of life. Many Americans are not going to give up cars and commuting. However, Americans are an aging population, and age has a way of redefining life goals. Can voters demand that their taxes support existing neighborhoods, with schools, libraries, and pedestrian centers, rather than raw subdivisions fifty miles farther out? Can suburban people, living in wide-ranging metropolitan areas, build housing without losing the face-to-face communication of suburban or small-town life, the attractions of generous yards and parks, and the pleasures of the sidewalk? The pedestrian centers of older suburban neighborhoods and small towns await rescue.

A more democratic definition of public planning supports equal citizenship as well as environmentally sustainable development. The role of federal, state, and local government should be to counterbalance the influence of the private market, to protect the young and the elderly, and to sustain decent shelter, services, jobs, and public places for all. The conservation of land, water, and air is necessary if the United States wants to house and feed citizens for decades to come in the suburban city. Conservation of energy can slow global warming and decrease reliance on foreign oil supplies. Preservation of existing buildings and landscapes can sustain people's social as well as environmental connections to local places. Planners and architects can engage the suburban city, with its seven historic landscapes, as a place for socially and environmentally responsible development. But first all citizens need to forge the political consensus for change.

NOTES

1. Richard Harris, "Introduction," special issue, *Journal of Urban History* 27 (March 2001): 261.

ONE: THE SHAPES OF SUBURBIA

1. The United States Census has a somewhat confusing system of classification. It identifies central cities, metropolitan areas (MA), and urbanized areas (UA). An MA must include at least one place of 50,000 people or a census-defined UA and a total MA population of at least 100,000 (75,000 in New England). A UA includes one or more central places and adjacent areas with a minimum population of 50,000. Within an MA, but outside the central city, the terms "suburban," "outer suburban," "metropolitan fringe," and "exurban" might be applied by social scientists, but these are also confusing and imprecise. U.S. Census Bureau, "American Housing Survey," revised Nov. 2002, counts 106.3 million occupied housing units, of which 31.7 million are in central cities, 53.6 million in suburbs within metropolitan areas, and 21 million outside metropolitan statistical areas (some of these are suburban also); see http://www.census.gov/hhes/www/housing/ahs/ahs01/tab1a1.html (March 31, 2003). Also see see Myron Orfield, *American Metropolitics: The New Suburban Reality* (Washington, D.C.: Brookings Institution Press, 2002); Peter Dreier, John Mollenkopf, and Todd Swanstrom, *Place Matters: Metropolitics for the Twenty-first Century* (Topeka: University of Kansas Press, 2002); G. Scott Thomas, *The United States of Suburbia: How the Suburbs Took Control of America*

and What They Plan to Do With It (Amherst, N.Y.: Prometheus Books, 1998); Bruce Katz and Robert E. Lang, eds., *Redefining Urban and Suburban America: Evidence from Census 2000* (Washington, D.C.: Brookings, 2003).

2. U.S. Census, "New Privately Owned Housing Units Started in the United States By Purpose and Design," http://www.census.gov/ftp/const/www/newresconstindex.html (June 20, 2001).

3. I have organized projects with aerial photographers Alex S. MacLean and Jim Wark to develop aerial documentation for scholarly study, teaching, and community land use debates. See Dolores Hayden, with photographs by Alex S. MacLean, "Aerial Photography on the Web: A New Tool for Community Debates in Land Use," *Lotus* 108 (Summer 2001): 118–31; Dolores Hayden, with photographs by Alex S. MacLean, "Flying Over Guilford," *Planning* 66 (September 2000): 10–15; Dolores Hayden, with photographs by Jim Wark, *A Field Guide to Sprawl* (New York: Norton, forthcoming).

4. Dolores Hayden, *Redesigning the American Dream* (New York: Norton, 1984), 55.

5. "Editorial," *National Real Estate Journal* 22 (March 28, 1921): 22, quoted in Carolyn S. Loeb, *Entrepreneurial Vernacular: Developers' Subdivisions in the 1920s* (Baltimore: Johns Hopkins University Press, 2001), 163; *American Architect and Building News,* quoted in Ben Eakeley, "Preserving the Picturesque," unpublished paper, 1999.

6. Cover by Constantin Alajálov, *New Yorker,* July 20, 1946.

7. Andrés Duany and Elizabeth Plater-Zyberk, "The Second Coming of the American Small Town," *Wilson Quarterly* 16 (Winter 1992): 19–50. D. J. Waldie, *Holy Land: A Suburban Memoir* (New York: St. Martin's, 1996).

8. John Rather, "Happiness Homes, Long Before Levitt," *New York Times,* May 21, 2000, section 11, 7.

9. Jacqueline Leavitt, "The Double Dream: The Single Family House and Community," unpublished survey based on *Ms.* magazine housing poll; Scott Donaldson, "City and Country: Marriage Proposals," *American Quarterly* 20 (Autumn 1968): 547–66; and Scott Donaldson, *The Suburban Myth* (New York: Columbia University Press, 1969). William Dobriner, *Class in Suburbia* (Englewood Cliffs, N.J.: Prentice-Hall, 1963), 8, quotes Harlan Douglas on "attachment to nature and the outdoor life," and Sylvia Fava on "neighboring."

10. Phyllis McGinley, "I Know a Village," *Times Three: Selected Poems 1932–60* (New York: Viking, 1960), 123. Also see "June in the Suburbs," 95, and "The 5:32," 137.

TWO: THE SUBURBAN CITY

1. Kenneth T. Jackson, *Crabgrass Frontier: The Suburbanization of the United States* (New York: Oxford University Press, 1985), 297–304.

2. Robert M. Fogelson, *Downtown: Its Rise and Fall, 1880–1950* (New Haven: Yale University Press, 2001).

3. For example, Adam Rome, *The Bulldozer in the Countryside: Suburban Sprawl and the Rise of American Environmentalism* (New York: Cambridge University Press, 2001); Oliver Gillham, *The Limitless City: A Primer on the Urban Sprawl Debate* (Washington, D.C.: Island Press, 2002). Also see Tom Daniels, *When City and Country Collide: Managing Growth in the Metropolitan Fringe* (Washington, D.C.: Island Press, 1999).

4. Pierce Lewis, "The Galactic Metropolis," in *Beyond the Urban Fringe: Land Use Issues in Nonmetropolitan America,* ed. Rutherford H. Platt and George Macinko (Minneapolis: University of Minnesota Press, 1983), 23–49; Peter Calthorpe and William Fulton, *The Regional City: Planning for the End of Sprawl* (Washington, D.C.: Island Press, 2001); Sam Bass Warner, Jr., "When Suburbs Are the City," in *Suburbia Re-Examined,* ed. Barbara M. Kelly (New York: Greenwood Press, 1989), 1–10.

5. Joel Schwartz, "The Evolution of the Suburbs," in *Suburbia: The American Dream and Dilemma,* ed. Philip C. Dolce (Garden City, N.Y.: Anchor Books, 1976), 6–8. He mentions early suburban working-class temperance communities including Morrisania in the Bronx and Temperanceville outside of Pittsburgh. Other scholars who explore class extensively include Bennett Berger, *Working-Class Suburb: A Study of Auto Workers in Suburbia* (Berkeley: University of California Press, 1960); Carol O'Connor, "Sorting Out the Suburbs," *American Quarterly* 37 (September 1985): 382–94; and Richard Harris, *Unplanned Suburbs: Toronto's American Tragedy, 1900–1950* (Baltimore: Johns Hopkins University Press, 1996), 286.

6. David W. Chen, "All Languages, All the Time, And All Over the Suburban Dial," *New York Times,* July 17, 2001, B1; Mary Rourke, "All That's Holy, and Then Some," *Los Angeles Times,* January 6, 2002, http://www.lats.com (January 6, 2002); Patricia Leigh Brown, "With an Asian Influx, Suburb Finds Itself Transformed," *New York Times,* May 25, 2001, A1.

7. Jo Becker, "Suburban Crowding Arouses Tension," *Washington Post,* May 3, 2002, A1; David Plotz, "A Suburb All Grown Up and Paved Over," *New York Times,* June 19, 2002, A23.

8. The subject of gender and suburbs now has a very large literature of its own, much of it discussed in Dolores Hayden, *Redesigning the American Dream,* rev. ed. (New York: Norton, 2002). In the mid-nineteenth century, affluent suburban women were the wives of homeowners who supervised hardworking female servants, or who did the necessary work of raising families themselves. In that era, working-class married women tended to take in boarders or find other ways to augment the family's income from the suburban house, while unmarried daughters might have paid jobs. By the late twentieth century, women of all classes became more likely to co-own their suburban residences or to own them as heads of households, although others continued to work as domestic servants. As women entered paid employment outside the home in increasing numbers in the late twentieth century, they commuted to urban and suburban jobs while continuing to care for spouses and children. The miles they drive have increased dramatically but their locational choices (for home and paid work) are still not well understood.

9. Mary Cahill, *Carpool* (New York: Fawcett Crest, 1991), 15.

10. *Roget's International Thesaurus,* 4th ed. (New York: Harper and Row, 1977), 183, 680.

11. Works on suburban housing patterns by architects, landscape architects, and planners include: David P. Handlin, *The American Home: Architecture and Society, 1815–1915* (Boston: Little, Brown, 1979); Gwendolyn Wright, *Moralism and the Model Home: Domestic Architecture and Cultural Conflict in Chicago, 1873–1913* (Chicago: University of Chicago Press, 1980); Dolores Hayden, *The Grand Domestic Revolution: A History of Feminist Designs for American Homes, Neighborhoods, and Cities* (Cambridge, Mass.: MIT Press, 1981); Gwendolyn Wright, *Building the Dream: A Social History of Housing in America* (New York: Pantheon, 1981); Robert A. M. Stern with John Massengale, eds., *The Anglo-American Suburb* (London: special issue of *Architectural Design,* 1981); Dolores Hayden, *Redesigning the American Dream: Gender, Housing, and Family Life,* rev. ed. (New York: Norton, 2002); Peter Rowe, *Making a Middle Landscape* (Cambridge, Mass.: MIT Press, 1991); Cynthia L. Girling and Kenneth I. Helphand, *Yard-Street-Park: The Design of Suburban Open Space* (New York: Wiley, 1994). Handlin, Wright, Helphand, and I were all students of John Brinckerhoff Jackson, the editor of *Landscape* magazine.

12. Among these are Andrés Duany and Elizabeth Plater-Zyberk, "The Second Coming of the American Small Town," *Wilson Quarterly* 16 (Winter 1992): 19–50; Peter Calthorpe, *The Next American Metropolis: Ecology, Community, and the American Dream* (Princeton: Princeton

Architectural Press, 1993); Andrés Duany, Elizabeth Plater-Zyberk, and Jeff Speck, *Suburban Nation: The Rise of Sprawl and the Decline of the American Dream* (New York: North Point/Farrar, Straus and Giroux, 2000).

13. Mark Gottdiener and Joe R. Feagin, "The Paradigm Shift in Urban Sociology," *Urban Affairs Quarterly* 24 (December 1988): 163–87 (special issue devoted to this topic).

14. Harvey Molotch, "The City as a Growth Machine: Toward a Political Economy of Place," *American Journal of Sociology* 82 (September 1976): 309–32.

15. Mark Gottdiener, *Planned Sprawl: Private and Public Interests in Suburbia* (Beverly Hills, Calif.: Sage, 1977); John R. Logan and Harvey L. Molotch, *Urban Fortunes: The Political Economy of Place* (Berkeley: University of California Press, 1987); John R. Logan, Rachel Bridges Whaley, and Kyle Crowder, "The Character and Consequences of Growth Regimes: An Assessment of Twenty Years of Research," *Urban Affairs Review* 32 (May 1997): 603–31; Andrew E. G. Jonas and David Wilson, eds., *The Urban Growth Machine: Critical Perspectives, Two Decades Later* (Albany: State University of New York Press, 1999); David Rusk, "The Sprawl Machine," in *Inside Game Outside Game: Winning Strategies for Saving Urban America* (Washington, D.C.: Brookings Institution, 1999), 82–100.

16. Eben Fodor, *Better Not Bigger: How to Take Control of Urban Growth and Improve Your Community* (Gabriola Island, B.C.: New Society Publishers, 1999), 30.

17. For example, policy analyst Anthony Downs has written: "Unlimited low-density development has dominated nearly all American policies affecting metropolitan area growth for more than four decades." The authors of a recent book quote him approvingly but state they are "concerned with the results rather than the causes of current development patterns." Anthony Downs, *New Visions for Metropolitan America* (Washington, D.C.: Brookings Institution and Lincoln Institute of Land Policy, 1994), 5, quoted in F. Kaid Benfield, Matthew D. Raimi, and Donald D. T. Chen, *Once There Were Greenfields: How Urban Sprawl Is Undermining America's Environment, Economy, and Social Fabric* (Washington, D.C.: Natural Resources Defense Council, 1999), 28, 24.

18. Robert Fishman, *Bourgeois Utopias: The Rise and Fall of Suburbia* (New York: Basic Books, 1987). For more general discussion see J. John Palen, *The Suburbs* (New York: McGraw-Hill, 1995); David Schuyler, *The New Urban Landscape: The Redefinition of Form in Nineteenth-Century America* (Baltimore: Johns Hopkins University Press, 1986);

Margaret Marsh, *Suburban Lives* (New Brunswick, N.J.: Rutgers University Press, 1990); Alan Gowans, *The Comfortable House: North American Suburban Architecture 1890–1930* (Cambridge, Mass.: MIT Press, 1986); Andrew Wiese, "The Other Suburbanites: African American Suburbanization in the North before 1950," *Journal of American History* 85 (March 1999): 1495–1524; Gail Radford, *Modern Housing in America: Policy Struggles in the New Deal Era* (Chicago: University of Chicago Press, 1996); Rosalyn Baxandall and Elizabeth Ewen, *Picture Windows: How the Suburbs Happened* (New York: Basic Books, 2000); Barbara M. Kelly, *Expanding the American Dream: Building and Rebuilding Levittown* (Albany: State University of New York Press, 1993).

19. The literature is vast. William Sharpe and Leonard Wallock, "Bold New City or Built-Up 'Burb? Redefining Contemporary Suburbia," *American Quarterly* 46 (March 1994): 1–30, is a review essay with responses.

20. Catharine E. Beecher, "How to Redeem Woman's Profession from Dishonor," *Harper's New Monthly Magazine* 31 (November 1865): 710; Dianne Harris, "Making Your Private World: Modern Landscape Architecture and *House Beautiful*, 1945–1965," in *The Architecture of Landscape, 1940–1960*, Marc Treib, ed. (Philadelphia: University of Pennsylvania Press, 2002), 182; Lizabeth Cohen, *A Consumers' Republic: The Politics of Mass Consumption in Postwar America* (New York: Knopf, 2003).

THREE: BORDERLANDS

1. John Stilgoe, *Borderland: Origins of the American Suburb, 1820–1939* (New Haven: Yale University Press, 1988); Joel Schwartz, "Evolution of the Suburbs," in *Suburbia: The American Dream and Dilemma*, ed. Philip C. Dolce (Garden City, N.Y.: Anchor Press/Doubleday, 1976), 1–36.

2. Henry Binford, *The First Suburbs: Residential Communities on the Boston Periphery, 1815–1860* (Chicago: University of Chicago Press, 1984), 43. For a comparative view of "City and Country: That Awkward Embrace," see John M. Merriman, *The Margins of City Life: Explorations on the French Urban Frontier, 1815–1851* (New York: Oxford University Press, 1991), 31–58.

3. Binford, *First Suburbs*, 149.

4. David Schuyler, *Apostle of Taste: Andrew Jackson Downing, 1815–1852* (Baltimore: Johns Hopkins University Press, 1996). Downing is also discussed in Robert Fishman, *Bourgeois Utopias: The Rise and Fall of Suburbia* (New York: Basic Books, 1987), 23–24, although Fish-

man overstates the importance of his architectural work in relation to Beecher. See also George William Curtis, foreword to *Rural Essays,* by Andrew Jackson Downing (New York: Leavitt and Allen, 1857); Kevin Baker, "The Improved Man," *Harper's* 300 (June 2000): 126–34.

5. Andrew Jackson Downing, *A Treatise on the Theory and Practice of Landscape Gardening, Adapted to North America, with a View to the Improvement of Country Residences 1841,* 6th ed. (New York: A. O. Moore, 1859); Alexander Jackson Davis, *Rural Residences* (1837–38, published in parts by the author), limited edition with color renderings, Beinecke Rare Book and Manuscript Library, Yale University.

6. Letter from Downing to Robert Donaldson, November 1841, quoted in Schuyler, *Apostle of Taste,* 55.

7. Schuyler, *Apostle of Taste,* 55.

8. Downing, *Treatise on Landscape Gardening,* 92–93.

9. Andrew Jackson Downing, *Cottage Residences, or A Series of Designs for Rural Cottages and Cottage-Villas, and Their Gardens and Grounds. Adapted to North America* (New York: Wiley and Putnam, 1842), 34ff.

10. *Ibid.,* 37.

11. *Ibid.,* 16–17, 22, 25.

12. Downing's "simple cottage" was a box cut up into rectangular rooms with a few traditional fireplaces. He said little about the interior, creating a closet for books off the parlor and an identical closet as a "pantry" for the kitchen, though storing books and storing food have little in common. The kitchen itself was otherwise identical to a first-floor bedroom. None of his five upstairs bedrooms was cross-ventilated. He did launch into a brief discussion of kitchen drainage and the need for a "smell-trap" for the cistern.

13. Downing, *Cottage Residences,* 47–49.

14. *Ibid.,* 49.

15. Downing, *Treatise on Landscape Gardening,* Appendix 2. Also see Virginia Scott Jenkins, *The Lawn: A History of an American Obsession* (Washington: Smithsonian Institution Press, 1994); Georges Teyssot, ed., *The American Lawn* (New York: Princeton Architectural Press, 1999); Michelle H. Bogart, "Lawns 'R' U.S.," *American Quarterly* 47 (September 1995): 556–62.

16. Andrew Jackson Downing, *The Architecture of Country Houses; Including Designs for Cottages, Farm-Houses and Villas, with Remarks on Interiors, Furniture, and the Best Modes of Warming and Ventilating,* reprint ed. (1850; New York: D. Appleton, 1852), 72–78, 213–53, 255–80, v.

17. Downing, *Cottage Residences,* 89.

18. Downing, *Architecture of Country Houses*, v–vi.

19. *Ibid.*, vi.

20. Downing, *Cottage Residences*, ii. A decade later a publisher was offering Downing's *Cheap Cottages and Farm Houses*, Part I of his *Country Houses*, with a $400 laborer's cottage.

21. Schuyler, *Apostle of Taste*, 88.

22. *Ibid.*, 222.

23. Catharine E. Beecher, *Treatise on Domestic Economy for the Use of Young Ladies at Home and at School* (Boston: Thomas H. Webb, 1842); Catharine E. Beecher and Harriet Beecher Stowe, *The American Woman's Home* (New York: J. B. Ford, 1869). The 1869 book was an expanded version of the *Treatise*, with her sister, a best-selling novelist, added as coauthor.

24. Beecher and Stowe, *American Woman's Home*, 24. Plans for an urban tenement and a single teacher's school and house combined with a chapel are interesting side projects, but the single-family detached suburban house is at the heart of her domestic proposals. For a detailed evaluation of all of these projects, see Dolores Hayden, "Catharine Beecher and the Politics of Housework," in *Women in American Architecture: Historic and Contemporary Perspectives*, ed. Susana Torre (New York: Whitney Library of Design, 1977). In this I differ with Margaret Marsh, who separates domesticity and the suburban impulse in her *Suburban Lives* (New Brunswick, N.J.: Rutgers University Press, 1990).

25. Kathryn Kish Sklar, *Catharine Beecher: A Study in American Domesticity* (New Haven: Yale University Press, 1973), 17–19.

26. Joseph Van Why, introduction to Beecher and Stowe, *American Woman's Home* (1869; reprint, Hartford: Stowe-Day Foundation, 1975).

27. For Beecher's place within broader nineteenth-century debates about issues of women's rights and the economic meaning of household work, see Dolores Hayden, *The Grand Domestic Revolution: A History of Feminist Designs for American Homes, Neighborhoods, and Cities* (Cambridge, Mass.: MIT Press, 1981), 54–63.

28. Catharine E. Beecher, "How to Redeem Woman's Profession from Dishonor," *Harper's New Monthly Magazine* 31 (November 1865): 710.

29. Reyner Banham, *The Architecture of the Well-Tempered Environment* (London: Architectural Press, 1969), 96–100.

30. Mira Engler, "Repulsive Matter: Landscapes of Waste in the American Middle-Class Residential Domain," *Landscape Journal* 16 (Spring 1997): 60–79.

31. Beecher and Stowe, *American Woman's Home*, 89.

32. Beecher, *Treatise on Domestic Economy*, 172.

33. Grace Duffield Goodwin, "The Commuter's Wife: A Sisterly Talk By One Who Knows Her Problems," *Good Housekeeping* 49 (October 1909): 363.

34. Frederick Law Olmsted, letter of 1860, quoted in Fishman, *Bourgeois Utopias,* 120–21.

35. Schuyler, *Apostle of Taste,* 218–19.

36. *Ibid.,* 204–8.

FOUR: PICTURESQUE ENCLAVES

1. Alexander Garvin, *The American City: What Works and What Doesn't* (New York: McGraw-Hill, 1996), 254–56.

2. Walter Muir Whitehill, *Boston: A Topographical History* (Cambridge, Mass.: Harvard University Press, 1969), 141–73.

3. Robert Fishman, *Bourgeois Utopias: The Rise and Fall of Suburbia* (New York: Basic Books, 1987), 18–73, discusses the Clapham Evangelicals and their influence at length.

4. All of these British developments are discussed in John Archer, "Country and City in the American Romantic Suburb," *Journal of the Society of Architectural Historians* 42 (May 1983): 140–47; Loudon quote, 144.

5. *Ibid.,* 150–51, discusses New Brighton and Ranlett's design for a village.

6. Albert Fein, "The American City: The Ideal and the Real," in *The Rise of an American Architecture,* ed. Edgar Kaufmann, Jr. (New York: Praeger, 1970), 81–101; Archer, "Country and City," 139. Theodore Tilton, in 1864, did praise a suburb as "Greenwood without the graves," in "Llewellyn Park," *The Independent,* May 26, 1864, quoted in Susan Henderson, "Llewellyn Park, Suburban Idyll," *Journal of Garden History* 7 (July/September 1987): 240.

7. Ellen Weiss, *City in the Woods: The Life and Design of An American Camp Meeting on Martha's Vineyard* (New York: Oxford University Press, 1987), 80. Also suggestive is John Reps's quotation from a sales brochure for burial plots in a picturesque cemetery in 1869. Selling interior lots to the living might not be very different from selling them as memorials: "In regard to the necessity of every burial lot fronting on an avenue, I will merely state that seclusion is more in unison with the feelings of many friends of the dead than publicity, glare, and notoriety. While persons engaged in the ordinary business of life might prefer front or corner lots, it may be questioned whether a cultivated and refined taste would prefer a more secluded spot for repose." John Reps, *The Making*

of Urban America: A History of City Planning in the United States (Princeton: Princeton University Press, 1965), 330.

8. Dolores Hayden, *Seven American Utopias: The Architecture of Communitarian Socialism, 1790–1975* (Cambridge, Mass.: MIT Press, 1976), 8–31.

9. Also flourishing in this period were the summer communities devoted to camp meetings and religious revivals, places like Oak Bluffs, Mass., where the beaches and dunes of Martha's Vineyard helped to inspire religious fervor. At this Methodist campground, tents were replaced by small Gothic cottages for the summer residents beginning in the 1850s. At meeting times, seven preachers spelled each other on the revival stand, allowing few breaks for the congregated parishioners during the heat of religious excitement. An 1859 site plan of concentric circles was elaborated over the next decades. By 1866 Robert Morris Copeland, a landscape architect, had laid out "Oak Bluffs," a rural subdivision with a park next to the camp meeting ground of the same name. Weiss, *City in the Woods*, 30–36.

10. Hayden, *Seven American Utopias*, 64–103.

11. *Ibid.*, 186–223.

12. George O. Beach and Joseph S. Wood, eds., *The Daily Eagle's Illustrated History of Mount Vernon* (Mount Vernon, N.Y.: F. T. Smiley, 1903), 5.

13. Modern Times, on Long Island, and Vineland, N.J., are other examples.

14. Jane B. Davies, "Works and Projects," in *Alexander Jackson Davis: American Architect 1803–1893*, ed. Amelia Peck (New York: Metropolitan Museum of Art, 1992), 115. Although Davies's definitive catalog of Davis's works lists this commission as "not executed," the structure was built as designed and survived into the twentieth century. For a photograph, see Hayden, *Seven American Utopias*, 148–85.

15. Carl J. Guarneri, *The Utopian Alternative: Fourierism in Nineteenth Century America* (Ithaca, N.Y.: Cornell University Press, 1991), 322–26, 396.

16. Schuyler, *Apostle of Taste*, 208–9, 273; Fredrika Bremer, *Homes of the New World*, 2 vols., tr. Mary Hewitt (New York, 1853); Hayden, *Seven American Utopias*, 180.

17. David Rothman, *The Discovery of the Asylum: Social Order and Disorder in the New Republic* (Boston: Little, Brown, 1971). In the 1840s architects and social reformers also began to apply themselves to the design of institutions for collective residential life, such as orphanages, asylums for the mentally ill, and penitentiaries for convicted criminals. For many of their founders, the architectural form of Fourier's

phalanx was appealing as a set of physical forms they believed could encourage and support social change. In this era the most fanatical enthusiasts believed that early admission to a well-designed asylum could help to cure insanity and confinement to a model penitentiary could help eliminate criminal inclinations. Often the spaces of these institutions referred to the model family residence or to the garden to justify their efficacy. Sometimes they were located in borderlands outside of cities, with closeness to nature cited as part of the curative regimen. John Haviland was famous for his design for the Eastern State Penitentiary outside Philadelphia in 1829, where every convict had a private cell and a private garden, as well as for his work on villas for the affluent at New Brighton.

18. This ideological mix existed in the work of Davis. His "social architecture" included a phalanx, a pauper lunatic asylum, a hospital for the insane, and two orphan asylums, as well as numerous suburban estates in Newburgh along the Hudson and in New Brighton on Staten Island. Davies, "Works and Projects," 105–19.

19. Alexander Jackson Davis, *Rural Residences* (New York: published by the author, 1837). Also see Richard Guy Wilson, "Idealism and the Origin of the First American Suburb: Llewellyn Park, New Jersey," *American Art Journal* (October 1979): 79–90; David Schuyler, *The New Urban Landscape: The Redefinition of Form in Nineteenth-Century America* (Baltimore: Johns Hopkins University Press, 1986), 149–66.

20. Henderson, "Llewellyn Park," 222.

21. Wilson, "Idealism," 79–90. Wilson mentions Swedenborgianism, Transcendentalism, and Fourierism as sources for Haskell, but does not discuss the close ties between this community and major characters involved in American Fourierism.

22. Henderson, "Llewellyn Park," 223.

23. *Ibid.*, 225.

24. Henry Winthrop Sargent, supplement to Downing, *Treatise on Landscape Gardening*, 1859 ed., 571.

25. Theodore Tilton, quoted in Henderson, *Llewellyn Park,* 225.

26. Short Hills, N.J., was a similar effort, a model suburb with extensive parkland and expensive architecture developed in 1877 by Stewart Hartshorn, a man who made his fortune as the inventor of the rolling window shade and believed that Adam and Eve could have walked in the lovely precincts of his town. I thank Benjamin Eakeley for drawing my attention to Short Hills in an unpublished paper for my class, "The American Suburb."

27. Wilson, "Idealism," 85.

28. Henderson, "Llewellyn Park," 240.

29. Frederick Law Olmsted, "Preliminary Report Upon the Proposed Suburban Village at Riverside Near Chicago," reprinted in *Landscape Architecture* 21 (July 1931): 262.

30. *Ibid.*, 275–76.

31. Riverside Improvement Company, *Riverside in 1871*, quoted in Garvin, *The American City*, 317.

32. Olmsted, "Preliminary Report," 274.

33. Henry Hubbard, "Land Subdivision Regulations," *Landscape Architecture* 16 (October 1925): 53, quoted in Cynthia L. Girling and Kenneth I. Helphand, *Yard-Street-Park: The Design of Suburban Open Space* (New York: Wiley, 1994), 54. This is a chart of twenty-nine Olmsted Brothers projects from 1883 to 1923.

34. Theodora Kimball Hubbard, introduction to "Riverside, Illinois," *Landscape Architecture* 22 (July 1931): 257.

35. Girling and Helphand, *Yard-Street-Park*, 52.

36. Witold Rybczynski, *A Clearing in the Distance: Frederick Law Olmsted and America in the Nineteenth Century* (New York: Scribner, 1999), 293.

37. Frederick Law Olmsted, letter to E. E. Childs, October 28, 1869, reprinted in *Landscape Architecture* 21 (July 1931): 287.

38. Fishman, *Bourgeois Utopias*, 130.

39. Olmsted to Edward Everett Hale, October 21, 1869, Olmsted Papers, Library of Congress, number 01916, quoted in Fishman, *Bourgeois Utopias*, 129.

40. Samuel Swift, "Community Life at Rochelle Park," *House and Garden* 5 (1904): 235–43; "Study of a New York Suburb, New Rochelle," *Architectural Record* 25 (April 1909): 235–48.

41. Samuel Swift, "Llewellyn Park, West Orange, Essex County New Jersey: The First American Suburban City," *House and Garden* 3 (June 1903): 331, quoted in Henderson, "Llewellyn Park," 243.

42. Hubbard, "Land Subdivision Regulations," in Girling and Helphand, *Yard-Street-Park*, 54.

43. Emily Post, "Tuxedo Park: An American Rural Community," *Century Magazine* 82 (October 1911): 795–805.

44. Michael Ebner, *Creating Chicago's North Shore, A Suburban History* (Chicago: University of Chicago Press, 1988), 195.

45. Margaret Marsh, *Suburban Lives* (New Brunswick, N.J.: Rutgers University Press, 1990): 172–73.

46. William S. Worley, *J. C. Nichols and the Shaping of Kansas City* (Columbia: University of Missouri Press, 1990), 38, 78.

47. John Archer, "Colonial Suburbs in South Asia, 1700–1850, and

the Spaces of Modernity," in *Visions of Suburbia,* ed. Roger Silverstone (London: Routledge, 1997), 52–53.

48. Fishman, *Bourgeois Utopias,* 4.

49. Mary Corbin Sies, "Paradise Retained: An Analysis of Persistence in Planned, Exclusive Suburbs, 1880–1980," *Planning Perspectives* 12 (1997): 165–91.

FIVE: STREETCAR BUILDOUTS

1. Robert A. Woods and Albert J. Kennedy, *The Zone of Emergence: Observations of the Lower, Middle, and Upper Working Class Communities of Boston, 1905–1919,* 2nd ed. (Cambridge, Mass.: MIT Press, 1969).

2. For Boston, see Sam Bass Warner, Jr., *Streetcar Suburbs* (Cambridge, Mass.: Harvard University Press, 1962); and Matthew Edel, Elliott D. Sclar, and Daniel Luria, *Shaky Palaces: Homeownership and Social Mobility in Boston's Suburbanization* (New York: Columbia University Press, 1984). On Chicago, see Gwendolyn Wright, *Moralism and the Model Home: Domestic Architecture and Cultural Conflict in Chicago, 1873–1913* (Chicago: University of Chicago Press, 1980). For Detroit, Olivier Zunz, *The Changing Face of Inequality: Urbanization, Industrial Development, and Immigrants in Detroit, 1880–1920* (Chicago: University of Chicago Press, 1982). For the trolleys themselves, see Scott Molloy, *Trolley Wars: Streetcar Workers on the Line* (Washington, D.C.: Smithsonian Institution Press, 1996); Mark S. Foster, *From Streetcar to Superhighway: American City Planners and Urban Transportation, 1900–1940* (Philadelphia: Temple University Press, 1981); and Brian J. Cudahy, *Cash, Tokens, and Transfers: A History of Urban Mass Transit in North America* (New York: Fordham University Press, 1990).

3. Jennifer Reese, "Streetcar Suburb," *Preservation* 51 (January/February 1999): 52–57; Natalie Cowan, "Carville, San Francisco's Oceanside Bohemia," *California History* 57 (1978): 308–19.

4. Judith Helm Robinson, "Chevy Chase: A Bold Idea, A Comprehensive Plan," in *Washington at Home: An Illustrated History of Neighborhoods in Our Nation's Capital,* ed. Kathryn Schneider Smith (Washington, D.C.: Windsor Publications, 1988), 200. The senators were in partnership with Colonel George Augustus Armes, a real estate speculator. Conductors on the line were helpful to residents, delivering prescriptions of medicine along the route.

5. Dolores Hayden, *The Power of Place: Urban Landscapes as Public History* (Cambridge, Mass.: MIT Press, 1995), 35.

6. Warner, *Streetcar Suburbs,* 22–26.

7. *Ibid.*, 27.

8. David E. Nye, *Electrifying America: Social Meanings of a New Technology* (Cambridge, Mass.: MIT Press, 1990), 86. Also see Mark H. Rose, *Cities of Light and Heat: Domesticating Gas and Electricity in Urban America* (University Park: Pennsylvania State University Press, 1995).

9. Kenneth T. Jackson, *Crabgrass Frontier: The Suburbanization of the United States* (New York: Oxford University Press, 1985), 106–7.

10. Warner, *Streetcar Suburbs,* 35–44.

11. Jackson, *Crabgrass Frontier,* 109–14; Edel, Sclar, and Luria, *Shaky Palaces,* 195–263.

12. Nye, *Electrifying America,* 91–92.

13. *Ibid.*, 97–104. On "sewer socialism," see Edel, Sclar, and Luria, *Shaky Palaces,* 264–90, for a discussion of the influence of Henry George's single-tax movement as well as of municipal socialism as promoted by the Socialist Party of America, and other responses to the need for worker housing.

14. Warner, *Streetcar Suburbs,* 127–29.

15. *Ibid.*, 67–79.

16. *Ibid.*, 103–16.

17. David P. Handlin, *The American Home: Architecture and Society, 1815–1915* (Boston: Little, Brown, 1979), 238–44.

18. Quoted in Clifford Edward Clark, Jr., *The American Family Home 1800–1960* (Chapel Hill: University of North Carolina Press, 1986), 96–97. See also W. A. Linn, "Co-operative Home Winning," *Scribner's Magazine* 7 (May 1890): 569–86.

19. *Tenth Annual Illustrated Catalog of S. E. Gross' Famous City Subdivisions and Suburban Towns* (Chicago: S. E. Gross, 1891), 72–73.

20. *Ibid.*, n.p.

21. Miles L. Berber, "Workingmen's Homes," *They Built Chicago: Entrepreneurs Who Shaped a Great City's Architecture* (Chicago: Bonus Books, 1992), 113–121; Emily Clark, "Own Your Own Home: S. E. Gross, the Great Domestic Promoter," in *The American Home: Material Culture, Domestic Space, and Family Life,* ed. Eleanor McD. Thompson (Hanover, N.H.: University Press of New England, 1998), 135–53; Emily Clark and Patrick Ashley, "The Merchant Prince of Cornville," *Chicago History* 21 (December 1992): 4–19.

22. *The Gross Cottages, Houses, and Lots* (Chicago: S. E. Gross, 1886), 12.

23. *Tenth Annual Illustrated Catalog,* n.p.

24. Clark and Ashley, "Merchant Prince," 6.

25. Clark, "Own Your Own Home," 147–50.

26. *Tenth Annual Illustrated Catalog*, 20.

27. *Ibid.*, 4.

28. *Ibid.*, 10.

29. According to Ann Durkin Keating in *Building Chicago*, Gross's brother lived in Grossdale and served as its mayor five times between 1888 and 1902. Ann Durkin Keating, *Building Chicago: Suburban Developers and the Creation of a Divided Metropolis* (Columbus: Ohio State University Press, 1988), 88.

30. Keating, *Building Chicago*, 142. Yerkes controlled the traction system in much of Chicago. His monopoly required a fair amount of bribery, satirized in Theodore Dreiser's 1914 novel *The Titan*.

31. Clark, "Own Your Own Home," 140.

32. Berger, "Workingmen's Homes," 17–120.

33. Edel, Sclar, and Luria, *Shaky Palaces*, 1.

34. Eugene Wood, "Why Pay Rent?" *Everybody's Magazine* 22 (June 1910): 765–74.

35. *Ibid.*, 769–71.

36. Nye, *Electrifying America*, ix–x.

37. Comment by an executive who worked for transit operator and real estate operator F. M. "Borax" Smith in Oakland, Calif., quoted in Jackson, *Crabgrass Frontier*, 121.

38. Rem Koolhaas, *Delirious New York: A Retroactive Manifesto for Manhattan* (New York: Oxford University Press, 1978), 50–51.

39. Nye, *Electrifying America*, 118.

40. The Lincoln Institute of Land Policy, *The Legacy and Works of Henry George*, CD-Rom, 2002, available from www.lincolninst.edu.

41. For a discussion of "The Collectivism of Urban Life" in comparative perspective, see Daniel T. Rodgers, *Atlantic Crossings: Social Politics in a Progressive Age* (Cambridge, Mass.: Harvard University Press, 1998), 112–30. For the American version of municipal socialism, see Amy Bridges, *Morning Glories: Municipal Reform in the Southwest* (Princeton, N.J.: Princeton University Press, 1997).

42. National Association of Realtors, "History," www.realtor.org/realtororg.nsf/pages/narhistory (May 6, 2002).

SIX: MAIL-ORDER AND SELF-BUILT SUBURBS

1. Alan Gowans, *The Comfortable House: North American Suburban Architecture, 1890–1930* (Cambridge, Mass.: MIT Press, 1986), 20. Gowans offers a complete stylistic analysis of many different kinds of

mail-order houses, but he has missed Catharine Beecher's contributions to the ideal of a comfortable house from the 1840s on, and dates the evolution of comfort quite a bit later. See also Alfred Bruce and Harold Sandbank, *A History of Prefabrication* (New York: John B. Pierce Foundation, 1944), especially 53–76 on wood and precut houses.

2. Linda E. Smeins, *Building an American Identity: Pattern Book Homes and Communities 1870–1900* (Walnut Creek, Calif.: Alta Mira, 1999). See also Dell Upton, "Pattern Books and Professionalism: Aspects of the Transformation of Domestic Architecture in America, 1800–1860," *Winterthur Portfolio* 19 (Summer/Autumn 1984): 107–50.

3. Smeins, *Building an American Identity,* 130.

4. Robert Schweitzer and Michael W. R. Davis, *America's Favorite Homes: Mail Order Catalogues as a Guide to Popular Early 20th Century Homes* (Detroit: Wayne State University Press, 1990), 59–60, 62. A New York firm called Skillings and Flint supplied the Union Army.

5. Carolyn Patricia Flynn, "Pacific Ready-Cut Homes: Mass Produced Bungalows in Los Angeles, 1908–1942," M.A. thesis, Urban Planning, University of California at Los Angeles, 1986; *Pacific's Book of Homes: A Notable Exhibition of California Architecture* (Los Angeles: Pacific Ready-Cut Homes, 1925).

6. The Aladdin Company, *Aladdin "Built in a Day" House Catalog, 1917* (New York: Dover, 1995), 4; *Small Houses of the Twenties: The Sears, Roebuck 1926 House Catalog* (Philadelphia: Athenaeum of Philadelphia and Dover, 1991), 18–19; Katharine Cole Stevenson and H. Ward Jandl, *Houses by Mail: A Guide to Houses from Sears, Roebuck and Company* (New York: Preservation Press and Wiley, 1986), 35; Schweitzer and Davis, *America's Favorite Homes,* 99–109. See also Marina Moskowitz, "Standard Bearers: Material Culture and Middle Class Communities at the Turn of the Century," (Ph.D. dissertation, American Studies, Yale University, 1999). The Aladdin company paid commissions to customers who recruited new buyers for the company.

7. Schweitzer and Davis, *America's Favorite Houses,* 70–72.

8. Stevenson and Jandl, *Houses by Mail,* 23; *Small Houses of the Twenties,* "Publisher's Note," n.p.

9. *Small Houses of the Twenties,* "Publisher's Note," n.p.

10. *Ibid.,* 1.

11. *Ibid.,* 7.

12. *Ibid.,* 144.

13. Stevenson and Jandl, *Houses by Mail,* 21–23.

14. Schweitzer and Davis, *America's Favorite Homes,* 121. In 1918 the price was $5,140, according to Stevenson and Jandl, *Houses by Mail,* 24.

15. Stevenson and Jandl, *Houses by Mail,* 179.

16. Gowans, *The Comfortable House,* 71.

17. *Ibid.,* 12.

18. Ring W. Lardner, *Own Your Own Home* (Indianapolis: Bobbs-Merrill, 1919).

19. Dolores Hayden, *The Power of Place: Urban Landscapes as Public History* (Cambridge, Mass.: MIT Press, 1995), 128–32.

20. Becky M. Nicolaides, *My Blue Heaven: Life and Politics in the Working-class Suburbs of Los Angeles, 1920–1965* (Chicago: University of Chicago Press, 2002).

21. Andrew Wiese, "Places of Our Own: Suburban Black Towns Before 1960," *Journal of Urban History* 19 (May 1992): 41.

22. Andrew Wiese, "The Other Suburbanites: African American Suburbanization in the North before 1950," *Journal of American History* 85 (March 1999): 1519. See also Richard Harris, "Self-Building in the Urban Housing Market," *Economic Geography* 67 (January 1991): 263–303.

23. Franklin D. Raines with Amy Zipkin, "Quarterback at the Lectern," *New York Times,* June 16, 2002, BU14.

24. Thomas J. Sugrue, *The Origins of the Urban Crisis: Race and Inequality in Postwar Detroit* (Princeton: Princeton University Press, 1996), 63–72.

25. Stevenson and Jandl, *Houses by Mail,* 11.

26. Mary Anne O'Boyle, Tacoma Park, Md., 1985, quoted in Stevenson and Jandl, *Houses by Mail,* 9.

27. Richard Harris, *Unplanned Suburbs: Toronto's American Tragedy, 1900 to 1950* (Baltimore: Johns Hopkins University Press, 1996), 271, 286. He mentions a "Magic Homes" program outside Stockholm, Sweden, in the 1930s, which offered sites and services in suburban locations to young couples willing to build, a much better planning solution than either the United States or Canada managed.

28. Harris, *Unplanned Suburbs,* 221.

29. Gowans, *The Comfortable House,* 20.

30. Flynn, "Pacific Ready-Cut Homes," 68.

31. Schweitzer and Davis, *America's Favorite Homes,* 109–15; Stevenson and Jandl, *Houses by Mail,* 21.

32. Gowans, *The Comfortable House,* 20.

33. *Ibid.,* 63–67.

34. Thomas Harvey, "Mail Order Architecture in the 1920s," *Landscape* 25 (Fall 1981): 6.

35. Harvey, "Mail Order Architecture," 9.

36. Janet Hutchinson, "The Cure for Domestic Neglect: Better Homes in America, 1922–1935," in *Perspectives in Vernacular Architecture II*, ed. Camille Wells (Columbia: University of Missouri Press, 1986), 168–78; Gowans, *The Comfortable House*, 141.

37. John Howard Payne, who wrote "Home, Sweet Home" in Europe in 1822, lived most of his life abroad.

38. Christine Frederick, *Selling Mrs. Consumer* (New York: Business Boursc, 1929), 388–94; Hayden, *The Grand Domestic Revolution*, 281–89.

39. Hutchinson, "The Cure for Domestic Neglect," 173.

40. Schweitzer and Davis, *America's Favorite Homes*, 99–109.

41. Joseph C. Bigott, *From Cottage to Bungalow: Houses and the Working Class in Metropolitan Chicago, 1869–1929* (Chicago: University of Chicago Press, 2001), offers a very detailed look at ethnic patterns in one city.

42. Matthew Edel, Elliott D. Sclar, and Daniel Luria, *Shaky Palaces: Homeownership and Social Mobility in Boston's Suburbanization* (New York: Columbia University Press, 1984), vii; Harris, *Unplanned Suburbs*, 286.

43. Joel Schwartz, "Evolution of the Suburbs," in *Suburbia: The American Dream and Dilemma*, ed. Philip C. Dolce (Garden City, N.Y.: Anchor Press/Doubleday, 1976), 14–15.

44. *Ibid.*, 14–21.

45. Carolyn S. Loeb, *Entrepreneurial Vernacular: Developers' Subdivisions in the 1920s* (Baltimore: Johns Hopkins University Press, 2001), 149–79.

46. Marc A. Weiss, *The Rise of the Community Builders: The American Real Estate Industry and Urban Land Use Planning* (New York: Columbia University Press, 1987), 1, 46–47.

47. Gwendolyn Wright, *Building the Dream* (New York: Pantheon, 1981), 197–98; Gail Radford, *Modern Housing in America: Policy Struggles in the New Deal Era* (Chicago: University of Chicago Press, 1996), 51–53.

48. Loeb, *Entrepreneurial Vernacular*, 157.

49. Jackson, *Crabgrass Frontier*, 194.

50. Ronald C. Tobey, *Technology as Freedom: The New Deal and the Electrical Modernization of the American Home* (Berkeley: University of California Press, 1996), 105.

51. Keller Easterling, *Organization Space: Landscapes, Highways, and Houses in America* (Cambridge, Mass.: MIT Press, 1999), 175–99.

52. Kenneth T. Jackson, *Crabgrass Frontier: The Suburbanization of*

the United States (New York: Oxford University Press, 1985), 190–218, traces HOLC "red-lining" influence on the FHA.

53. John Hancock, "The New Deal and American Planning: The 1930s," *Two Centuries of American Planning,* ed. Daniel Schaffer (Baltimore: Johns Hopkins University Press, 1988), 197–230.

54. An excellent overview of the housing activists' work in this era is Daniel T. Rogers, *Atlantic Crossings: Social Politics in a Progressive Age* (Cambridge, Mass.: Harvard University Press, 1998), 391–408.

55. Paul Conklin, *Tomorrow a New World: The New Deal Community Program* (Ithaca, N.Y.: Cornell University Press, 1959); Joseph L. Arnold, *The New Deal in the Suburbs: A History of the Greenbelt Town Program, 1935–1954* (Columbus: Ohio State University Press, 1971); Cathy D. Knepper, *Greenbelt, Maryland: A Living Legacy of the New Deal* (Baltimore: Johns Hopkins University Press, 2002); Arnold R. Alanen and Joseph A. Eden, *Main Street Ready-Made: The New Deal Community of Greendale, Wisconsin* (Madison: State Historical Society of Wisconsin, 1987); Diane Ghirardo, *Building New Communities: New Deal America and Fascist Italy* (Princeton: Princeton University Press, 1989).

56. Radford, *Modern Housing,* 188; Catherine Bauer, *Modern Housing* (Boston: Houghton Mifflin, 1934); Richard Pommer, "The Architecture of Urban Housing in the United States During the Early 1930s," *Journal of the Society of Architectural Historians* 37 (December 1978): 235–64.

57. Knepper, *Greenbelt, Maryland,* 21.

58. Schwartz, "Evolution of the Suburbs," 31.

SEVEN: SITCOM SUBURBS

1. Sarah Jo Peterson, "Bombers, But No Bomber City," unpublished paper delivered to the OAH Midwestern Regional Conference, August 2000; "The Town of Willow Run," *Architectural Forum* (March 1943): 37–54.

2. D. J. Waldie, *Holy Land: A Suburban Memoir* (New York: St. Martin's, 1996), 161.

3. Dolores Hayden, *Redesigning the American Dream: Gender, Housing, and Family Life* (New York: Norton, 2002), 3–12; Margaret Crawford, "Daily Life on the Home Front: Women, Blacks, and the Struggle for Public Housing," in *World War II and the American Dream: How Wartime Building Changed a Nation,* ed. Donald Albrecht (Washington, D.C.: National Building Museum, 1995), 90–143.

4. Rosalyn Baxandall and Elizabeth Ewen, *Picture Windows: How the Suburbs Happened* (New York: Basic Books, 2000), 87–116.

5. *Ibid.*, 91.

6. Radford, *Modern Housing*, 189, 253 n.49; Barry Checkoway, "Large Builders, Federal Housing Programs, and Postwar Suburbaniza-tion," in *Critical Perspectives on Housing*, ed. Rachel G. Bratt, Chester Hartman, and Ann Meyerson (Philadelphia: Temple University Press, 1986), 129–31.

7. Baxandall and Ewen, *Picture Windows*, 107.

8. *Ibid.*, 90.

9. Jackson, *Crabgrass Frontier*, 233. Gregory C. Randall, *America's Original GI Town: Park Forest, Illinois* (Baltimore: Johns Hopkins University Press, 2000), 183.

10. Richard Harris, *Unplanned Suburbs: Toronto's American Tragedy, 1900–1950* (Baltimore: Johns Hopkins University Press, 1996), 221; Weiss, *Rise of the Community Builders*, 161; Jackson, *Crabgrass Frontier*, 233; Checkoway, "Large Builders," 121–23; Christopher Tunnard and Boris Pushkarev, *Man-made America: Chaos or Control?* (New Haven: Yale University Press, 1963), 78.

11. Waldie, *Holy Land*, 160.

12. Alfred Levitt, "A Community Builder Looks at Community Plan-ning," *Journal of the American Institute of Planners* 17 (Spring 1951): 81.

13. The developments of Fritz B. Burns for aircraft workers in Los Angeles in the late 1930s anticipated postwar projects. Burns pioneered turning the housing site into "a continuous production process" at West-side Village in Mar Vista, California. He built 788 units, using identical plans for two-bedroom, 885-square-foot houses, with variation in the garage placement and the rooflines, on 5,400-to-6,000-square-foot lots. Burns established a staging area on National Boulevard where suppliers delivered materials. Workers precut and preassembled parts of houses there for trucking throughout the site. Other teams of workers moved down the streets, "grading and grubbing, preparing and pouring founda-tions, framing and sheathing the building envelope, and applying finish materials." Greg Hise, "Homebuilding and Industrial Decentralization in Los Angeles: The Roots of the Post–World War II Urban Region," in *Planning the Twentieth Century American City*, ed. Mary Corbin Sies and Christopher Silver (Baltimore: Johns Hopkins University Press, 1996), 240–61.

Two points should be underlined. First, the transformation of airframe manufacture from craft work to a continuous process handled by opera-tives, two-thirds of whom were unskilled, was already occurring inside many of Southern California's aircraft factories between 1935 and 1943. Burns simply applied the same logic to provide housing for Douglas Aircraft operatives and others.

Second, Burns kept costs down by emphasizing sweat equity. He left unfinished both site work, such as driveway paving, and finish work, such as exterior painting. He also sold material for fences, trees, shrubs, and perennials to his buyers at wholesale prices. The houses cost $2,990, that is, $150 down and $29.90 per month on an FHA-insured mortgage. After 1945 prices would double or triple, and subdivisions would be twenty or thirty times larger. Burns himself moved on to develop Panorama City outside Los Angeles.

14. Joseph B. Mason, "Levitt and Sons of Virginia Set New Standards in Title VI War Homes," *American Builder* (June 1942): 48–53ff., cited in Peter S. Reed, "Enlisting Modernism," in Albrecht, *World War II and the American Dream,* 30.

15. "Housing: Up from the Potato Fields," *Time,* 56 (July 3, 1950): 67, 72.

16. Eric Larrabee, "The Six Thousand Houses That Levitt Built," *Harper's* 197 (September 1948): 84. For an account of the transformations of the houses see Barbara M. Kelly, *Expanding the American Dream: Building and Rebuilding Levittown* (Albany: State University of New York Press, 1993).

17. Jackson, *Crabgrass Frontier,* 241. He reports that by 1980 it was 38 percent African-American.

18. Baxandall and Ewen, *Picture Windows,* 125, quoting testimony at McCarthy hearings.

19. "Levitt's Progress," *Fortune* 46 (October 1952): 158. See also "The Most House for the Money" *Fortune* 46 (October 1952): 151–54.

20. When other developers began to build larger shopping facilities on the Sunrise Highway, the small Levitt commercial strips were in trouble, and vacant stores have remained a problem, according to Alexander Garvin, *The American City: What Works and What Doesn't* (New York: McGraw-Hill, 1996), 337.

21. Charles E. Redfield and others, "The Impact of Levittown on Local Government," *Journal of the American Institute of Planners* 17 (Summer 1951): 130–41.

22. *Ibid.,* 137.

23. Adam Rome, *The Bulldozer in the Countryside: Suburban Sprawl and the Rise of American Environmentalism* (New York: Cambridge University Press, 2001), 96–97.

24. Redfield and others, "Impact of Levittown," 134.

25. "The Most House for the Money," 154.

26. A. Levitt, "A Community Builder, " 81–88.

27. In 1960 the company became publicly held; in 1969 Levitt sold out to ITT, which later sold the firm to Starrett. Jackson, *Crabgrass Frontier,* 371, n. 19.

28. Waldie, *Holy Land,* 91. See also John S. Todd, *A History of Lakewood, 1949–1954* (Lakewood, Calif.: Lakewood City Hall, 1984).

29. Waldie, *Holy Land,* 89.

30. *Ibid.,* 35–36.

31. *Ibid.,* 37.

32. *Ibid.,* 101–2.

33. "The Lakewood Story," http://www.lakewoodcity.org/history/contract_city.html (June 20, 2002); "Lakewood," http://www.colapublib.org/history/lakewood (June 20, 2002); William Fulton, *The Reluctant Metropolis: The Politics of Urban Growth in Los Angeles* (Point Arena, Calif.: Solano Press, 1997), 13. See also Ann Durkin Keating, "Real Estate Developers: Creators of Improved Subdivisions, Mentors of Suburban Government," in *Suburbia Re-examined,* ed. Barbara M. Kelly (New York: Greenwood Press, 1989), 199–206.

34. Waldie, *Holy Land,* 164–70; "The Lakewood Story"; "Lakewood."

35. *Collier's,* February 14, 1948, quoted in Randall, *America's Original GI Town,* 157.

36. Klutznick wanted to avoid the Greenbelt towns' problem, where renters of public housing couldn't overrule the political decision-making of the federal government, according to Randall, *America's Original GI Town,* 50.

37. *Ibid.,* 18–19. Randall thinks that Manilow didn't need the lecture.

38. *Ibid.,* 69. Over eighty oral history interviews, photographs, and other materials are available through the Park Forest Public Library, "Park Forest: An Illinois Planned Community," http://www.pfpl.org. There is also a preserved "50th Anniversary House Museum" at 397 Forest Boulevard, Park Forest, Ill.

39. Randall notes that Peets's plan for neighborhoods was attacked by both Reginald Isaacs, a regional planner, who said the neighborhood concept was elitist and racist, and by Henry Churchill, a conservative FHA supporter.

40. Checkoway, "Large Builders," 123.

41. U.S. Census Bureau, "Homeownership Rates by Race and Ethnicity of Householder," http://www.census.gov/hhes/www/housing/hvs/annual00/annt20.html (June 21, 2001); U.S. Census Bureau, "Home-

ownership Rates for the United States," http://www.census.gov/hhes/www/housing/hvs/annual001/annoot20.html (June 21, 2001).

42. John Keats, *The Crack in the Picture Window* (Boston: Houghton Mifflin, 1957), 112–22; Sloan Wilson, *The Man in the Gray Flannel Suit* (New York: Simon and Schuster, 1955).

43. Karal Ann Marling, *As Seen on TV: The Visual Culture of Everyday Life in the 1950s* (Cambridge, Mass.: Harvard University Press, 1994), 6.

44. *Ibid.,* 242–83.

45. Ella Taylor, *Prime-Time Families: Television Culture in Postwar America* (Berkeley: University of California Press, 1989), 20.

46. Eric Hodgins, *Mr. Blandings Builds His Dream House* (New York: Simon and Schuster, 1946); film by RKO and Vanguard Films, starring Cary Grant and Myrna Loy, 1948.

47. Catherine Jurca, "Hollywood, the Dream House Factory," *Cinema Journal* 37 (Summer 1998): 22.

48. *Ibid.,* 29.

49. Vicky Kemper, "Home Inequity," *Common Cause Magazine* 20 (Summer 1994): 14–18. In 2002, $100 billion.

50. Cushing Dolbeare, "How the Income Tax System Subsidizes Housing for the Affluent," in Bratt, Hartman, and Meyerson, eds., *Critical Perspectives on Housing,* 269.

51. Checkoway, "Large Builders," 119–38.

52. Radford, *Modern Housing,* 180–98.

53. Weiss, *Rise of the Community Builders,* 142–43.

EIGHT: EDGE NODES

1. Mary Konsoulis and Mary Corbin Sies, curator and historical consultant, *Metropolitan Perspectives: Smart Growth and Choices for Change* (Washington, D.C.: National Building Museum, 2000), https://nbm.org/Exhibits/Metropolitan_Perspectives.html (February 18, 2001).

2. Joel Garreau, *Edge City: Life on the New Frontier* (New York: Doubleday, 1991), 6–7; Robert E. Lang, *Edgeless Cities: Exploring the Elusive Metropolis* (Washington, D.C.: Brookings Institution, forthcoming), distinguishes three types of metropolitan growth counties.

3. Garreau, 347–422. On the edge city see: Peter O. Muller, *The Outer City: Geographical Consequences of the Urbanization of the Suburbs,* resource paper No. 75-2 (Washington, D.C.: Association of American Geographers, 1976), expanded as Peter O. Muller, *Contemporary Suburban America* (Englewood Cliffs, N.J.: Prentice-Hall, 1981); Robert Fish-

man, *Bourgeois Utopias: The Rise and Fall of Suburbia* (New York: Basic Books, 1987), 184; William Sharpe and Leonard Wallock, "Bold New City or Built-Up 'Burb? Redefining Contemporary Suburbia," *American Quarterly* 46 (March 1994): 1–30.

4. F. Kaid Benfield, Matthew D. Raimi, and Donald D. T. Chen, *Once There Were Greenfields: How Urban Sprawl Is Undermining America's Environment, Economy, and Social Fabric* (New York: Natural Resources Defense Council and Surface Transportation Policy Project, 1999), 40.

5. Bank of America, *Beyond Sprawl: New Patterns of Growth to Fit the New California* (San Francisco: Bank of America and others, 1995). For extensive review of the "sprawl" literature see Transit Cooperative Research Program, *The Costs of Sprawl—Revisited,* Report 39 (Washington, D.C.: National Academy Press, 1998).

6. Glenn Frankel and Steven C. Fehr, "As the Economy Grows, the Trees Fall," *Washington Post,* March 23, 1997, A1, 20–21.

7. Tom Daniels, *When City and Country Collide: Managing Growth in the Metropolitan Fringe* (Washington, D.C.: Island Press, 1999), 1. According to Garreau, *Edge City,* 403–21, Hazel finally found himself outmaneuvered in 1988 when he battled for "Disney's America," a theme park and mall complex next to historic Civil War battlefields in northern Virginia. The land Hazel finally sold to the U.S. government as an addition to the Manassas Battlefield National Park—bought for $11 million, sold for $81 million—never became a mall.

8. James J. Flink, *The Automobile Age* (Cambridge, Mass.: MIT Press, 1988), 37.

9. Chester H. Liebs, *Main Street to Miracle Mile: American Roadside Architecture* (1985; Baltimore: Johns Hopkins University Press, 1995); Catherine Gudis, *Buyways: Automobility, Billboards, and the American Cultural Landscape* (New York: Routledge, forthcoming); John A. Jakle and Keith A. Sculle, *The Gas Station in America* (Baltimore: Johns Hopkins University Press, 1994).

10. Los Angeles entrepreneurs invented the superservice station, offering "a wide range of auto-related goods and services, organized around a sizable forecourt." These places sold auto accessories and tires as well as gas and oil, and included technicians offering to service cars or "monkey-wrench" them. Some grew to include vast "auto-laundries," such as the Western Auto Wash, designed by Morgan, Walls, and Clements on Western Avenue in 1927, "festooned with Spanish classical details but composed as if it were an ancient Greek stoa with a line of cars rather than pedestrians entering its portals." Richard Longstreth, *The Drive-In, the Supermarket, and the Transformation of Commercial Space in Los Ange-*

les, 1914–1941 (Cambridge, Mass.: MIT Press, 1999): xv, 3, 24. See also his *City Center to Regional Mall: Architecture, the Automobile, and Retailing in Los Angeles, 1920–1950* (Cambridge, Mass.: MIT Press, 1997).

11. In the 1920s the "drive-in" appeared, an automobile-oriented food market modeled on the superservice station, offering groceries, meat, poultry, and baked goods. Los Angeles had a tradition of street-front public food markets, stretching back to its founding by colonists from Mexico, but Longstreth shows how the drive-in tied the food market to automobile circulation, becoming a distinctive Southern California form. By the 1930s the drive-in gave way to the supermarket. Longstreth, *The Drive-In*, 111.

12. Liebs, *Main Street,* covers these building types.

13. Eric Schlosser, *Fast Food Nation: The Dark Side of the American Meal* (New York: HarperCollins, 2001), 20–21. Liebs, *Main Street,* attributes the building design to architect Stanley Meston in 1952, 213–14.

14. Peter Blake, *God's Own Junkyard: The Planned Deterioration of America's Landscape,* rev. ed. (1964; New York: Holt, Rinehart and Winston, 1979), 23.

15. *Ibid.,* 44.

16. Seymour Freedgood, "The Motel Free-For-All," *Fortune* 59 (June 1959): 163–71, quoted in Thomas Hanchett, "U.S. Tax Policy and the Shopping-Center Boom of the 1950s and 1960s," *American Historical Review* 101 (October 1996): 1108.

17. Schlosser, *Fast Food Nation,* 96.

18. Hanchett, "U.S. Tax Policy," 1082–1110.

19. The term "tomorrowland" derived from an attraction in Walt Disney's Orange County theme park. When Disneyland opened in 1955, Tomorrowland included corporate exhibits to promote consumption and a ride with miniature cars on mock freeways called "Autopia." For a discussion of Disneyland as both television show and theme park, see Karal Ann Marling, *As Seen on TV: The Visual Culture of Everyday Life in the 1950s* (Cambridge, Mass.: Harvard University Press, 1994), 86–126.

20. Charles F. Floyd and Peter J. Shedd, *Highway Beautification: The Environmental Movement's Greatest Failure* (Boulder: Westview Press, 1979), 113–17.

21. Thomas Hanchett, "U.S. Tax Policy," 1099. See also Kenneth T. Jackson, "All the World's a Mall: Reflections on the Social and Economic Consequences of the American Shopping Center," *American Historical Review* 101 (October 1996): 1111–21.

22. Daniels, *When City and Country Collide,* 22.

23. Joseph Interrante, "You Can't Go to Town in a Bathtub: Automobile Movement and the Reorganization of American Rural Space, 1900–1930," *Radical History Review* 21 (Fall 1979): 151–68.

24. Flink, *The Automobile Age*, 368–73.

25. Schlosser, *Fast Food Nation*, 16–17; Stephen B. Goddard, *Getting There: The Epic Struggle Between Road and Rail in the American Century* (New York: Basic Books, 1994), 134–35.

26. Flink, *Automobile Age*, 371.

27. Lewis Mumford, quoted in Jackson, *Crabgrass Frontier*, 250.

28. Helen Leavitt, *Superhighway—Superhoax* (Garden City, N.Y.: Doubleday, 1970), 187–88.

29. Mark H. Rose, *Interstate: Express Highway Politics, 1939–1989*, rev. ed. (1979; Knoxville: University of Tennessee Press, 1990), 116.

30. Flink, *Automobile Age*, 371–72; Rose, *Interstate*, 69–95.

31. Tom Lewis, *Divided Highways: Building the Interstate Highways, Transforming American Life* (New York: Viking, 1997), photograph opposite p. 210.

32. Jane Holtz Kay, *Asphalt Nation: How the Automobile Took Over America and How We Can Take It Back* (New York: Crown, 1997), 258. Truckers benefited as well as motorists, of course.

33. Victor Gruen and Larry Smith, *Shopping Towns USA: The Planning of Shopping Centers* (New York: Reinhold, 1960); also see Howard Gillette, Jr., "The Evolution of the Planned Shopping Center in Suburb and City," *American Planning Association Journal* 51 (Autumn 1985): 449–60.

34. Mark Jeffrey Hardwick, *The Mallmaker: Cities, Suburbs, and Architect Victor Gruen* (Philadelphia: University of Pennsylvania Press, forthcoming).

35. Margaret Crawford, "The World in a Shopping Mall," in *Variations on a Theme Park: The New American City and the End of Public Space*, ed. Michael Sorkin (New York: Hill and Wang, 1992), 3–30. On market segmentation and characterizations of malls, see Michael J. Weiss, *The Clustered World: How We Live, What We Buy, and What It All Means About Who We Are* (Boston: Little, Brown, 2000).

36. Hanchett, "U.S. Tax Policy," 1108.

37. A comic example of this is described in William Fulton, *The Reluctant Metropolis: The Politics of Urban Growth in Los Angeles* (Point Arena, Calif.: Solano Press, 1997), 255–82.

38. Mark Gottdiener, *Planned Sprawl: Private and Public Interests in Suburbia* (Beverly Hills, Calif.: Sage, 1977), 103.

39. Morton Paulson, *The Great Land Hustle* (Chicago: Henry Reg-

nery, 1972); Leonard Downie, *Mortgage on America* (New York: Praeger, 1974).

40. International Council of Shopping Centers, http://www.icsc.com (March 23, 2002); William Leach, *Country of Exiles: The Destruction of Place in American Life* (New York: Pantheon, 1999), 55. On the design of malls and how they can work in Main Street situations, especially in Australia, see Ann Forsyth, "Variations on a Main Street; When a Mall is an Arcade," *Journal of Urban Design* 2 (Fall 1997): 297–307.

41. Lizabeth Cohen, "From Town Center to Shopping Center: The Reconfiguration of Community Marketplaces in Postwar America," *American Historical Review* 101 (October 1996): 1050–81; Lizabeth Cohen, *A Consumers' Republic:* The Politics of Mass-Consumption in Postwar America (New York: Knopf, 2003), 257–344.

42. Frank Jossi, "Rewrapping the Big Box," *Planning* 64 (August 1998): 16–18.

43. Benfield, Raimi, and Chen, *Once There Were Greenfields,* 15.

44. "Mall of America," http://www.mallofamerica.com (March 23, 2002).

45. Garreau, *Edge City,* 113–16.

46. Bettina Drew, *Crossing the Expendable Landscape* (Minneapolis: Graywolf, 1998), 11–31.

47. Ann Forsyth, personal communication, August 2002; Ann Forsyth, *Reforming Suburbia: Building New Communities in Irvine, Columbia, and The Woodlands* (Berkeley: University of California Press, forthcoming). She notes that The Woodlands was "the only one of the thirteen 'Title VII' new towns to be largely completed."

48. Muller, *Contemporary Suburban America,* 164.

49. Patricia Leigh Brown, "Megachurches as Minitowns," *New York Times,* May 9, 2002, F1. This recalls attempts around 1900 to make churches resemble urban settlement houses, with spaces for sports and meetings.

50. Benfield, Raimi, and Chen, *Once There Were Greenfields,* 36–40.

51. Douglas Kelbaugh, article in *Urban Land,* June 1999, quoted in Konsoulis and Sies, *Metropolitan Perspectives,* n.p.

52. Al Norman, *Slam-Dunking Wal-Mart* (Atlantic City, N.J.: Raphael Marketing, 1999); Bill Saporito and Jacqueline M. Graves, "And the Winner is Still . . . Wal-Mart," *Fortune* 129 (May 2, 1994): 62ff.

53. Constance E. Beaumont, *How Superstore Sprawl Can Harm Communities and What Citizens Can Do About It* (Washington, D.C.: National Trust for Historic Preservation, 1994); Constance E. Beaumont,

Better Models for Superstores (Washington, D.C.: National Trust for Historic Preservation, 1997).

54. Al Norman, "The Case Against Sprawl," www.sprawlbusters.com (May 10, 2002).

55. Keller Easterling, *Organization Space: Landscapes, Highways, and Houses in America* (Cambridge, Mass.: MIT Press, 1999).

56. Leach, *Country of Exiles,* 32–35.

57. Schlosser, *Fast Food Nation,* 6–10, condemns McDonald's massive monopoly of beef and potatoes, processed according to the rules of headquarters, who freeze a standard product complete with flavor additives and "mouthfeel" texture.

58. *Ibid.,* 59–88; Steven Greenhouse, "Suits Say Wal-Mart Forces Workers to Toil Off the Clock," *New York Times,* June 25, 2002, A18.

59. Robert Davis, "Postscript," in Congress for the New Urbanism, *Charter of the New Urbanism* (New York: McGraw-Hill, 2000), 182.

60. Garreau, *Edge City,* 14–15.

61. Timothy Egan, "Retail Darwinism Puts Old Malls in Jeopardy," *New York Times* (January 1, 2000), A20.

NINE: RURAL FRINGES

1. Tom Daniels, *When City and Country Collide: Managing Growth in the Metropolitan Fringe* (Washington, D.C.: Island Press, 1999), 40; F. Kaid Benfield, Matthew D. Ramie, and Donald D. T. Chen, *Once There Were Greenfields: How Urban Sprawl Is Undermining America's Environment, Economy, and Social Fabric* (Washington, D.C.: Natural Resources Defense Council, 1999), 6, 9. Note that greater Phoenix is the size of Delaware, and greater Los Angeles the size of Connecticut.

2. "Schaumburg," http://www.villageprofile.com/illinois/schaumburg/location/topic.html (March 27, 2002).

3. Dirk Johnson, "Town Sired by Autos Seeks Soul Downtown," *New York Times,* August 7, 1996, 8. See also Bob Thall, *The New American Village* (Baltimore: Johns Hopkins University Press, 1999), for a documentary photographer's look at Schaumburg.

4. Johnson, "Town Sired by Autos," 8.

5. Village of Schaumburg, "Progress Through Thoughtful Planning," http://www.ci.schaumburg.il.us (March 27, 2002).

6. "Crystal Lake," http://www.crystallake.org/About CL (March 27, 2002).

7. Benfield, Ramie, and Chen, *Once There Were Greenfields,* 91, 178 n. 12.

8. Valerie Berton, "Harvest or Homes?" *American Farmland* 16 (Fall

1995): 14, quoted in Benfield, Ramie, and Chen, *Once There Were Greenfields*, 69.

9. Benfield, Ramie, and Chen, *Once There Were Greenfields*, 20.

10. Daniels, *When City and Country Collide*, xiii.

11. *Ibid.*, xiv.

12. Julie Campoli, Elizabeth Humstone, and Alex MacLean, *Above and Beyond: Visualizing Change in Small Towns and Rural Areas* (Chicago: American Planning Association, 2002); also see Vermont Forum on Sprawl, http://www.vtsprawl.org (May 10, 2002).

13. Pierce F. Lewis, "The Galactic Metropolis," in *Beyond the Urban Fringe: Land Use Issues in Nonmetropolitan America*, ed. Rutherford H. Platt and George Macinko (Minneapolis: University of Minnesota Press, 1983), 23–49. This book is the proceedings of a conference held in 1980.

14. John Herbers, *The New Heartland: America's Flight Beyond the Suburbs and How It Is Changing Our Future* (New York: Times Books, 1986).

15. Lisa W. Foderaro, "No Beaches, No Boondocks, No Problem," *New York Times*, April 5, 2002, F1. Interestingly, some of the people she interviewed were escaping the city, some fleeing the edge nodes, and some leaving houses in places too remote for neighboring because children were isolated.

16. Herbers, *New Heartland*, 197.

17. Daniels, *When City and Country Collide*, 144.

18. Patricia Leigh Brown, "In 'the Other California' a Land Rush Continues," *New York Times*, December 27, 2000, A14.

19. Benfield, Ramie, and Chen, *Once There Were Greenfields*, 30.

20. In 1998 Americans owned 131,838,538 passenger vehicles, according to the Bureau of Transportation Statistics, http://www.bts.gov/publications/pocketguide/html/table7.html (June 9, 2002). In 2000 there were 72.3 million children under age eighteen, according the Population Reference Bureau's report, *Kid Count*, based on the 2000 Census, http://www.prb.org/AmeristatTemplate.cfm?section=children1&template=/contentmanagement/contentDisplay.cfm&contentID=5655 (June 9, 2002).

21. Benfield, Ramie, and Chen, *Once There Were Greenfields*, 30–32.

22. Jane Holtz Kay, *Asphalt Nation: How the Automobile Took Over America and How We Can Take It Back* (New York: Crown, 1997), 14.

23. *Ibid.*, 120–23. Philip Langdon suggests that car costs could be commemorated on April Fool's Day, one-quarter of the way through the year, according to Andrés Duany, Elizabeth Plater-Zyberk, and Jeff Speck, *Suburban Nation: The Rise of Sprawl and the Decline of the American Dream* (New York: North Point Press, 2000), 127.

24. *The New Spatial Order? Technology and Urban Development,*

Lincoln Institute of Land Policy Annual Roundtable (Cambridge, Mass: Lincoln Institute of Land Policy, 2001); Frank Swoboda and Kirstin Downey Grimsley, "OSHA Covers At-Home Workers," *Washington Post,* January 4, 2000, A1.

25. Verizon advertisement, *New York Times,* November 23, 2000, B14.

26. Robert Kraut and others, "Internet Paradox: A Social Technology That Reduces Social Involvement and Psychological Well-Being?" *American Psychologist* 53 (September 1998): 1017–31.

27. Arlie Hochschild, with Anne Machung, *The Second Shift: Working Parents and the Revolution at Home,* 2d ed. (1989; New York: Avon, 1997).

28. Laura C. Johnson, *The Co-Workplace: Teleworking in the Neighborhood* (Vancouver: University of British Columbia Press, 2002).

29. *Telecommuting: The Road to Success,* video (New Haven and Hartford: Telecommute Connecticut! and Connecticut Department of Transportation, 2000).

30. Debra A. Dinnocenzo, *101 Tips for Telecommuters: Successfully Manage Your Work, Team, Technology and Family* (San Francisco: Berrett-Koehler, 1999), 76, 39–41. Also see Alice Bredin, *The Virtual Office Survival Handbook* (New York: Wiley, 1996); Swoboda and Grimsley, "OSHA Covers At-Home Workers," A1.

31. William M. Dobriner, "The Natural History of a Reluctant Suburb," *Class in Suburbia* (Englewood Cliffs, N.J.: Prentice-Hall, 1963), 132–33.

32. *Ibid.,* 136.

33. Peter Wolf, *Hot Towns: The Future of the Fastest Growing Communities in America* (New Brunswick, N.J.: Rutgers University Press, 1999).

34. Michael Pollan, "Living at the Office," *New York Times,* March 14, 1997, A33.

35. Joel Kotkin, *The New Digital Geography: How the Digital Revolution Is Reshaping the American Landscape* (New York: Random House, 2000).

36. U.S. Bureau of the Census, "Characteristics of New Single Family Homes, 1987–99," compiled by NAHB Economics Department. In 1999 1,307,000 new single-family homes were built; 34 percent were 2,400 square feet or more; http://www.nahb.com/facts/forecast/sf.html (June 6, 2001).

37. Blaine Harden, "Big, Bigger, Biggest: The Supersize Suburb . . . ," *New York Times,* June 20, 2002, F1ff.

38. Andrea Strickley and Rasa Gustaitis, "Teardowns of the Techno-Riche" (Palo Alto and Carmel), *Preservation* 52 (August 2000): 18–20; Tracie Rozhon, "Boxes Full of the Past, But Loved By So Few," *New York Times,* October 19, 2000, F1ff. For planning advice, see Lincoln Institute of Land Policy and American Planning Association, "Tear Downs, Monster Houses, and Appropriate Infill," audio conference training program (December 5, 2001), http://www.planning.org.

39. Tamar Lewin, "Now a Majority: Families with 2 Parents Who Work," *New York Times,* October 24, 2000, A20.

40. Dolores Hayden, *Redesigning the American Dream: Gender, Housing, and Family Life,* rev. ed. (New York: Norton, 2002).

41. Sandra Rosenbloom, "Trends in Women's Travel Patterns," in *Women's Travel Issues: Proceedings from the Second National Conference,* October 1996, http://www.fhwa.dot.gov/ohim/womens/chap2/pdf (June 6, 2001).

42. Lisa Belkin, "A Silent Drain on Time: Children's Sports," *New York Times,* April 28, 2002, WC1.

43. Barbara Ehrenreich, "Maid to Order: The Politics of Other Women's Work," *Harper's* 300 (April 2000): 59–70.

44. Tod Papageorge, *Robert Adams—What We Bought: The New World* (New Haven: Yale University Art Gallery, 2002), 28.

45. Real Estate Research Corporation, *The Costs of Sprawl: Environmental and Economic Costs of Alternative Residential Development Patterns at the Urban Fringe,* 2 vols. (Washington, D.C.: U.S. Government Printing Office, 1974); Transit Cooperative Research Program, *The Costs of Sprawl—Revisited,* Report 39 (Washington, D.C.: National Academy Press, 1998).

46. For a discussion of these initiatives see Daniels, *When City and Country Collide,* 185–209.

47. National Association of Home Builders, *Smart Growth: Building Better Places to Live, Work, and Play* (Washington, D.C.: NAHB, 1999); Urban Land Institute, *Smart Growth: Myth and Fact* (Washington, D.C.: Urban Land Institute, 1999).

48. Jane S. Shaw and Ronald D. Utt, eds., *A Guide to Smart Growth: Shattering Myths, Providing Solutions* (Washington, D.C.: Heritage Foundation, 2000).

49. National Association of Home Builders, "The Next Decade for Housing," http://www.nahb.com/facts/nextdecade~forecast.pdf (June 6, 2001).

50. HUD-FHA advertisement, *New York Times,* December 3, 2000, section 4:20.

51. "Sprawl Tops List of Concerns," *Population Today* 28 (April 2000): 5; "Straight Talk from America—2000," http://www.pewcenter.org/doingcj/research/index.html (May 2002).

TEN: NOSTALGIA AND FUTURISM

1. Andrés Duany, Elizabeth Plater-Zyberk, and Jeff Speck, *Suburban Nation: The Rise of Sprawl and the Decline of the American Dream* (New York: North Point Press, 2000), 243.

2. "Seaside . . . Still the One, Twenty Years Later," and "Seaside: Environmentally Sound," *Seaside Times,* Extra Special 20th Anniversary Issue, 2001, 7; *A Walking Tour of Seaside* (Seaside, Fla.: Seaside Cottage Rental Agency, n.d.); David Mohney and Keller Easterling, eds., *Seaside: Making a Town in America* (New York: Princeton Architectural Press, 1991).

3. Drummond Buckley, "A Garage in the House," in *The Car and the City: The Automobile, the Built Environment, and Daily Urban Life,* ed. Martin Wachs and Margaret Crawford (Ann Arbor: University of Michigan Press, 1992), 124–40; Raymond Arsenault, "The End of the Long Hot Summer: The Air Conditioner and Southern Culture," *Journal of Southern History* 50 (November 1984): 597–628.

4. "Seaside: Environmentally Sound," *Seaside Times,* 7.

5. Seaside Community Realty, Seaside, Fla., brochure, March 9, 2001. A brochure of March 13, 2002, indicated prices might be down slightly.

6. Congress for the New Urbanism, *Charter of the New Urbanism* (New York: McGraw-Hill, 2000). It was adopted in 1996. The Ahwanee Principles of 1991 are reprinted in Tom Daniels, *When City and Country Collide: Managing Growth in the Metropolitan Fringe* (Washington, D.C.: Island Press, 1999), 91–92. See also Douglas Kelbaugh, ed., *The Pedestrian Pocket Book: A New Suburban Design Strategy* (New York: Princeton Architectural Press, 1989); and Douglas Kelbaugh, *Common Place: Toward Neighborhood and Regional Design* (Seattle: University of Washington Press, 1997). Emily Talen, "The Social Goals of New Urbanism," *Housing Policy Debate* 13 (2002): 165–88, evaluates the aims in the *Charter.*

7. Peter Calthorpe, in Congress for the New Urbanism, *Charter,* 178.

8. Joel Garreau, *Edge City: Life on the New Frontier* (New York: Doubleday, 1991), 433, lists downtown, the Maitland Center area, the airport area, and the University of Central Florida area.

9. Joel Schwartz, "Evolution of the Suburbs," in *Suburbia: The American Dream and Dilemma,* ed. Philip C. Dolce (Garden City, N.Y.: Anchor

Press/Doubleday, 1976), 27. Prather was the developer of Highland Park and River Oaks in Texas.

10. Sales information based on Celebration brochures, 1996–2001; "Celebration," http://www.celebrationfl.com (January 2002); *Celebration News* (March 2001); *Celebration Independent* (March 2001); author interview with Robert A. M. Stern, July 2002.

11. Alex Marshall, *How Cities Work: Suburbs, Sprawl, and the Roads Not Taken* (Austin: University of Texas Press, 2000), 6.

12. Osceola County Building and Development, The Celebration Company, "DRI 02-0009 and PD02-00017 Celebration, Map H, Density Map, and Support Document," revised June 26, 2002.

13. Andrew Ross, *The Celebration Chronicles: Life, Liberty, and the Pursuit of Property Value in Disney's New Town* (New York: Ballantine, 1999), 36–44; Douglas Frantz and Catherine Collins, *Celebration, U.S.A.: Living in Disney's Brave New Town* (New York: Marian Wood/Henry Holt, 1999), 82–101.

14. Marlena Morton, "Class Action Suit Filed Regarding School," *Celebration Independent*, March 2001, 1.

15. Andrew Ross, *The Celebration Chronicles*, 13; David L. Kirp, "Pleasantville," *New York Times Book Review*, September 19, 1999, section 7, 22–23.

16. Some of the momentum established in these two enclaves was not to be sustained. DPZ went on to design Rosemary Beach, another Panhandle beach community which abandoned indigenous landscaping and local vernacular architecture for the Dutch Colonial Revival style with lawns.

17. Evan MacKenzie, *Privatopia: Homeowner Associations and the Rise of Residential Private Government* (New Haven: Yale University Press, 1994); Edward J. Blakely and Mary Gail Snyder, *Fortress America: Gated Communities in the United States* (Washington, D.C.: Brookings Institution and Lincoln Institute of Land Policy, 1997).

18. Setha Low, *Behind the Gates: The New American Dream* (New York: Routledge, 2003), 15–16.

19. Patricia Leigh Brown, "Megachurches as Minitowns," *New York Times*, May 9, 2002, F6. The private managers who run all kinds of Community of Interest Developments (CIDs) tend to be conservative. While they believe that they can make rules for their residents as private managers, they have a lot in common with private-property rights activists who dislike federal, state, and local government. The private-property rights advocates—also on the rise in 2000—belong to groups demanding an end to any kind of government regulation of land. Both

groups are involved in withdrawing from the public realm. See Harvey M. Jacobs, ed., *Who Owns America? Social Conflict Over Property Rights* (Madison: University of Wisconsin Press, 1998); Charles Geisler and Gail Daneker, eds., *Property and Values: Alternatives to Public and Private Ownership* (Washington, D.C.: Island Press, 2000).

20. Brian Horrigan, "The Home of Tomorrow, 1927–1945," in *Imagining Tomorrow: History, Technology, and the American Future*, ed. Joseph J. Corn (Cambridge, Mass.: MIT Press, 1986); Lynn Spigel, *Welcome to the Dreamhouse: Popular Media and Postwar Suburbs* (Durham, N.C.: Duke University Press, 2001), 381–408.

21. Dolores Hayden, *Redesigning the American Dream: Gender, Housing, and Family Life,* rev. ed. (New York: Norton, 2002), 81–119.

22. Hariri and Hariri, "The Digital-House," 1997–98 information sheet, 18 E. 12th Street, New York, NY 10003, n.p.

23. Terence Riley, *The Un-Private House* (New York: Museum of Modern Art, 1999), 36–39. Also see Eduard Bru, *Nuevos territorios, nuevos paisajes/New Territories, New Landscapes* (Barcelona: Museu d'Art Contemporani de Barcelona, 1997); Jaime Salazar and Manuel Gausa, *Single Family Housing: The Private Domain* (Basel: Birkhauser and Actar, 1999).

24. Hariri and Hariri, "The Digital-House," n.p.

25. *Ibid.,* n.p.

26. Riley, *The Un-Private House,* 40–145.

27. Among these futurists, only the husband-and-wife team of Charles and Ray Eames explored the house for the two-worker family and the live/work house. Most of the Case Study architects designed for stereotypical stay-at-home housewives and commuting husbands. Dolores Hayden, "Model Houses for the Millions: Architects' Dreams, Builders' Boasts, Residents' Dilemmas," in *Blueprints for Modern Living: History and Legacy of the Case Study Houses,* ed. Elizabeth A. T. Smith (Los Angeles: Museum of Contemporary Art and MIT Press, 1989), 197–212.

28. "The MIT Home of the Future," http://web.mit.edu/emunguia/www/research.html (November 13, 2001); Sara Hart, "Home Work," *architecture* 9 (September 1999): 133–37; Kent Larson, "The Home of the Future," *A+U* (June 1, 2000), on the House_*n* website.

29. Larson, "The Home of the Future."

30. "The MIT Home of the Future."

31. *Idem.*

32. Anna Bowman Dodd, *The Republic of the Future, or, Socialism a Reality* (New York: Cassell, 1887), 40; Dolores Hayden, *The Grand Domestic Revolution: A History of Feminist Designs for American*

Homes, Neighborhoods, and Cities (Cambridge, Mass.: MIT Press, 1981), 137.

33. "House_n: The MIT Home of the Future," http://architecture.mit .edu/house_n (November 13, 2001).

34. The research questions include: "What influences how people adjust to new environments?" and "What new innovations for the home would most fundamentally alter the way we live our everyday lives?" The organizers boast, "The Living Laboratory will be a unique, world-class tool that will be used for unique, world-class research on the home previously not possible." http://architecture.mit.edu/house_n/web/livinglab/ livinglaboratory.htm (November 13, 2001).

35. Larson, "The Home of the Future."

36. It follows in the tradition of architecture designed to make surveillance of inmates easy, such as Jeremy Bentham's "Panopticon" (all-seeing building), proposed for poorhouses, schools, and penitentiaries. While its designers present it as beneficent, since it is connected to manufacturers, supermarkets, and pharmacies, this is naive.

37. As opposed to modernist architects, most local builders had always been building frame houses in eclectic styles: ranch, Tudor, Mediterranean, colonial.

38. William J. Mitchell, *City of Bits: Space, Place, and the Infobahn* (Cambridge, Mass.: MIT Press, 1995); Nicholas Negroponte, *Being Digital* (New York: Random House, 1995).

39. Spigel, *Welcome to the Dreamhouse*, 383.

40. Adam Rome, *The Bulldozer in the Countryside: Suburban Sprawl and the Rise of American Environmentalism* (New York: Cambridge University Press, 2001), 45–64.

41. "Test House Heated Only By Solar Heat," *Architectural Record* 105 (March 1949): 136–37.

42. Rome, *Bulldozer in the Countryside*, 49, 55.

43. *Ibid.*, 38.

44. Doris Kearns Goodwin, *Wait Till Next Year: A Memoir* (New York: Simon and Schuster, 1997), 76–77.

45. Rome, *Bulldozer in the Countryside*, 68–69.

46. *Ibid.*, 77–80.

47. "William McDonough," http://www.mcdonough.com (May 22, 2002).

48. F. Herbert Bormann, Diana Balmori, and Gordon T. Geballe, *Redesigning the American Lawn: A Search for Environmental Harmony*, 2d ed. (New Haven: Yale University Press, 2001).

49. Susan Sully, "Up on a Tree on an Island of Green," *New York*

Times, May 23, 2002, F1. See also the Rocky Mountain Institute website, http://www.rmi.org, for information on green developments. Village Homes in Davis, Calif., is an early example of a green community.

50. Green Seal, "Who We Are and What We Do," http://www.greenseal.org/about.htm (May 20, 2002).

51. "The Hannover Principles: Design for Sustainability," http://www.mcdonoughpartners.com/projects/p_hannover.html (May 20, 2002); William McDonough and Michael Braungart, *Cradle to Cradle: Remaking the Way We Make Things* (New York: North Point Press, 2002).

52. U.S. Green Building Council, "Mission Statement," http://www.usgbc.org/AboutUs/mission_facts.asp (January 18, 2003).

ELEVEN: THE IMPORTANCE OF OLDER SUBURBS

1. Robert D. Bullard, Glenn S. Johnson, and Angel O. Torres, *Sprawl City: Race, Politics, and Planning in Atlanta* (Washington, D.C.: Island Press, 2000); Myron Orfield, *Metropolitics: A Regional Agenda for Community and Stability,* rev. ed. (Washington, D.C.: Brookings Institution and Lincoln Institute for Land Policy, 1998). See also William H. Lucy and David L. Phillips, *Confronting Suburban Decline: Strategic Planning for Metropolitan Renewal* (Washington, D.C.: Island Press, 2000).

2. Robert D. Yaro, talk at Lincoln Institute of Land Policy and Institute of Urban Design conference, Pocantico Conference Center, May 2000. It is difficult to overestimate the responsibility of the growth machines for the poor condition of the American built environment in both city and suburb. See John R. Logan, Rachel Bridges Whaley, and Kyle Crowder, "The Character and Consequences of Growth Regimes: An Assessment of Twenty Years of Research," *Urban Affairs Review* 32 (May 1997): 603–31. Many writers have chronicled the self-interest, incompetence, racism, fraud, and corruption involved in the making of Interstate highways. There is no comparable investigative reporter's book about the real estate interests behind the growth machines.

3. Tom Daniels, *When City and Country Collide: Managing Growth in the Metropolitan Fringe* (Washington, D.C.: Island Press, 1999), 36–37.

4. Vicky Kemper, "Home Inequity," *Common Cause Magazine* 20 (Summer 1994): 14–26; William Goldsmith, "Revisiting the Reality of Race," http://www.lincolninstitute.edu (March 31, 2003).

5. David Cay Johnston, "The Pitfall in the Flat Tax," *New York Times,* January 12, 1996, D1.

6. National Association of Realtors, "Famous American Homewreckers," advertisement, *New York Times,* March 4, 1996, A9.

7. NAHB includes 205,000 members, one-third construction firms, the rest mortgage lenders or building products suppliers. "About NAHB," http://nahb.com/builders/default.htm (May 31, 2002).

8. Urban Land Institute, "Institute History," http://uli.org (May 31, 2002).

9. "History of the National Association of Realtors," http://www .realtor.org/realtor.org.nsf/pages/narhistory (May 6, 2002). The NAR began its lobbying career in 1913, trying to exempt landlord's rents from taxation. In the 1920s it successfully lobbied for the mortgage interest deduction, which it has been defending and expanding ever since.

10. Donella H. Meadows, "If We Don't Like Sprawl, Why Do We Go on Sprawling?" *Boca Sierra* (January 2000): 1.

11. Eben Fodor, *Better Not Bigger: How to Take Control of Urban Growth and Improve Your Community* (Gabriola Island, B.C.: New Society Publishers, 1999); Grady Clay, "Sprawl Machine," text of public radio broadcast, *Morning Edition,* WFPL, Louisville, Ky., February 28, 2001; Planners Network, "The Seventh Generation: Alternatives to the Growth Machine," *Planners Network Online* 137 (September/October 1999), http://www.plannersnetwork.org/137/seventh.htm; *Planners Network Online* 138 (November/December 1999), http://www.plannersnetwork.org/138/seventh.htm.

12. Torie Osborn, "Rebuilding a City One Block at a Time," *New York Times,* April 29, 2002, A25.

13. John O. Calmore, "Metropolitan America and Racism," *Poverty and Race* 2 (May/June 1993): 11–12.

14. "The promised land," Daniels, *When City and Country Collide,* 261–73; "the brighter dream," F. Kaid Benfield, Matthew D. Raimi, and Donald D. T. Chen, *Once There Were Greenfields: How Urban Sprawl Is Undermining America's Environment, Economy, and Social Fabric* (New York: Natural Resources Defense Council and Surface Transportation Policy Project, 1999), 161; "solving sprawl," F. Kaid Benfield, Jutka Terris, and Nancy Vorsanger, *Solving Sprawl: Models of Smart Growth in Communities Across America* (New York: Natural Resources Defense Council, 2001); "the new urbanism," http://www.cnu.org (June 1, 2002), which includes "the transect," by Andrés Duany. "The regional city" and "the new American metropolis" are phrases of Peter Calthorpe's.

15. Martha Farnsworth Riche, "America's Diversity and Growth: Signposts for the 21st Century," *Population Bulletin* 55 (June 2000): 3, 5.

16. Orfield, *Metropolitics,* 1–15.

17. Timothy Egan, "Portland Voters Endorse Curbs on City Growth," *New York Times,* May 23, 2002, A24.

18. Robert D. Yaro and Tony Hiss, *A Region at Risk: The Third Regional Plan for the New York–New Jersey–Connecticut Metropolitan Area* (Washington, D.C.: Island Press, 1996), 19, notes that there are nearly 1,600 cities, towns, and villages in the tristate metro region.

19. http://www.oua-adh.org/centerEdge_project.htm (June 10, 2002).

20. Kevin Lynch, *What Time Is This Place?* (Cambridge, Mass.: MIT Press, 1972).

21. The Location Efficient Mortgage (LEF) is one example of a smart-growth idea supported by architects and planners. The concept is that bankers might give bigger mortgages to buyers who are in inner-city locations or near transit, because their location will enable them to cut their automobile expenses. LEF enables people to buy bigger or more expensive houses as a trade-off for fewer or smaller cars, but it leaves the federal machinery for subsidizing houses intact. It does little to make housing more affordable for lower-income groups or the poor. In the long term it might strengthen the property tax base (which is used to pay for schools) in older suburbs.

22. "The Burnham Building," http://www.rose-network.com (August 2002); Jane Gross, "Not-So-Rich Get a Hand on Housing in Westchester," *New York Times,* April 3, 2000, B1.

23. Benfield, Terris, and Vorsanger, *Solving Sprawl,* 91–95.

24. Jonathan F. P. Rose, "Solutions: Under Development," *Amicus Journal* (Fall 1996): 23.

25. Gayle Epp, "Emerging Strategies for Revitalizing Public Housing Communities," *Housing Policy Debate* 7 (1996): 582; U.S. Department of Housing and Urban Development, "Hope VI Fact Sheet" (February 4, 1997).

26. Toby Eckert, "Placing Hopes in Hope VI," *Indianapolis Business Journal,* December 9–15, 1996, 1; author interview with Daniel Glenn, 2000.

27. Dolores Hayden, *The Power of Place: Urban Landscapes as Public History* (Cambridge, Mass.: MIT Press, 1995).

28. "Park Forest: An Illinois Planned Community," http://www.pfpl.org (January 10, 2003).

29. Alexander Garvin, *The American City: What Works and What Doesn't* (New York: McGraw-Hill, 1996), 3.

30. Laura Mansnerus, "McGreevey to Legislators: Fight Sprawl," *New York Times* (January 15, 2003): B1.

SELECTED BIBLIOGRAPHY

This brief general bibliography is offered for the reader's convenience. Many more works are cited in the Notes.

BOOKS AND CHAPTERS IN BOOKS

Archer, John. "Colonial Suburbs in South Asia, 1700–1850, and the Spaces of Modernity." In *Visions of Suburbia,* edited by Roger Silverstone. London: Routledge, 1997.

Bank of America. *Beyond Sprawl: New Patterns of Growth to Fit the New California.* San Francisco: Bank of America and others, 1995.

Bauer, Catherine. *Modern Housing.* Boston: Houghton Mifflin, 1934.

Baxandall, Rosalyn, and Elizabeth Ewen. *Picture Windows: How the Suburbs Happened.* New York: Basic Books, 2000.

Beaumont, Constance E. *Better Models for Superstores.* Washington D.C.: National Trust for Historic Preservation, 1997.

———. *How Superstore Sprawl Can Harm Communities and What Citizens Can Do About It.* Washington, D.C.: National Trust for Historic Preservation, 1994.

Beecher, Catharine E. *Treatise on Domestic Economy.* Boston: Thomas H. Webb, 1842.

Beecher, Catharine E., and Harriet Beecher Stowe. *The American Woman's Home.* New York: J. B. Ford, 1869.

Benfield, F. Kaid, Matthew D. Raimi, and Donald D. T. Chen. *Once There Were Greenfields: How Urban Sprawl Is Undermining America's Environment, Economy, and Social Fabric.* New York: Natural Resources Defense Council and Surface Transportation Policy Project, 1999.

Benfield, F. Kaid, Jutka Terris, and Nancy Vorsanger. *Solving Sprawl:*

Models of Smart Growth in Communities across America. New York: Natural Resources Defense Council, 2001.

Berger, Miles L. *They Built Chicago: Entrepreneurs Who Shaped a Great City's Architecture.* Chicago: Bonus Books, 1992.

Bigott, Joseph C. *From Cottage to Bungalow: Houses and the Working Class in Metropolitan Chicago, 1869–1929.* Chicago: University of Chicago Press, 2001.

Binford, Henry. *The First Suburbs: Residential Communities on the Boston Periphery, 1815–1860.* Chicago: University of Chicago Press, 1984.

Blackmar, Elizabeth. *Manhattan for Rent, 1785–1850.* Ithaca, N.Y.: Cornell University Press, 1989.

Blake, Peter. *God's Own Junkyard: The Planned Deterioration of America's Landscape.* Rev. ed. New York: Holt, Rinehart and Winston, 1979.

Blakely, Edward J., and Mary Gail Snyder. *Fortress America: Gated Communities in the United States.* Washington, D.C.: Brookings Institution and Lincoln Institute of Land Policy, 1997.

Bormann, F. Herbert, Diana Balmori, and Gordon T. Geballe. *Redesigning the American Lawn: A Search for Environmental Harmony.* 2d ed. New Haven: Yale University Press, 2001.

Bremer, Fredrika. *Homes of the New World.* Translated by Mary Hewitt. 2 vols. New York: Harper and Brothers, 1853.

Bridges, Amy. *Morning Glories: Municipal Reform in the Southwest.* Princeton, N.J.: Princeton University Press, 1997.

Bru, Edward. *Nuevos territorios, nuevos paisajes/New Territories, New Landscapes.* Barcelona: Museu d'Art Contemporani de Barcelona, 1997.

Bruce, Alfred, and Harold Sandbank. *A History of Prefabrication.* New York: John B. Pierce Foundation, 1944.

Buckley, Drummond. "A Garage in the House." In *The Car and the City: The Automobile, The Built Environment, and Daily Urban Life,* edited by Martin Wachs and Margaret Crawford. Ann Arbor: University of Michigan Press, 1992.

Bullard, Robert D., Glenn S. Johnson, and Angel O. Torres. *Sprawl City: Race, Politics, and Planning in Atlanta.* Washington, D.C.: Island Press, 2000.

Burgess, Patricia. *Planning for the Private Interest: Land Use Controls and Residential Patterns in Columbus, Ohio, 1900–1970.* Columbus: Ohio State University Press, 1994.

Calthorpe, Peter. *The Next American Metropolis: Ecology, Community, and the American Dream.* New York: Princeton Architectural Press, 1993.

Calthorpe, Peter, and William Fulton. *The Regional City: Planning for the End of Sprawl*. Washington, D.C.: Island Press, 2001.

Campoli, Julie, Elizabeth Humstone, and Alex MacLean. *Above and Beyond: Visualizing Change in Small Towns and Rural Areas*. Chicago: American Planning Association, 2002.

Checkoway, Barry. "Large Builders, Federal Housing Programs, and Postwar Suburbanization." In *Critical Perspectives on Housing*, edited by Rachel G. Bratt, Chester Hartman, and Ann Meyerson. Philadelphia: Temple University Press, 1986.

Chow, Renee. *Suburban Space: The Fabric of Dwelling*. Berkeley: University of California Press, 2003.

Clark, Clifford Edward, Jr., *The American Family Home 1800–1960*. Chapel Hill: University of North Carolina Press, 1986.

Clark, Emily. "Own Your Own Home: S. E. Gross, the Great Domestic Promoter." In *The American Home: Material Culture, Domestic Space, and Family Life*, edited by Eleanor McD. Thompson. Hanover, N.H.: University Press of New England, 1998.

Cohen, Lizabeth. *A Consumers' Republic: The Politics of Mass Consumption in Postwar America*. New York: Knopf, 2003.

Congress for the New Urbanism. *Charter of the New Urbanism*. New York: McGraw-Hill, 2000.

Corn, Joseph J., ed. *Yesterday's Tomorrows: Past Visions of the American Future*. 1984. Reprint, Baltimore: Johns Hopkins University Press, 1996.

Crawford, Margaret. "Daily Life on the Home Front: Women, Blacks, and the Struggle for Public Housing." In *World War II and the American Dream: How Wartime Building Changed a Nation*, edited by Donald Albrecht. Washington, D.C.: National Building Museum, 1995.

———. "The World in a Shopping Mall." In *Variations on a Theme Park: The New American City and the End of Public Space*, edited by Michael Sorkin. New York: Hill and Wang, 1992.

Curtis, George William. Foreword to *Rural Essays*, by Andrew Jackson Downing. New York: Leavitt and Allen, 1857.

Daniels, Tom. *When City and Country Collide: Managing Growth in the Metropolitan Fringe*. Washington, D.C.: Island Press, 1999.

Davies, Jane B. "Works and Projects." In *Alexander Jackson Davis: American Architect 1803–1893*, edited by Amelia Peck. New York: Metropolitan Museum of Art, 1992.

Davis, Alexander Jackson. *Rural Residences*. New York: published by the author, 1837.

Dobriner, William M. *Class in Suburbia*. Englewood Cliffs, N.J.: Prentice-Hall, 1963.

Dolbeare, Cushing. "How the Income Tax System Subsidizes Housing for the Affluent." In *Critical Perspectives on Housing*, edited by Rachel G. Bratt, Chester Hartman, and Ann Meyerson. Philadelphia: Temple University Press, 1986.

Dolce, Philip C., ed. *Suburbia: The American Dream and Dilemma*. Garden City, N.Y.: Anchor Press/Doubleday, 1976.

Douglas, Harlan Paul. *The Suburban Trend*. New York: Century, 1925.

Downing, Andrew Jackson. *The Architecture of Country Houses; Including Designs for Cottages, Farm-Houses and Villas, with Remarks on Interiors, Furniture, and the Best Modes of Warming and Ventilating*. 1850. Reprint, New York: D. Appleton, 1852.

—————. *Cottage Residences, or A Series of Designs for Rural Cottages and Cottage-Villas, and Their Gardens and Grounds. Adapted to North America*. New York: Wiley and Putnam, 1842.

—————. *A Treatise on the Theory and Practice of Landscape Gardening, Adapted to North America, with a View to the Improvement of Country Residences*. 1841. 6th ed. New York: A. O. Moore, 1859.

Drew, Bettina. *Crossing the Expendable Landscape*. Minneapolis: Graywolf, 1998.

Duany, Andrés, Elizabeth Plater-Zyberk, and Jeff Speck. *Suburban Nation: The Rise of Sprawl and the Decline of the American Dream*. New York: North Point Press, 2000.

Easterling, Keller. *Organization Space: Landscapes, Highways, and Houses in America*. Cambridge, Mass.: MIT Press, 1999.

Ebner, Michael. *Creating Chicago's North Shore, A Suburban History*. Chicago: University of Chicago Press, 1988.

Edel, Matthew, Elliott D. Sclar, and Daniel Luria. *Shaky Palaces: Homeownership and Social Mobility in Boston's Suburbanization*. New York: Columbia University Press, 1984.

Eichler, Ned. *The Merchant Builders*. Cambridge, Mass.: MIT Press, 1982.

Feagin, Joe R., and Robert Parker. *Building American Cities: The Urban Real Estate Game*. 2d ed. Englewood Cliffs, N.J.: Prentice-Hall, 1990.

Fein, Albert. "The American City: The Ideal and the Real." In *The Rise of an American Architecture*, edited by Edgar Kaufmann, Jr. New York: Praeger, 1970.

Fishman, Robert. *Bourgeois Utopias: The Rise and Fall of Suburbia*. New York: Basic Books, 1987.

Flink, James J. *The Automobile Age*. Cambridge, Mass.: MIT Press, 1988.

Fodor, Eben. *Better Not Bigger: How to Take Control of Urban Growth and Improve Your Community.* Gabriola Island, B.C.: New Society Publishers, 1999.

Forsyth, Ann. *Constructing Suburbs: Competing Voices in a Debate Over Urban Growth.* Amsterdam: Gordon and Breach, 1999.

————. *Reforming Suburbia: Building New Communities in Irvine, Columbia, and The Woodlands.* Berkeley: University of California Press, forthcoming.

Frantz, Douglas, and Catherine Collins. *Celebration, U.S.A.: Living in Disney's Brave New Town.* New York: Marian Wood/Henry Holt, 1999.

Frederick, Christine. *Selling Mrs. Consumer.* New York: Business Bourse, 1929.

Gans, Herbert. *The Levittowners: Ways of Life and Politics in a New Suburban Community.* Reprint with a new preface by the author. New York: Columbia University Press, 1982.

Gardiner, John A. "Corruption and Reform in Land-Use and Building Regulation: Incentives and Disincentives." In *Ethics in Planning,* edited by Martin Wachs. New Brunswick, N.J.: Center for Urban Policy Research, 1985.

Garreau, Joel. *Edge City: Life on the New Frontier.* New York: Doubleday, 1991.

Geisler, Charles, and Gail Daneker, eds. *Property and Values: Alternatives to Public and Private Ownership.* Washington, D.C.: Island Press, 2000.

Gelfand, Mark J. *A Nation of Cities: The Federal Government and Urban America, 1933–1965.* New York: Oxford, 1975.

Girling, Cynthia L., and Kenneth I. Helphand. *Yard-Street-Park: The Design of Suburban Open Space.* New York: Wiley, 1994.

Goddard, Stephen B. *Getting There: The Epic Struggle Between Road and Rail in the American Century.* New York: Basic Books, 1994.

Gottdiener, Mark. *Planned Sprawl: Private and Public Interests in Suburbia.* Beverly Hills, Calif.: Sage, 1977.

Gowans, Alan. *The Comfortable House: North American Suburban Architecture, 1890–1930.* Cambridge, Mass.: MIT Press, 1986.

The Gross Cottages, Houses, and Lots. Chicago: S. E. Gross, 1886.

Gruen, Victor, and Larry Smith. *Shopping Towns USA: The Planning of Shopping Centers.* New York: Reinhold, 1960.

Guarneri, Carl J. *The Utopian Alternative: Fourierism in Nineteenth Century America.* Ithaca, N.Y.: Cornell University Press, 1991.

Gudis, Catherine. *Buyways: Automobility, Billboards, and the American Cultural Landsape.* New York: Routledge, forthcoming.

Hancock, John. "The New Deal and American Planning: The 1930s."

In *Two Centuries of American Planning,* edited by Daniel Schaffer. Baltimore: Johns Hopkins University Press, 1988.

Handlin, David P. *The American Home: Architecture and Society, 1815–1915.* Boston: Little, Brown, 1979.

Hardwick, Mark Jeffrey. *The Mallmaker: Cities, Suburbs, and Architect Victor Gruen.* Philadelphia: University of Pennsylvania Press, forthcoming.

Harris, Dianne. "Making Your Private World: Modern Landscape Architecture and *House Beautiful,* 1945–1965." In *The Architecture of Landscape, 1940–1960,* edited by Mark Treib. Philadelphia: University of Pennsylvania Press, 2002.

Harris, Richard. *Unplanned Suburbs: Toronto's American Tragedy, 1900 to 1950.* Baltimore: Johns Hopkins University Press, 1996.

Hayden, Dolores. "Catharine Beecher and the Politics of Housework." In *Women in American Architecture: Historic and Contemporary Perspectives,* edited by Susana Torre. New York: Whitney Library of Design, 1977.

———. *The Grand Domestic Revolution: A History of Feminist Designs for American Homes, Neighborhoods, and Cities.* Cambridge, Mass.: MIT Press, 1981.

———. "Model Houses for the Millions: Architects' Dreams, Builders' Boasts, Residents' Dilemmas." In *Blueprints for Modern Living: History and Legacy of the Case Study Houses,* edited by Elizabeth A. T. Smith. Los Angeles: Museum of Contemporary Art and MIT Press, 1989.

———. *The Power of Place: Urban Landscapes as Public History.* Cambridge, Mass.: MIT Press, 1995.

———. *Redesigning the American Dream: Gender, Housing, and Family Life.* New York: Norton, 1984. Rev. ed., New York: Norton, 2002.

———. *Seven American Utopias: The Architecture of Communitarian Socialism, 1790–1975.* Cambridge, Mass.: MIT Press, 1976.

Haynes, Bruce. *Red Lines, Black Space: The Politics of Race and Space in a Black Middle-Class Suburb.* New Haven: Yale University Press, 2001.

Herbers, John. *The New Heartland: America's Flight Beyond the Suburbs and How It Is Changing Our Future.* New York: Times Books, 1986.

Hise, Greg. "Homebuilding and Industrial Decentralization in Los Angeles: The Roots of the Post–World War II Urban Region." In *Planning the Twentieth Century American City,* edited by Mary Corbin Sies and Christopher Silver. Baltimore: Johns Hopkins University Press, 1996.

———. *Magnetic Los Angeles: Planning the Twentieth-Century Metropolis.* Baltimore: Johns Hopkins University Press, 1997.

Hochschild, Arlie, with Anne Machung. *The Second Shift: Working Parents and the Revolution at Home.* 2d ed. New York: Viking, 1997.

Horrigan, Brian. "The Home of Tomorrow 1927–1945." In *Imagining Tomorrow: History, Technology, and the American Future,* edited by Joseph J. Corn. Cambridge, Mass.: MIT Press, 1986.

Hutchinson, Janet. "The Cure for Domestic Neglect: Better Homes in America, 1922–1935." In *Perspectives in Vernacular Architecture II,* edited by Camille Wells. Columbia: University of Missouri Press, 1986.

Jackson, John Brinckerhoff. *Landscape in Sight: Looking at America.* Edited by Helen Lefkowitz Horowitz. New Haven: Yale University Press, 1997.

Jackson, Kenneth T. *Crabgrass Frontier: The Suburbanization of the United States.* New York: Oxford University Press, 1985.

Jacobs, Harvey M., ed. *Who Owns America? Social Conflict Over Property Rights.* Madison: University of Wisconsin Press, 1998.

Jakle, John A., and Keith A. Sculle. *The Gas Station in America.* Baltimore: Johns Hopkins University Press, 1994.

Jenkins, Virginia Scott. *The Lawn: A History of an American Obsession.* Washington, D.C.: Smithsonian Institution Press, 1994.

Johnson, Laura A. *The Co-Workplace: Teleworking in the Neighborhood.* Vancouver: University of British Columbia Press, 2002.

Jonas, Andrew E. G., and David Wilson, eds. *The Urban Growth Machine: Critical Perspectives Two Decades Later.* Albany: State University of New York Press, 1999.

Jurca, Catherine. *White Diaspora: The Suburbs and the Twentieth-Century American Novel.* Princeton: Princeton University Press, 2001.

Kay, Jane Holtz. *Asphalt Nation: How the Automobile Took Over America and How We Can Take It Back.* New York: Crown, 1997.

Keating, Ann Durkin. *Building Chicago: Suburban Developers and the Creation of a Divided Metropolis.* Columbus: Ohio State University Press, 1988.

Keats, John. *The Crack in the Picture Window.* Boston: Houghton Mifflin, 1957.

Kelbaugh, Douglas. *Common Place: Toward Neighborhood and Regional Design.* Seattle: University of Washington Press, 1997.

———, ed. *The Pedestrian Pocket Book: A New Suburban Design Strategy.* New York: Princeton Architectural Press, 1989.

Kelly, Barbara M. *Expanding the American Dream: Building and Rebuilding Levittown.* Albany: State University of New York Press, 1993.

———, ed. *Suburbia Re-examined.* New York: Greenwood Press, 1989.

Knepper, Cathy D. *Greenbelt Maryland: A Living Legacy of the New Deal.* Baltimore: Johns Hopkins University Press, 2001.

Kotkin, Joel. *The New Digital Geography: How the Digital Revolution Is Reshaping the American Landscape.* New York: Random House, 2000.

Kowinski, William Severini. *The Malling of America: An Inside Look at the Great Consumer Paradise.* New York: Morrow, 1985.

Lang, Robert E. *Edgeless Cities: Exploring the Elusive Metropolis.* Washington, D.C.: Brookings Institution, forthcoming.

Langdon, Philip. *A Better Place to Live: Reshaping the American Suburb.* Amherst: University of Massachusetts Press, 1994.

Lardner, Ring W. *Own Your Own Home.* Indianapolis: Bobbs-Merrill, 1919.

Leach, William. *Country of Exiles: The Destruction of Place in American Life.* New York: Pantheon, 1999.

Leavitt, Helen. *Superhighway—Superhoax.* Garden City, N.Y.: Doubleday, 1970.

Lewis, Pierce F. "The Galactic Metropolis." In *Beyond the Urban Fringe: Land Use Issues in Nonmetropolitan America,* edited by Rutherford H. Platt and George Macinko. Minneapolis: University of Minnesota Press, 1983.

Lewis, Tom. *Divided Highways: Building the Interstate Highways, Transforming American Life.* New York: Penguin, 1997.

Liebs, Chester H. *Main Street to Miracle Mile: American Roadside Architecture.* Baltimore: Johns Hopkins University Press, 1985. Rev. ed., 1995.

Lincoln Institute of Land Policy. *The New Spatial Order? Technology and Urban Development.* Annual Roundtable, 2000. Cambridge, Mass: Lincoln Institute of Land Policy, 2001.

Loeb, Carolyn S. *Entrepreneurial Vernacular: Developers' Subdivisions in the 1920s.* Baltimore: Johns Hopkins University Press, 2001.

Logan, John R., and Harvey Molotch. *Urban Fortunes: The Political Economy of Place.* Berkeley: University of California Press, 1987.

Longstreth, Richard. *City Center to Regional Mall: Architecture, the Automobile, and Retailing in Los Angeles, 1920–1950.* Cambridge, Mass.: MIT Press, 1997.

———. *The Drive-In, the Supermarket, and the Transformation of Commercial Space in Los Angeles, 1914–1941.* Cambridge, Mass.: MIT Press, 1999.

Low, Setha. *Behind the Gates.* New York: Routledge, 2003.

Lucy, William H., and David L. Phillips. *Confronting Suburban De-*

cline: Strategic Planning for Metropolitan Renewal. Washington, D.C.: Island Press, 2000.

Lynch, Kevin. *What Time Is This Place?* Cambridge, Mass.: MIT Press, 1972.

Marling, Karal Ann. *As Seen on TV: The Visual Culture of Everyday Life in the 1950s.* Cambridge, Mass.: Harvard University Press, 1994.

Marsh, Margaret. *Suburban Lives.* New Brunswick, N.J.: Rutgers University Press, 1990.

Marshall, Alex. *How Cities Work: Suburbs, Sprawl, and the Roads Not Taken.* Austin: University of Texas Press, 2000.

Martinson, Tom. *American Dreamscape: The Pursuit of Happiness in Postwar Suburbia.* New York: Carroll and Graf, 2000.

Mattingly, Paul. *Suburban Landscapes: Culture and Politics in a New York Metropolitan Community.* Baltimore: Johns Hopkins University Press, 2001.

May, Elaine Tyler. *Homeward Bound: American Families in the Cold War Era.* New York: Basic Books, 1988.

McDonough, William, and Michael Braungart. *Cradle to Cradle: Remaking the Way We Make Things.* New York: North Point Press, 2002.

McKenzie, Evan. *Privatopia: Homeowner Associations and the Rise of Residential Private Government.* New Haven: Yale University Press, 1994.

Merriman, John M. *The Margins of City Life: Explorations on the French Urban Frontier, 1815–1851.* New York: Oxford University Press, 1991.

Mitchell, William J. *City of Bits: Space, Place, and the Infobahn.* Cambridge, Mass.: MIT Press, 1995.

———. *e-topia: "urban life, Jim, but not as we know it."* Cambridge, Mass.: MIT Press, 1999.

Muller, Peter O. *Contemporary Suburban America.* Englewood Cliffs, N.J.: Prentice-Hall, 1981.

———. *The Outer City: Geographical Consequences of the Urbanization of the Suburbs.* Resource paper no. 75-2. Washington, D.C.: Association of American Geographers, 1976.

National Association of Home Builders. *Smart Growth: Building Better Places to Live, Work, and Play.* Washington, D.C.: NAHB, 1999.

Negroponte, Nicholas. *Being Digital.* New York: Random House, 1995.

Nicolaides, Becky M. *My Blue Heaven: Life and Politics in the Working-class Suburbs of Los Angeles, 1920–1965.* Chicago: University of Chicago Press, 2002.

Norman, Al. *Slam Dunking Wal-Mart.* Atlantic City, N.J.: Raphel Marketing, 1999.

Nye, David E. *Electrifying America: Social Meanings of a New Technology.* Cambridge, Mass.: MIT Press, 1990.

Orfield, Myron. *Metropolitics: A Regional Agenda for Community and Stability.* Rev. ed. Washington, D.C.: Brookings Institution and Lincoln Institute for Land Policy, 1998.

———. *American Metropolitics: The New Suburban Reality.* Washington, D.C.: Brookings Institution, 2002.

Pacific's Book of Homes: A Notable Exhibition of California Architecture. Los Angeles: Pacific Ready-Cut Homes, 1925.

Papageorge, Tod. *Robert Adams—What We Bought: The New World.* New Haven: Yale University Art Gallery, 2002.

Paulson, Morton. *The Great Land Hustle.* Chicago: Henry Regnery, 1972.

Prigge, Walter. *Peripherie ist Überall.* Frankfurt: Campus, 1998.

Radford, Gail. *Modern Housing in America: Policy Struggles in the New Deal Era.* Chicago: University of Chicago Press, 1996.

Randall, Gregory C. *America's Original GI Town: Park Forest, Illinois.* Baltimore: Johns Hopkins University Press: 2000.

Real Estate Research Corporation. *The Costs of Sprawl: Environmental and Economic Costs of Alternative Residential Development Patterns at the Urban Fringe.* 2 vols. Washington, D.C.: U.S. Government Printing Office, 1974.

Reps, John William. *The Making of Urban America: A History of City Planning in the United States.* Princeton: Princeton University Press, 1965.

Riley, Terence. *The Un-Private House.* New York: Museum of Modern Art, 1999.

Robinson, Judith Helm. "Chevy Chase: A Bold Idea, A Comprehensive Plan." In *Washington at Home: An Illustrated History of Neighborhoods in Our Nation's Capital,* edited by Kathryn Schneider Smith. Washington, D.C.: Windsor, 1988.

Rogers, Daniel. *Atlantic Crossings: Social Politics in a Progressive Age.* Cambridge, Mass.: Belknap Press of Harvard University Press, 1998.

Rome, Adam. *The Bulldozer in the Countryside: Suburban Sprawl and the Rise of American Environmentalism.* New York: Cambridge University Press, 2001.

Rose, Mark H. *Cities of Light and Heat: Domesticating Gas and Electricity in Urban America.* University Park: Pennsylvania State University Press, 1995.

————. *Interstate: Express Highway Politics, 1939–1989*. Rev. ed. Knoxville: University of Tennessee Press, 1990.

Rosenzweig, Roy, and Elizabeth Blackmar. *The Park and the People: A History of Central Park*. Ithaca, N.Y.: Cornell University Press, 1992.

Ross, Andrew. *The Celebration Chronicles: Life, Liberty, and the Pursuit of Property Value in Disney's New Town*. New York: Ballantine, 1999.

Rothman, David. *The Discovery of the Asylum: Social Order and Disorder in the New Republic*. Boston: Little, Brown, 1971.

Rybczynski, Witold. *A Clearing in the Distance: Frederick Law Olmsted and America in the Nineteenth Century*. New York: Scribner, 1999.

Salazar, Jaime, and Manuel Gausa. *Single Family Housing: The Private Domain*. Basel: Birkhauser and Actar, 1999.

Schlosser, Eric. *Fast Food Nation: The Dark Side of the American Meal*. New York: HarperCollins, 2001.

Schuman, Tony, and Elliott Sclar. "The Impact of Ideology on American Town Planning." In *Planning the Twentieth Century American City*, edited by Mary Corbin Sies and Christopher Silver. Baltimore: Johns Hopkins University Press, 1996.

Schuyler, David. *Apostle of Taste: Andrew Jackson Downing, 1815–1852*. Baltimore: Johns Hopkins University Press, 1996.

————. *The New Urban Landscape: The Redefinition of Form in Nineteenth-Century America*. Baltimore: Johns Hopkins University Press, 1986.

Schwartz, Joel. "Evolution of the Suburbs." In *Suburbia: The American Dream and Dilemma*, edited by Philip C. Dolce. Garden City, N.Y.: Anchor Press/Doubleday, 1976.

Schweitzer, Robert, and Michael W. R. Davis. *America's Favorite Homes: Mail Order Catalogues as a Guide to Popular Early 20th Century Homes*. Detroit: Wayne State University Press, 1990.

Shaw, Jane S., and Ronald D. Utt, eds. *A Guide to Smart Growth: Shattering Myths, Providing Solutions*. Washington, D.C.: Heritage Foundation, 2000.

Sies, Mary Corbin. " 'God's Very Kingdom on the Earth': The Design Program for the American Home, 1877–1917." In *Modern Architecture in America: Visions and Revisions*, edited by Richard Guy Wilson and Sidney K. Robinson. Ames: Iowa State University Press, 1991.

Sklar, Kathryn Kish. *Catharine Beecher: A Study in American Domesticity*. New Haven: Yale University Press, 1973.

Small Houses of the Twenties: The Sears, Roebuck 1926 House Catalog. Philadelphia: Athenaeum of Philadelphia and Dover, 1991.

Smeins, Linda E. *Building an American Identity: Pattern Book Homes and Communities 1870–1900*. Walnut Creek, Calif.: Alta Mira, 1999.

Spigel, Lynn. *Welcome to the Dreamhouse: Popular Media and Post-war Suburbs.* Durham, N.C.: Duke University Press, 2001.

Stevenson, Katharine Cole, and H. Ward Jandl. *Houses by Mail: A Guide to Houses from Sears, Roebuck and Company.* New York: Preservation Press and Wiley, 1986.

Stilgoe, John. *Borderland: Origins of the American Suburb, 1820–1939.* New Haven: Yale University Press, 1988.

Sugrue, Thomas J. *The Origins of the Urban Crisis: Race and Inequality in Postwar Detroit.* Princeton: Princeton University Press, 1996.

Szold, Terry, and Armando Carbonell, eds. *Smart Growth: Form and Consequences.* Cambridge, Mass.: Lincoln Institute of Land Policy, 2002.

Tenth Annual Illustrated Catalog of S. E. Gross' Famous City Subdivisions and Suburban Towns. Chicago: S. E. Gross, 1891.

Teyssot, Georges, ed. *The American Lawn.* New York: Princeton Architectural Press, 1999.

Thomas, G. Scott. *The United States of Suburbia.* Amherst, N.Y.: Prometheus Books, 1998.

Thrall, Bob. *The New American Village.* Baltimore: Johns Hopkins University Press, 1999.

Tobey, Ronald C. *Technology as Freedom: The New Deal and the Electrical Modernization of the American Home.* Berkeley: University of California Press, 1996.

Transit Cooperative Research Program. *The Costs of Sprawl—Revisited.* Report 39. Washington, D.C.: National Academy Press, 1998.

Urban Land Institute. *Smart Growth: Myth and Fact.* Washington, D.C.: ULI, 1999.

Waldie, D. J. *Holy Land: A Suburban Memoir.* New York: St. Martin's, 1996.

Walker, Richard. "A Theory of Suburbanization: Capitalism and the Construction of Urban Space in the United States." In *Urbanization and Urban Planning,* edited by Michael Dear and Allen J. Scott. London: Methuen, 1981.

Warner, Sam Bass, Jr. *Streetcar Suburbs: The Process of Growth in Boston, 1870–1900.* Cambridge, Mass.: Harvard University Press, 1962.

Weiss, Ellen. *City in the Woods: The Life and Design of an American Camp Meeting on Martha's Vineyard.* New York: Oxford University Press, 1987.

Weiss, Marc A. *The Rise of the Community Builders: The American Real Estate Industry and Urban Land Use Planning.* New York: Columbia University Press, 1987.

Weiss, Michael J. *The Clustered World: How We Live, What We Buy, and What It All Means About Who We Are.* Boston: Little, Brown, 2000.

Whitehill, Walter Muir. *Boston: A Topographical History.* Cambridge, Mass.: Harvard University Press, 1969.

Wilson, Sloan. *The Man in the Gray Flannel Suit.* New York: Simon and Schuster, 1955.

Wolf, Peter. *Hot Towns: The Future of the Fastest Growing Communities in America.* New Brunswick, N.J.: Rutgers University Press, 1999.

Wood, Charles B., III. "Asher Benjamin, Andrew Jackson Downing: Two Divergent Forms of Bookmaking." In *American Architects and Their Books to 1848,* edited by Kenneth Hafertepe and James F. O'Gorman. Amherst: University of Massachusetts Press, 2001.

Woods, Robert A., and Albert J. Kennedy. *The Zone of Emergence: Observations of the Lower, Middle, and Upper Working Class Communities of Boston, 1905–1919.* 2d ed. Cambridge, Mass.: MIT Press, 1969.

Worley, William S. *J. C. Nichols and the Shaping of Kansas City.* Columbia: University of Missouri Press, 1990.

Wright, Gwendolyn. *Building the Dream: A Social History of Housing in America.* New York: Pantheon, 1981.

———. *Moralism and the Model Home: Domestic Architecture and Cultural Conflict in Chicago, 1873–1913.* Chicago: University of Chicago Press, 1980.

Yaro, Robert D., and Tony Hiss. *A Region at Risk: The Third Regional Plan for the New York–New Jersey–Connecticut Metropolitan Area.* Washington, D.C.: Island Press, 1996.

Zunz, Olivier. *The Changing Face of Inequality: Urbanization, Industrial Development, and Immigrants in Detroit, 1880–1920.* Chicago: University of Chicago Press, 1982.

ARTICLES

Archer, John. "Country and City in the American Romantic Suburb." *Journal of the Society of Architectural Historians* 42 (May 1983): 140–47.

Arsenault, Raymond. "The End of the Long Hot Summer: The Air Conditioner and Southern Culture." *Journal of Southern History* 50 (November 1984): 597–628.

Baker, Kevin. "The Improved Man." *Harper's* 300 (June 2000): 126–34.

Beecher, Catharine E. "How to Redeem Woman's Profession from Dishonor." *Harper's New Monthly Magazine* 31 (November 1865): 710–16.

Brooks, David. "Patio Man and the Sprawl People: America's Newest Suburbs." *The Weekly Standard,* August 12–19, 2002, 19–29.

Brown, Patricia Leigh. "In 'the Other California' a Land Rush Continues." *New York Times,* December 27, 2000, A14.

————. "Megachurches as Minitowns." *New York Times,* May 9, 2002, F1ff.

Calmore, John O. "Metropolitan America and Racism." *Poverty and Race* 2 (May/June 1993): 11–12.

Clark, Emily, and Patrick Ashley. "The Merchant Prince of Cornville." *Chicago History* 21 (December 1992): 4–19.

Cohen, Lizabeth. "From Town Center to Shopping Center: The Reconfiguration of Community Marketplaces in Postwar America." *American Historical Review* 101 (October 1996): 1050–81.

Cowan, Natalie. "Carville, San Francisco's Oceanside Bohemia." *California History* 57 (1978): 308–19.

Ehrenreich, Barbara. "Maid to Order: The Politics of Other Women's Work." *Harper's* 300 (April 2000): 59–70.

Engler, Mira. "Repulsive Matter: Landscapes of Waste in the American Middle-Class Residential Domain." *Landscape Journal* 16 (Spring 1997): 60–79.

Forsyth, Ann. "Variations on a Main Street: When a Mall Is an Arcade." *Journal of Urban Design* 2 (Fall 1997): 297–307.

Gillette, Howard, Jr. "The Evolution of the Planned Shopping Center in Suburb and City." *Journal of the American Planning Association* 51 (Autumn 1985): 449–60.

Hanchett, Thomas. "U.S. Tax Policy and the Shopping-Center Boom of the 1950s and 1960s." *American Historical Review* 101 (October 1996): 1082–1110.

Harris, Richard. "Self-Building in the Urban Housing Market." *Economic Geography* 67 (January 1991): 263–303.

————, and Robert Lewis. "The Geography of North American Cities and Suburbs, 1900–1950: A New Synthesis." *Journal of Urban History* 27 (March 2001): 262–92.

Hart, Sara. "Home Work." *Architecture* 9 (September 1999): 133–37.

Harvey, Thomas. "Mail Order Architecture in the 1920s." *Landscape* 25 (Fall 1981): 1–9.

Henderson, Susan. "Llewellyn Park, Suburban Idyll." *Journal of Garden History* 7 (July/September 1987): 221–43.

Hubbard, Henry. "Land Subdivision Regulations." *Landscape Architecture* 16 (October 1925): 53–54.

Interrante, Joseph. "You Can't Go to Town in a Bathtub: Automobile Movement and the Reorganization of American Rural Space, 1900–1930." *Radical History Review* 21 (Fall 1979): 151–68.

Jackson, Kenneth T. "All the World's a Mall: Reflections on the Social and Economic Consequences of the American Shopping Center." *American Historical Review* 101 (October 1996): 1111–21.

Jossi, Frank. "Rewrapping the Big Box." *Planning* 64 (August 1998): 16–18.

Jurca, Catherine. "Hollywood, the Dream House Factory." *Cinema Journal* 37 (Summer 1998): 19–36.

Kemper, Vicky. "Home Inequity." *Common Cause Magazine* (Summer 1994): 14–18.

Kraut, Robert, and others. "Internet Paradox: A Social Technology That Reduces Social Involvement and Psychological Well-Being?" *American Psychologist* 53 (September 1998): 1017–31.

Levitt, Alfred. "A Community Builder Looks at Community Planning." *Journal of the American Institute of Planners* 17 (Spring 1951): 80–88.

Linn, W. A. "Co-operative Home Winning." *Scribner's Magazine* 7 (May 1890): 569–86.

Logan, John R., Rachel Bridges Whaley, and Kyle Crowder. "The Character and Consequences of Growth Regimes: An Assessment of Twenty Years of Research." *Urban Affairs Review* 32 (May 1997): 603–31.

Mohl, Raymond A. "City and Region: The Missing Dimension in U.S. Urban History." *Journal of Urban History* 25 (November 1998): 3–21.

Molotch, Harvey. "The City as a Growth Machine: Toward a Political Economy of Place." *American Journal of Sociology* 82 (September 1976): 309–32.

Morton, Marian J. "The Suburban Ideal and Suburban Realities: Cleveland Heights, Ohio, 1860–2001." *Journal of Urban History* 28 (September 2002): 671–98.

Muller, Peter O. "The Suburban Transformation of the Globalizing American City." *Annals of the American Academy of Political and Social Science* 551 (May 1997): 44–58.

Olmsted, Frederick Law. "Preliminary Report Upon the Proposed Suburban Village at Riverside Near Chicago." Reprinted in *Landscape Architecture* 21 (July 1931): 257–89.

Post, Emily. "Tuxedo Park: An American Rural Community." *Century Magazine* 82 (October 1911): 795–805.

Redfield, Charles E., and others. "The Impact of Levittown on Local Government." *Journal of the American Institute of Planners* 17 (Summer 1951): 130–41.

Reese, Jennifer. "Streetcar Suburb." *Preservation* 51 (January/February 1999): 52–57.

Riche, Martha Farnsworth. "America's Diversity and Growth: Signposts for the 21st Century." *Population Bulletin* 55 (June 2000): 1–41.

Rosenbloom, Sandra. "Trends in Woman's Travel Patterns." In *Women's Travel Issues: Proceedings from the Second National Conference,* October 1996, http://www.fhwa.dot.gov/ohim/womens/chap2/pdf (June 2001).

Sharpe, William, and Leonard Wallock. "Bold New City or Built-Up 'Burb? Redefining Contemporary Suburbia." *American Quarterly* 46 (March 1994): 1–30.

Sies, Mary Corbin. "North American Suburbs, 1880–1950: Cultural and Social Reconsiderations." *Journal of Urban History* 27 (March 2001): 313–46, 355–61.

———. "Paradise Retained: An Analysis of Persistence in Planned, Exclusive Suburbs, 1880–1980." *Planning Perspectives* 12 (1997): 165–91.

Upton, Dell. "Pattern Books and Professionalism: Aspects of the Transformation of Domestic Architecture in America, 1800–1860." *Winterthur Portfolio* 19 (Summer/Autumn 1984): 107–50.

Wiese, Andrew. "Black Housing, White Finance": African American Housing and Home Ownership in Evanston, Illinois, before 1940." *Journal of Social History* 33 (Winter 1999): 429–60.

———. "The Other Suburbanites: African American Suburbanization in the North before 1950." *Journal of American History* 85 (March 1999): 1495–1525.

———. "Places of Our Own: Suburban Black Towns Before 1960." *Journal of Urban History* 19 (May 1992): 30–55.

Wilson, Richard Guy. "Idealism and the Origin of the First American Suburb: Llewellyn Park, New Jersey." *American Art Journal* (October 1979): 79–90.

Wood, Eugene. "Why Pay Rent?" *Everybody's Magazine* 22 (June 1910): 765–74.

THESES AND DISSERTATIONS

Flynn, Carolyn Patricia. "Pacific Ready-Cut Homes: Mass Produced Bungalows in Los Angeles, 1908–1942." M.A. thesis, Urban Planning, University of California at Los Angeles, 1986.

Moskowitz, Marina. "Standard Bearers: Material Culture and Middle Class Communities at the Turn of the Century." Ph.D. dissertation, American Studies. Yale University, 1999.

Peterson, Sarah Jo. "The Politics of Land Use and Housing in World War II Michigan: Building Bombers and Communities." Ph.D. dissertation. History. Yale University, 2002.

Wilson, Leslie E. "Dark Spaces: An Account of Afro-American Suburbanization, 1890–1950." Ph.D. dissertation. City University of New York, 1992.

INDEX

Abrashkin, Raymond, 217
accelerated depreciation, 162–64
  See also subsidies, federal
Adams, Robert, 194
aerial photography, 5
Affordable Housing Development
  Corporation, 239–40
Agriculture, U.S. Department of,
  and road building, 165
air conditioning, 227
Aladdin Company, 102–03,
  110–11, 116
Alajálov, Constantin, 6
American Architect and Building
  News, 6
American Association of State
  Highway Officials (AASHO),
  165
American Community Builders
  (ACB), 132, 141–46
"American dream"
  as a business, 3
  Fannie Mae, mortgage
    slogan, 3
  triple focus, home, nature, com-
    munity, 7–9
American Institute of Architects
  (AIA), 116–18

American Quarterly, 16
American Safety Foundation
  (ASF), 165
American Scenery, 23, 24, 25
American Woman's Home, The,
  21, 35–37, 40–42
amusement parks, suburban
  Coney Island, 94
  in malls, 172
  trolley parks and electricity,
    93–94
Archer, John, 47, 50
architecture
  Architects' Small House Bureau
    (ASHB), 117–18
  modern, 130
  Seaside, Fl., 207
  styles, vernacular, 106–10
  women, in, 103–04
  See also American Institute of
    Architects and names of indi-
    vidual architects.
Architecture of Country Houses,
  The, 33
asbestos, 135
"Association," Fourierist theory
  of, 51–52, 62
asylums, design of, 259n. 17

Automobile Manufacturers Association (AMA), 165
automobiles
and roadside construction, 158–68
automobile lobby, 165–8
automobile travel, 185
ownership, 159, 165, 185, 190–01
See also highways, Road Gang

Bachelor in Paradise, 149
Baltz, Lewis, 194
Bank of America, 157
bankruptcy, 88
barbecues, at land sales, 98–100
Barber, Donn, 117
Barrett, Nathan, 65
Bartlett, W.H., 24–25
Bauer, Catherine, 125–27, 130, 245
Baumann, Eugene, 59
Bay City, Mich., 104
Bechtel, engineering firm, 166
Beecher, Catharine, 17, 25, 35–43, 216
Beecher, Lyman, 37
Bellamy, Edward, 202
Benjamin, Asher, 101
Bennett, Richard, 144
Berger, Bennett, 146
Better Homes in America, Inc., 117–18, 122
big box stores, 175–79
locational practices, 196–97
See also Wal-Mart, Target, category killer
Bigelow, Jacob, 48
billboards, 120, 164
Binford, Henry, 22

Blake, Peter, 162–63
Blakely, Edward, 215
Blanding's Way, 150–51
Blast From The Past, 148
"Bomber City" (Willow Run, Mich.), 130
borderlands, 20–44
economy of the periphery, 22
farmers in, 23
focus on house and yard, 43–44
manuals for settlers, 24–44
preservation in, 235
retreat from city, 1820s, 20–22
vulnerable to development, 43–44
Boston, Mass.
Back Bay, 46
Beacon Hill, 46
infrastructure investment in, 77
South End, 46
Boyar, Lewis, 133, 140–41
Braungart, Michael, 228
Bremer, Fredrika, 53
Brisbane, Albert, 51–52
Brook Farm, West Roxbury, Mass., 50
Brookfield, Ill. (formerly Grossdale), 86–87.
Brooklyn, N.Y.
Brooklyn Heights, 46
cemetery, 48
ferry, 24, 25
Brown, Lancelot "Capability," 27
Brown, Patricia Leigh, 185, 216
builders, *see* housing industry
building and loan associations, 78
building code, model, 121
Bullard, Robert D., 230
Bunner, Henry Cuyler, 89–92

Burnham Building, Irvington, N.Y., 239–41
Burns, Fritz, 133, 134, 268–69n. 13
Bush, George W., 195

Cahill, Mary, 14
Cairo, Ill., 104, 110
Calthorpe, Peter, 207
Cambridge, Mass., 22, 48, 74
camp meeting grounds, 258n. 9
Camp Snoopy, Mall of America, 172
Carbonell, Armando, 201
carpenters, 77
    "Carpetects," 116–18
    union, 116
Case Study House Program, 220
"category-killer" stores, 175–79
Celebration, Osceola Co., Fl., 7, 209–15
cemeteries, 46, 48–50, 257n. 7
Center Edge Coalition, 234
Cervero, Robert, 175
Chagrin Falls Park, Oh., 111
Chatlos, William F., 6
Checkoway, Barry, 151
Chestnut Hill, Penn., 69
Chevy Chase, Md., 73
children in suburbia, 13–14
    childcare, 13–14, 190–93
    digital technology and, 216–17,
    home and school work, 222–3
    manuals and, 43
    orphanages, suburban, 12
    taxi parents, 14, 193
    telecommuters and, 185–87
Childs, Emory E., 64
churches, freeway, 174, 175

city
    center, 14
    downtowns, losing population and jobs, 3, 10–11, 14–15
    in 1820, 20–22
    focus for urban history, 14–15
    inner, 10
    suburban city, 10–18
    See also metropolitan region, suburbia
Clapham, London, 47
classes
    in borderlands, 23
    in picturesque enclaves, 46, 52, 59–60, 65–70
    in rural fringes, 185–88, 190, 192–93
    in self-built suburbs, 97, 115, 119–20, 125–27
    in sitcom suburbs, 146–48, 161–62
    in streetcar buildouts, 72–73, 77–79
    and suburban economic development, 238–43
    in suburbs, 5
Cleveland, Oh., 127
Cohen, Lizabeth, xii, 17, 170–71
Commerce, U.S. Department of, 117
    Division of Building and Housing, 121–25
Columbia, Md., 173
Communitarian movement, 45–46
Communitarian settlements, 18, 50–54
Community of Interest developments, 28ln. 19
commuters, *see* transportation
"complex marriage," 51

Concord Village, Indianapolis, Ind., 241–44
concurrency, 195
    See also planning
Coney Island, N.Y., 94
Congress of the New Urbanism, 207, 209
consumption and suburbs, 41–42, 118, 148–51, 175–76, 224–26
    "Consumer's Republic," 17
    frugal patterns, 17–18
    See also shopping malls
continuous production process, 268n. 13
Copeland, Morris, 258n. 8
Cottage Residences, 27, 30–32
Country Club Plaza, Kansas City, Mo., 68–69, 168
Crack in the Picture Window, The, 89–92
Crystal Lake, McHenry Co., Ill., 182
curbstoners, 97, 123–25

Daniels, Howard, 59
Daniels, Tom, xii, 231, 233
Davis, A.J., 26, 35, 52–61, 69, 259n. 18
Davis, Cal., Village Homes, 228
Davis, Robert, 203, 206, 215
deed restrictions, 68–69 *See also* racial segregation
defense, and highway design, 166
Detriot, Mich., 127
    Eight-Mile-Wyoming neighborhood, 111–14
Dewees Island, S.C., 228
Digital-House, 217–20
Dobriner, William M., 188–89

Dodd, Anna Bowman, 222
do-it-yourself, *See* self-built houses
Dolbeare, Cushing, 151
domestic feminism, *see* feminism
Dorchester, Mass., 76–77
Dotsun, Olon, 242
Douglas, Harlan, 10
Downing, Andrew Jackson, approach to landscape and architecture, 25–35, 39
    influence, 43–44, 51, 53, 78, 101, 239, 255n.12
Downs, Anthony, 253n. 17
downtown, *see* city
Dreiser, Theodore, 71
driving, cost of, 168
    See also automobiles
Druid Hills, Atlanta, Ga., 65
Duany, Andrés, 6, 202

Eagleswood, N.J., 52–53
Eakeley, Benjamin, 259n. 26
Eames, Charles and Ray, 282n. 27
Edel, Matt, 88
edge nodes, 154–80
    building types in, 159–61, 163, 174–75
    definition of, 154–55
    developed around malls, 172–75
    "edge cities," 154–55
    "edgeless cities," 155
    housing in, 180
    improvements needed, 237
    Schaumburg, Ill., 181–82
    Tysons Corner, Va., 154–58
Edison, Thomas, 60
Eisenhower, Dwight D., 163
Eisner, Michael, 209
electric generating plants, 93–94
electrification, 93

Emerson, Ralph Waldo, 50
EPCOT, 209
Epp, Gayle, 241
Ethnic diversity in suburbs, 12–13
   in Columbia, Md., 173
   in streetcar suburbs; 72–73
   in suburbs after 1945, 12–13,
      146–47
   See also racial segregation
Eugene, Ore., 16
Everybody's Magazine, 88–91
Eyre, Wilson, 65

Fairfax Co, Va., 13, 154, 158
"family" values, 17
   See also gender
Fannie Mae, 111
farmhouses, gentrification of,
      27–29
fast food, 174–75
   See also franchises, McDonald's
Federal government, subsidizes
      private development, 4
Federal Highway Act, 165
Federal Highway Administration
      (FHWA), 167–68
Federal Home Loan Bank Act, 123
Federal Housing Administration
      (FHA), 66, 123–25, 131–33,
      135, 140–41, 149, 151–52,
      196, 227
Federal tax deductions for hous-
      ing, 231–32
   See also subsidies
feminism, domestic, social and
      material, 38
Fisher Hill, Brookline, Mass., 65
Fishman, Robert, xii, 16, 64
Fodor, Eben, 15–16
food market, drive-in, 273n. 11

foreclosures, 105, 119
   See also home ownership, mort-
      gages
Fourier, Charles, 50, 51,
      258n. 17
franchises
   fast food, 161
   maids and child care, 197
Frederick, Christine, 118
Freeport, Long Island, 13
Fremont, Cal., 13
Fulton, Robert, 46
Fulton, William, 140

Gans, Herbert J., 146
garages, 110, 115
garage suburbs, 115
Garnett, William, 139, 194
Garreau, Joel, 154–55, 173, 179,
      209
gas stations, 159–60, 272n. 10
gated communities, 66–69,
      215–16
gender roles, female, 39–43,
      50–51, 89–92, 114–15,
      252n. 8
   "family" values, 5–6, 17
   maids and childcare, 197
   paid and unpaid work, 13–14,
      147–48, 192–93, 216–17,
      224
   servants, 13–14, 42, 55
   "taxi parents," 14, 193
   "trail of errands," 14
   volunteer work, 152
gender roles, male, 8–9, 91–92
   furnace repair, 92
   housework, 14, 192–93
   sweat equity, 110–15, 133–35
   yard work, 32–33, 93

General Electric Company, 6, 8, 135, 150, 216, 226–27
General Motors, 165–66, 225
George, Henry, 95
Girling, Cynthia, 64
"GI Town" (Park Forest, Ill.), 146
Glenn, Daniel, 242
Godwin, Parke, 95
Gordon, Elizabeth, 17
Gottdiener, Mark, 169–70
Gowans, Alan, 97
Greeley, Horace, 52
Greenbelt, Md., 126–27
greenbelt towns, 18, 125–27
green building
    Green Building Council, 228
    "green" houses, 225–29
    Green Seal, 228–29
Green-Wood Cemetery, Brooklyn, N.Y., 48
Greystone Foundation, 239
Grimké, Angelina and Sarah, 52–53
Gross, Samuel E., 6–7, 73, 78–88, 105, 122, 246
    Grossdale, Ill., *see* Brookfield, Ill.
    Gross Park (subdivision), 87
growth boundaries, 237–38
growth machine, xii, 4, 15, 232
Gruen, Victor, 168
Guilford, Conn., 235

Hall, John, 102
Hamilton, Erastus, 51
Hanchett, Thomas, 164, 169
Hancock, Mass. (Shaker community), 51
Handlin, David, 78
Hannover Principles, 228

Hariri, Gisue and Mojgan, 217–20
Harlem River Houses, New York City, 126
Harris, Richard, xi, 114–15, 119–20
Hartshorn, Stewart, 259n. 26
Haskell, Llewellyn, 54–61, 69
Haviland, John, 47, 48, 259n. 17
Hazel, Til, 155, 158
heating, 39
    See also air conditioning
Helphand, Kenneth, 64
Henderson, Susan, 57, 59–61
Herbers, John, 183–84
Heritage Foundation, 195
Highway Beautification Act, 164
highways, 176
    Federal support for, 4, 165–68
    in Llewellyn Park, N.J., 61
    in rural areas, 184
    Interstate system, 165–68
    See also Road Gang, subsidies, federal
historic preservation in suburbia, 235–45
Hodgkins, Eric, 92
home ownership, 78–79
    by ethnicity, 147
    by female-headed households, 147
    See also "Why pay rent?" campaigns
Home Owners Loan Corporation (HOLC), 124–25
Home Owners Service Institute (HOSI), 117–18
Hoover, Herbert, 118, 121–25, 127, 225, 246
HOPE VI, 236, 241, 242
horsecars, 71, 74–76

hotels, resort, in suburbs, 47–48, 69
House Beautiful, 17, 217
household composition, and gender roles, 13–14
House_*n*, 220–223
house sizes, 190–92
housework, *see* gender roles, kitchens
Housing Acts, 130–31
  See also legislation
housing industry, 76–78
  as a business including subdivision, construction, and lending, 97–100
  conflict between owners and developers, 95–96
  furnishing of houses, 118
  manufactured, share of housing starts, 190
  multifamily, 18
  rental, 144–45
  scale of industry reorganized, 131–32
  shortage after 1945, 131–32
  single-family, units built p.a., 4
  war workers' housing, 129–30
Howard, Ebenezer, 202
Huntington, Henry, 76

Indianapolis, Ind., 241
Industrial Home Association, Number 1, 52
industries, in borderlands, 22
inequality and suburban growth, 230–31
Intermodal Surface Transportation Efficiency Act (ISTEA), 234

Interstate Highway Act, 1956, 166–68
Irvine, Cal., 173
Irvington, N.Y., 44, 239, 244
  public library and affordable housing, 239

Jackson, Kenneth T., xii, 10, 16, 76, 135
Johnson, Glenn S., 230
Johnson, Laura C., 186
Johnson, Philip, 157, 210
Jones, Eugene, 241
Jones, Robert Trent, Sr. and Jr., 210
Jurca, Catherine, 149–50

Kaiser, Henry J., 130
Kampen, Owen, 217
Kansas City, Mo., 68
Kay, Kane Holtz, 168, 181
Keats, John, 92, 147
Keck, George, 226
Kelbaugh, Douglas, 207
King of Prussia, Penn., 174–75, 180
Kitchen Debate between Nixon and Khrushchev, 148
kitchen design, 39–42, 216
  virtual chef, 221–22
  See also gender roles, female
Klutznick, Philip M., 128, 132, 141–46
Kotkin, Joel, 189–90

Labor Housing Conference, 125–27
Lake Forest, Ill., 68, 168

Lakewood, Cal., 6, 128, 138–41, 145, 152, 226
  employment near, 162
  Lakewood system (government services on contract), 140
Landia (planned community), 137–38
landlords, 95–96
landscape, American, 3–5
landscape architecture at Llewellyn Park, 59–61
landscape gardening, 89–91
Lane, Richard, 47
Lang, Robert E., 155
Lanham Act, 130
Larchmont, N.Y., 8
Lardner, Ring W., 110
Larson, Kent, 221, 223
lawns
  lawnmower, 33, 205
  pesticide use, 228
Leamington, U.K., 47
leapfrogging, 182–83
Leavitt, Helen, 166
Leeds, Lewis W., 51
Leen, Nina, 147
legislation, *see* Federal Highway Act, Federal Home Loan Bank Act, Wagner Act, Interstate Highway Act, Lanham Act, etc.
Levitt and Sons, 145
  Levitt, Abraham, 136–38
  Levitt, Alfred, 133–34, 136–38, 145, 225
  Levitt, William J., 82, 131–38, 225, 246
Levittowns
  Bucks County, Pa., 138
  employment near, 162

Nassau County, N.Y., 128–29, 162, 226
  Puerto Rico, 138
  Willingboro, N.J., 138
Lewis, Adna G., 103
Lewis Manufacturing Company, 103
Lewis, Pierce, 183
Lewis, Russell, 242
Liverpool, U.K.
  Birkenhead Park, 47
  Prince's Park, 47
Llewellyn Park, West Orange, New Jersey, 45, 69, 207, 236
  See also borderlands, landscape architecture
lobby, growth, 232, 246
  See also growth machine, real estate, automobiles
Location Efficient Mortgage, 236, 286n. 21
Loebl, Jerrold, and Norman Schlossman, 141–44
Lof, George, 226
London, U.K., Regent's Canal Village, 47
Los Angeles, Cal., 13, 98–100
  Boyle Heights, diversity, 13
  L.A., East, 13
Loudon, John Claudius, 26, 47
Low, Setha, 215
Luce publications, 134–35
lumber interests, 97–98, 119
Luria, Daniel, 88

MacDonald, Thomas H., 166
MacKaye, Benton, 126
MacKenzie, Evan, 215
MacLean, Alex S., 11, 12, 72, 171, 177, 178, 183

mail-order and self-built suburbs,
97–127
demands for planning, 120
mail-order houses, 225
preservation in, 236–37
See also Aladdin Company, gender roles, Lewis Manufacturing Company, Sears, Roebuck
and Co., Pacific Ready-Cut
Homes, sweat equity
male work in house and yard, *see*
gender
malls, shopping
and accelerated depreciation,
163, 168–72
Cherry Hill, N.J., 170
Connecticut Post Mall, Milford,
Conn., 171
conversion of, 237
dead malls, 179
history of, 168–72
Lakewood Center, Lakewood,
Cal., 140
Mall of America (MOA),
Bloomington, Minn., 171
South Coast Mall, Orange
County, Cal., 171
Southdale Mall, Minn., 168
types of, 170
Tysons Corner Center, Va.,
156–57
Woodfield Mall, Schaumburg,
Ill., 181
Manchester, U.K., 47
Manilow, Nathan, 141
Mansfield, La., 103
Marshall, Alex, 212
Mar Vista, Cal., 133
material feminism, *see* feminism
McCarthy, Joseph, 130–31,
246

McDonald's, 160–61, 163–64
McDonough, William, 228
McGinley, Phyllis, 8
McGreevey, James, 247
Meadows, Donella, 232
Meloney, Marie, 118
See also Better Homes in Amer-
ica, Inc.
metropolitan regions
planning for, 234
suburban cities, 10–18
See also city, suburbia, suburban
city
Metuchen, N.J., 13
*Mr. Blandings Builds His Dream
House*, 92, 149–51
Molotch, Harvey, 15, 232
Morgan, James, 47
Moore, Charles, 211
Morrisett, Mary, 239
mortgages
amortizing, 78
balloon, 89, 104
mortgage subsidy, *see* subsidies,
federal government
See also home ownership
Mount Auburn Cemetery, Cam-
bridge, Mass., 48
Mount Vernon, N.Y., 52
Muller, Peter, 174
Mumford, Lewis, 125–26, 149,
166

Nash, John, 47
National Association of Home
Builders (NAHB), 131,
195–96, 229, 232
National Association of Real
Estate Exchanges (NAREE),
96

National Association of Real Estate Boards (NAREB), 95–96, 122–25, 130–31, 232, 246

National Association of Realtors (NAR), 96, 231

National Conference on Home-building and Homeowner-ship, 123–27

National Highway Users Conference (NHUC), 165

National Real Estate Journal, 6

Natural Resources Defense Council (NRDC), 194

neighborhood context, loss of, 225

Nelson, Herbert U., 131

neo-traditional houses, 223–24

New Land Marks, 243

Newbold Comyn Estate, Leamington, U.K., 47

New Brighton, Staten Island, N.Y., 47–49

Newburgh, N.Y., 26, 44, 53

New Haven, Conn., 13

New Gloucester, Maine (Shaker community), 54

Newlands, Francis G., 73

New Lebanon, N.Y. (Shaker community), 51

New Urbanism, Charter of the, 215

new urbanists (architects and planners), 15, 201, 215

new urbanist sociology, 15

New York, N.Y., 24, 46–47

New Yorker, 6

Nichols, J.C., 68–9, 122, 246

Nicoll, Jane, 245

North American Phalanx, 50, 52

Norfolk, Va., 133

North Haven, Conn., 12

Norwood, Ohio, 104

Noyes, John Humphrey, 51

nurseryman, 89–91 *See also* landscape gardener

Nye, David, 93

Oak Bluffs, Mass., 258n. 9

office parks, 174–5
   See also edge nodes

Olmsted, Frederick Law, 45, 53–4, 61–6, 245

Olmsted, Frederick Law, Jr., 68

omnibus, 23, 73–4
   See also transportation

Oneida, N.Y., 51

Oneida Perfectionists, 50, 51

Orfield, Myron, 231, 234

Orlando, Fla., 209

Osceola County, Fla., 209–12

Otis, Elisha, 60

Own Your Own Home, 78

Pacific Ready-Cut Homes, 103, 105, 115–16
   See also mail order suburbs

Paine, Robert Treat, 78

Palliser, George, 101

Palos Verdes, Cal., 68

panelized buildings, 102, 115
   See also garage suburbs, mail-order houses

Park Forest, Ill., 132, 141–6, 226

Park Forest Public Library, public history, 245

parks in suburbs, 46, 136

Paxton, Joseph, 47

Peets, Elbert, 142–45, 246

Peirce, Melusina Fay, 38

Pelli, Cesar, 210

Pennethorne, James, 47
Phoenix, Ariz., 216
picturesque enclaves, 45–70
    communitarian models, 50–54
    gated, 61, 67
    Haskell, Llewellyn, 54–61
    Llewellyn Park, N.J., 54–61
    market for property in, 69–70
    origins, 45–54
    picturesque cemeteries and
        parks, 48–50
    preservation in, 236
    resort hotels in, 48, 69
    villa parks, 47
Pierrepont, Hezekiah, 46
Place Matters, 243
planning, urban, history of
    demands for, 120
    Planned Sprawl, 168–72
    *Planning Profitable Neighbor-
        hoods* (FHA), 66
    See also city, metropolitan
        region, new urbanists, subur-
        bia, suburban city, zoning,
        and names of towns
Plater-Zyberk, Elizabeth, 6,
    202–09
Pleasantville, N.Y. (Sears, Roebuck
    Hill), 113
Pleasantville, 148
Pollan, Michael, 189
Pomona, N.Y., 13
population increase, U.S., 233–34
porches, 205
    See also air conditioning, auto-
        mobiles
Portland, Ore., 237
Post, Emily, 67
Power of Place, The, 243
precut buildings, 102–04
Price, Bruce, 67

printing techniques, role in mail-
    order houses, 100–02
public history of suburbs, 243–45
Public Works Administration
    (PWA) Hosiery Workers'
    Housing, 126
Pullman, George, 60
Purcell, William Gray, 117

race, and highway location,
    166–68
racial segregation and suburbs, 16,
    65–70
    African American suburbs,
        111–14
    Celebration, Osceola County,
        Fla., 211
    deed restrictions, 68–69
    federal government policy,
        111–114, 123–25, 135
    Lakewood, Cal., 139
    Levittown, Nassau County,
        N.Y., 135
    mechanisms, 12
    practices, 5, 124–125
    sprawl and segregation, 197
    See also ethnic diversity, Home
        Owners Loan Corporation,
        walls
Radford, Gail, 151–2
railroads, 23, 94
Randall, Gregory, 141
Ranlett, William H., 48–49
Raritan Bay Union, 52–53, 55
Raymond, Eleanor, 226, 246
real estate
    real estate and construction
        lobby, 4
    Real Estate Investment Trusts
        (REITs), 179

real estate (*continued*)
  Realtors' Political Action Committee, 232
  Realtors' Washington Committee (NAREB), 125, 131
  See also housing industry, National Association of Real Estate Boards, National Association of Realtors
Reconstruction Finance Corporation (RFC), 123
Red Bank, N.J., 50, 52
red-lining, *see* racial segregation, practices
Reedy Creek Improvement District, 210
Regional Plan Association (RPA), 138
Regional Planning Association of America (RPAA), 125–27
religion, use in promotion of suburbs, 5–7
  Prayer for America's Road Builders, 134
  religious authority for gender roles, 5–6
  sites in heaven or Eden, 5–7
"reluctant suburb" (older town), 188–89
Reps, John, 257 n. 7
Resettlement Administration (RA), 125–27
restricted community *See* racial segregation, deed restrictions
Riley, Terence, 220
Riverside, Ill., 45, 61–66, 83, 119
Riverside Improvement Company, 62
  scandal with Chicago embezzlement, 65

Road Gang, *see* automobiles, highways, trucking.
Robertson, Jacquelin, 209, 213
Rochelle Park, New Rochelle, N.Y., 65, 236
Roland Park, Md., 168
Rome, Adam, 227
Roosevelt, Franklin Delano, 125–26
Rose, Jonathan F.P., 239
Rose, Mark, 167
Rossi, Aldo, 210
Rouse, James, 170, 173
Roxbury, Mass., 76
Rural Free Delivery, role in mail-order houses, 102
rural fringes, 181–97
  commuters, long-haul, 185
  preservation in, 238
  rapid growth of, 181–84
  relation to edge nodes, 181–82
  telecommuters, 185–88
Rural Residences, 26

scale, architectural, of big box stores, 177–79
Schaumburg, Ill., 181–83, 196
Schwartz, Joel, 120, 127
Sclar, Elliot, 88
Sears, Roebuck and Co., 97, 103–10, 115, 225, 246
  store locations on roadside, 161
  testimony of residents who bought houses, 113–14
  See also mail order suburbs
Seaside, Fla., 6, 203–09
septic tanks, 137
  See also sewers

self-built houses, 110–15
  See also gender roles, male,
    sweat equity
servants, 13–14, 42, 55
  See also gender roles, women,
    paid work
sewers, 86, 137, 139
sewer socialism, 76
Shakers, 50, 51, 60
Shoppell, Robert, 101
Short Hills, N.J., 6, 236, 259n. 26
Sierra Club, 194
Silver Spring, Md., 13
Sies, Mary Corbin, 69–70
single-family housing, *see* housing
sitcom (situation comedy), 128
sitcom suburbs, 128–53
  citizen activists in, 152–53
  confusion of city and subdivi-
    sion, 128
  Lakewood, Cal., 138–41
  Levittown, Nassau County,
    N.Y., 132–37
  lobbying behind, 128–29
  Park Forest, Ill., 141–46
  preservation of, 237
  public space lacking in, 152
  relation to local government,
    136–37
  scale of, 128, 131–32
  true cost of, 152–53
  See also classes in suburbia,
    consumption, sprawl, televi-
    sion
small town, quality of life, 176,
  184
"smart" appliances, 216–226
smart growth, 195
Smart House, 217
"smart" houses, 216–26
Smith, Borax, 76

Snyder, Mary Gail, 215
social feminism, *see* feminism
Socialist Party, U.S., 95
  See also sewer socialism
solar houses, 227–28
Somerville, Mass., 22, 74
sprawl, 11, 193–94, 232, 247
  definition of, 11
  New Jersey, governor's "war on
    sprawl," 247
  rise of the big builders, 121–25
  "sprawl machine," xii
  unregulated houses in
    unplanned areas, 118–20
  vast platted areas, empty,
    96–97
  See also growth machine
Spring, Marcus, 52–53
Stamford, Conn., 173
Stanton, Elizabeth Cady, 53
Staten Island, N.Y., 47–49
steamboats, 34–35
Steen, Jessica, 217
Stein, Clarence, 125–26, 245
Stern, Robert A.M., 210, 213
Stevens, John, 52
Stewart, Martha, 34
Stewart, William M., 73
Stowe, Harriet Beecher, 37
streetcars, 23, 71–76, 88, 92–94,
  120
  electric, bought up by automo-
    tive interests, 165–66
  interurban, 92–94
  See also transportation
streetcar buildouts, 71–96
  final expansion with interur-
    bans, 92–94
  home ownership in, 77–92
  preservation in, 236
  sweat equity in, 72

streetcar buildouts (*continued*)
    variety in dwellings and yards,
        71–73
    vast platted areas, 96
street lighting, 86
strip mall, *see* mall
strips, roadside, and accelerated
    depreciation, 163–64
subsidies, federal government
    cost of, 231
    for commercial real estate, xii,
        4, 162–64, 168–70, 230–31
    for highways, 165–8
    for residential real estate, xii, 4,
        121–27, 131–32, 140–41,
        151–52, 230–31
Suburban Gardener, The, 47
*Suburban Gardener and Villa
    Companion, The,* 26
suburbia
    definition, 3, 11, 16
    ethnic diversity in, 12–13
    job growth, 3, 10–11
    proportion of U.S. population
        residing in, 10
    segregation in, *see* racial segre-
        gation
    seven patterns of suburban con-
        struction, 4, 5, 11, 17, 234
    suburban city, 10–18
    See also borderlands, picturesque
        enclaves, streetcar buildouts,
        mail-order and self-built
        suburbs, sitcom suburbs, edge
        nodes, rural fringes
Sudbrook Park, Md., 65
Sugrue, Thomas J., 111–12
supermarkets, 159–61
sustainability, *see* green building
sweat equity, *see* self-built houses
Sweet, Carroll F., Jr., 128

Taft-Ellender Wagner Act (1949
    Housing Act), 130–31
Taper, Mark, 138
Target Stores, 177
taxes and subsidies, federal, state,
    and local, 4
    See also subsidies, federal gov-
        ernment
taxi-parent, 14, 192–93
Taylor, Ella, 149
Taylor, Horace, 89–91
telecommuting, 184–89
television, 135, 148
Telkes, Maria, 226, 246
tenements, 71, 120
Tise, Stephen and Stephen, Jr.,
    241–42
Title VII communities, 173
Torres, Angel O., 230
traction, *see* streetcars
trade unions
    AFL/CIO, 130–31
    Labor Housing Congress,
        125–27, 130–31
    non-union workers, Wal-Mart
        and, 178
    non-union workers, William
        Levitt and, 134
tram, *see* streetcars
transit, public, *see* streetcars, rail-
    roads
transportation, 23, 73–76
    and degree of urbanization, 23
    categorizing suburbs by, prob-
        lems of, 5
    commuters, 24–25, 73–74, 185
    discomfort of commuting,
        73–74
    fares, 23
    impact on built environment,
        74–78

transportation technologies and suburban development, 23

Treatise on Domestic Economy for the Use of Young Ladies at Home and at School, 35

Treatise on the Theory and Practice of Landscape Gardening, 26–29

triple-decker, 71–72

triple dream, 66

trolleys, *see* streetcars

trucking industry
demands for road widening, 176
Road Gang, 165–68
part of highway lobby, 165–66

The Truman Show, 148, 207

Tugwell, Rexford, 126–27

Tuxedo Park, N.Y., 67, 191–92, 215

Tysons Corner, Va., 154–58, 180, 196, 209
See also edge nodes

unincorporated areas, chosen for mall development, 171–73

United States Census, American Housing Survey, 249n. 1

urban growth boundary, 182–83, 195

Urban Land Institute (ULI), 195, 229, 232

urban planning, *see* planning, zoning

Vachon, John, 112–13, 159

Vanport City, Ore., war workers' housing, 130

Vaux, Calvert, 35, 61–66

Veterans Administration (VA) mortgages, 135

Victoria Park, Manchester, U.K., 47

villa parks, 46–47

Wagner Act (U.S. Housing Act, 1937), 125–27

Waldie, D.J., 6, 140

walls, between neighborhoods, 111–14
See also racial segregation

Wal-Mart, 175–79

Walt Disney Company, The, 7, 209–15

Warner, Sam Bass, Jr., 11, 77

waste removal, 137, 139

Weehawken, N.J., 24

Weingart, Ben, 138, 140–41

Weiss, Marc A., 122, 152

Weld, Theodore, 53

West Bloomfield, N.J., 55

West Haven, Conn., 11

West Roxbury, Mass., 50, 77

West Side Village, Mar Vista, Cal., 268n. 13

Whitney, Henry M. and William, 74, 76

Why-pay-rent? campaigns, 88–92

Whyte, William, 146

Wick, Whitman S., 117

Widener, Peter, 76

Willard, Frances, 38

Williams, Jay, 217

Williams, Raymond, 230

Willingboro, N.J., *see* Levittowns

Willis, Nathaniel Parker, 23–25

Williston Park, Nassau County, N.Y., 6

Wilshyre of McLean (tract), 158

Wilson, Sloan, 147
Wolf, Peter, 189–90
wood construction, 78
    wood, sustainably harvested,
        228
    wood, treated (CCA), 228
    See also lumber interests
Wood, Edith Elmer, 125–26
Wood, Eugene, 89
Woodlands, The, outside Houston,
        Tex., 173
    See also Title VII communities

Woods, Clyde, 241–42
Wrenn, Raymond F., 154
Wright, Gwendolyn, xii, 78
Wright, Henry, 125–26

Yaro, Robert, 231, 233
Yerkes, Charles Tyson, 76, 88

zoning, model ordinance, Depart-
        ment of Commerce, 121